SPEAKING TO PERSUADE

Fourth Edition

Barbara L. Breaden

Kendall Hunt
publishing company

Cover image © Shutterstock, Inc

Kendall Hunt
publishing company

www.kendallhunt.com
Send all inquiries to:
4050 Westmark Drive
Dubuque, IA 52004-1840

CONTENTS

CHAPTER 3
DISCOVERING ARGUMENTS: USING THE COMMON TOPICS   67

CHAPTER 4

DISCOVERING ARGUMENTS: ANALYZING AND REPAIRING YOUR CREDIBILITY

CHAPTER 5

ANALYZING THE AUDIENCE

CHAPTER 7

REASONING AND REFUTATION

CHAPTER 8

VERBAL STYLE IN PERSUASIVE SPEAKING

Part Four
Memory and Delivery: Speech Presentation **217**

Part Five
Beyond the Speech: Adaptation and Analysis

CHAPTER 11
ADAPTING THE PERSUASIVE SPEECH

CHAPTER 12
ASSESSING SPEECH EFFECTIVENESS

PREFACE

What constitutes democracy? As we know, starting with the geographic roots of *dēmokratia* in ancient Athens, democracy's defining characteristic merges *dēmos* or people with *kratos* or rule: that is, rule by the people—directly or through their chosen representatives. Clearly a democratic political system is difficult to achieve when governments rule millions of people. Still, in 2017 the Pew Research Center found that nearly 60%, of the world's largest countries (population 500,000+) function as democracies.

How does a government discover the will of so many people? The people must make their will known, by the vote or by speech or by both. The fundamental premise of *Speaking to Persuade*, then, is that each individual's perspective in a democratic society calls for a speaking role. Unless we speak, our unique vantage point is lost to time. Citizens in a democracy must set aside natural reticence to express their positions. They must speak to persuade. This book explores from start to finish how to approach this vital participation.

We frame our approach to persuasion as **a cooperative act**. Persuasion as cooperation requires a **dialectical interchange** between speakers and listeners, where we come to know, exchange, and integrate diverse perspectives. That is, through our dialectic, we discover mutually acceptable values and policies.

Of course, in speaking to persuade we are inviting others to share our conclusions. We use the art of rhetoric to discover ways to persuade, and this discovery works best informed by past and present practitioners in both **classical and contemporary theories of persuasion**. Finally, to formulate messages, we draw on some durable building blocks—the **classical rhetorical canons** of invention, organization, style, memory, and delivery.

This classical backdrop to a contemporary view of persuasion as cooperation offers brief theoretical excursions in each chapter's popular *Since You Asked* feature—tackling short theoretical questions, without detracting from the book's essential simplicity, practicality, and user-friendliness.

We have retained the same features that readers valued previously:

- theory informing practice
- emphasis on invention and critical thinking to formulate ideas
- awakening vivid language and dependable memory for dynamic speech delivery
- practice in reasoning and refuting arguments

- options in organizing coherent and convincing messages
- guidelines for adapting basic persuasive principles to public advocacy, sales, informal debate, social commentary, and legal practice.

Whether you use this book as a textbook for developing and presenting simple persuasive speeches, as a self-help workbook for effective professional presentations, or as a guide to professional speechwriting, the following features should augment your progress:

- Chapter previews (*To Make a Long Story Short*) and summaries highlight key concepts and terms
- *Theory into Practice* exercises apply each chapter's principles.
- A variety of annotated *sample speeches* demonstrate real persuasive appeals applied to diverse circumstances.
- *Ethics Watch* segments pose ethical dilemmas within each canon of persuasion.

This fourth edition also

- Considers how to think about and manage polarized audiences.
- Expands guidelines for assessing the accuracy and authenticity of evidence.
- Addresses the relationship between freedom of speech and sensitive language usage.
- Considers social commentary as a distinct genre of persuasion.
- Extensively updates examples, theories, and resources, particularly in issues surrounding social media and online information.
- Offers a variety of supplemental materials, from assessment tools and test banks to chapter-by-chapter slides for instructional use.

ACKNOWLEDGEMENTS

Speaking to Persuade has been conceived all along as a bridgework between text and practical guide. Its readers have included lawyers, engineers, health care workers, teachers, communication consultants, speechwriters, and students, who have expressed appreciation for its readability and relevance. Those professors who have requested updated editions note the scarcity of practical guides to persuasive speech.

For this revision of *Speaking to Persuade*, I am fortunate to have had the assistance of Daniel Henry, a distinguished scholar, author, and teacher at Lane Community College. Nearly every one of the suggestions in his extensive and insightful review of the third edition inspired new material for the fourth.

Additional thanks go to the those colleagues who generously contributed their endorsements: Jay Frasier, Lane Community College; Dr. David Frank, University of Oregon; Dr. Molly Mayhead, Western Oregon University; Stephen Zwickel, University of Wisconsin/Madison; and Dana Rubin, Rubin&Co and VizibilityLab, New York, New York.

Editor Lara McCombie and Project Coordinator Noelle Henneman at Kendall Hunt must be two of the most agreeable and supportive women in the publishing industry. Deepest thanks to both for their consistently positive and intelligent direction in seeing this project through.

Ron Breaden, my wise and well read husband, has a knack for seeing connections that have escaped me and deserves credit for his smart and steady input. His confidence in the importance of rhetoric and the democratic ideals embedded in this book energized its execution. To him once again my work is dedicated.

ABOUT THE AUTHOR

Educated in Rhetoric and Communication at the University of Illinois (Champaign-Urbana) and the University of Oregon, Barbara Breaden has taught on-site and online Speech and Communication Studies courses in higher education for more than thirty-five years. As part of the Northwest Forensics Conference, she founded a successful debate team at Lane Community College, Eugene, Oregon. Aside from rhetorical theory and free speech issues, Breaden's research interests have included the elements of attention and memory in listening and critical thinking.

Part One

Perspectives on Persuasion

1 The Whys and Whats of Persuasion

To Make a Long Story Short...

We persuade often and for good reason.

Key Concepts

- Persuasion springs from conviction.
- A dialectical approach to persuasion explores opposing positions to formulate and advance sound ideas.
- Persuasion is neither propaganda nor coercion.
- Persuasion is most common to free societies.
- Effective persuasion requires thought about the controversy, the audience, and the speech's context.

Key Terms

dialectic

polarization

tribalism

persuasion

beliefs

attitudes

actions

cognitive dissonance

brainwashing

propaganda

disinformation

misinformation

coercion

rhetoric

Why Persuasion?

Imagine for a moment a world without disagreement. As a child, you wouldn't wrestle with your playmate over a toy. As a student, you would neither question a rule nor dispute the correct answer on an exam. As an adult in the work force, you would never challenge the wisdom of your boss's decisions, nor would you complain of unjust treatment. We could go on to depict parents and children in perfect harmony, baseball fans and umpires in a perpetual atmosphere of mutual affection, but you get the idea. This is no real world; this is Utopia. Or is it?

Would our lives be more satisfying if we never disagreed and we had no need for the art of persuasion? Brett Stephens, a foreign policy writer for the *New York Times*, wrote a rousing piece about "The Dying Art of Disagreement,"[1] in which he calls disagreement "the most vital ingredient of any society." It's true. We build community and the relationships that sustain us through agreement, but to say, "I disagree" defines us as free people. To disagree makes healthy democracies work. Since we are each unique, we possess different looks, voices, personalities, perspectives, and doctrines. In a world of people, disagreement is inevitable. We can respond to our familial, social, and public disagreements with silence or by speaking our minds—that is, by speaking to persuade.

Figure 1.1 As long as humans diverge in their perspectives, disagreement will persist.
© bikeriderlondon/Shutterstock, Inc.

The Importance of Persuasion

Democracy and Polarization

By some accounts, twenty-first-century global populations have been characterized by heightened **polarization**. The Pew Research Center documented a widening gap and increased animosity between right and left political positions in the United States between 1994 and 2014.[2] As political positions become more staunchly partisan, people gravitate toward more entrenched opposition. The political climate becomes *polarized*. We know that with electromagnetic force, positive and negative charges attract; they are drawn together. But politically opposed people *repel* one another.

Harvard psychology professor, Joshua Greene, attributes the tendency toward polarization to the problem of moral **tribalism**. Each "moral tribe" (e.g., a party or political affiliation) has its own common sense that differs from the common sense of other "tribes." Although humans use their particular common sense to cooperate *within* a tribe, tribes tend not to cooperate *with other* tribes. People become both selfish and intensely loyal at the tribal level, favoring *us* over *them*, effectively pushing *them* away, rather than conjoining into intertribal commonality and community.[3]

Throughout the history of humankind, tribal loyalties, those *us*-versus-*them* instincts, have led people away from cooperation and toward domination or destruction of the other. In 1939, Adolf Hitler's determination to square off against the world ignited one of many twentieth-century genocides that upturned countries from Turkey and Russia to Cambodia and Bosnia.

Considering the state of our polarized world and its brazenly dysfunctional disagreement, can we reasonably expect to overcome differences to achieve constructive ends? Although this was the aspiration of a new American democracy in 1787, within twenty years of the newly adopted US Constitution, founder Alexander Hamilton nearly despaired that the country might not survive. In a letter, he referred to the confounding "disease" of democracy.[4] But Hamilton did *not* despair. So must we not. Hamilton's perseverance speaks to the value of maintaining a level head in a polarized world and of working one's way around tribal impulses.

A distinguished historian of early America, Gordon Wood, has pointed out that polarization in Hamilton's day was easily more highly pitched than today.[5] In fact, history shows that persuasion exists *because of* opposition, and that societies can survive polarized times, but it takes grit and a good number of steady hands to maintain the mechanism of democracy.

We have no silver bullets for managing social conflict in democratic systems. Living in a democracy is not for the faint of heart. Rather than shrinking from political polarization, we need to confront it. We must acknowledge tribal impulses and transcend them to perform the responsibilities of civic life. US Citizenship and Immigration Services[6] articulate several such responsibilities in a democracy: supporting and defending the Constitution, staying informed on the issues of your community, and participating in the democratic process. And eventually we need to reach for that fundamental tool of a democratic society: the art of persuasion.

Benefits of Persuasion

Can persuasion benefit individuals and societies? Celebrities and sports heroes seem to think so; they persuade youth to stay in school and steer clear of drugs. Legislators and lawyers spend their lives persuading constituents, colleagues, and judges. And what about us? We join organizations and attend meetings to impact public policy. We urge family members to quit smoking and city councilors to fix our streets. As students, we prod a professor to put off an exam from Wednesday to Friday, defend our interpretation of a poem, or organize a lobby for more healthful food in the cafeteria. We attempt persuasion when we speak on behalf of a friend who has been unjustly treated and when we appeal at our job for sick pay or family leave. We attempt persuasion because we feel that our way of seeing things has some value or may do some good.

Persuasion is a common form of human interaction, but it is also a valuable and necessary practice. Persuasion makes strong leaders, such as the founder of Nike, Bill Bowerman, who moved a population to improve their well being by taking up jogging, influencing generations of footwear customers. On Bowerman's death, the *New York Times* reported that

> On a trip to New Zealand in the 1960's, Bowerman saw how Arthur Lydiard, a well-known coach, *had persuaded* many people to jog. In 1967, Bowerman wrote *Jogging*, a book credited with inspiring the running boom in America.[7]

Persuasion is a means of making peace. In 1953, President Dwight Eisenhower delivered to the United Nations a speech known as "Atoms for Peace." According to Jim Walsh, Former Executive Director of the Project on Managing the Atom, Eisenhower's speech "was one of the defining moments of the nuclear age." At the time, the United States was facing off against communism.

> The United States *had to convince* governments that there was some benefit to nuclear restraint . . . Countries *would have to be persuaded* even as the world's great powers were building their own nuclear weapons. Eisenhower proposed that the United States share the benefits of

nuclear science—energy, medical isotopes, and the like—with countries that chose peaceful rather than military applications of the atom. This idea was later incorporated into the Nuclear Nonproliferation Treaty.[8]

Persuasion is an art available to any point on the political spectrum and it is practiced by good and bad alike. As Bower Aly, the "Father of High School Debate" in the United States once said, public speakers are not always successful, good, or great. "On the contrary, we may observe [them] sometimes to be unsuccessful, evil, and mean."[9] But, as eighteenth-century British Parliamentarian Edmund Burke purportedly said, the only way to assure the triumph of evil is for good people to remain silent. You might say we speak to persuade when we know we ought not remain silent.

Persuasion through Dialectic

If the persuader may be "unsuccessful, evil, and mean," how can the "art" of persuasion be a positive force? People have raised this question since scholars first discussed and wrote about persuasion. Marcus Fabius Quintilianus, a first century Spaniard raised in Rome and professor of oratory, wrote twelve books on the subject of persuasive speech, and in the second he raises the controversy.

'It is eloquence,' [some] say 'that snatches criminals from penalties of the law, eloquence that from time to time secures the condemnation of the innocent . . . that stirs up wars beyond all expiation.'[10]

Still, Quintilian contends that

Although the weapons of oratory may be used either for good or ill, it is unfair to regard as an evil that which can be employed for good . . . .[11]

For this reason, Quintilian claims that to speak well, the persuasive speaker must be a good person. According to Quintilian, then, unless we possess good character traits, we cannot be eloquent.

So the most useful persuasion requires good people advocating good things. How do we discover what is good? Through conversation and cooperation. Speech scholar Lance Bennett claims that with effective persuasion, we engage *equality* and *consensus* through talk.[12] We prepare to speak by talking and reflecting with diverse people to understand a variety of perspectives and to seek feasible solutions to problems. Classicists called this pre-speech deliberation **dialectic**,[13] a process by which you generate sound ideas through discussion, questioning, and conflicting perspectives.

According to Cass Sunstein, a close advisor to former President Barack Obama, the President had internalized the values of dialectic or what Sunstein called "deliberative democracy." In deliberative democracy, adults converse and listen to one another. They "attempt to persuade one another by means of argument and evidence, and . . . remain open to the possibility that they could be wrong."[14]

As an example, in a remarkable interview with the late PBS newswoman Gwen Ifill in 2007, Ehud Olmert, then Prime Minister of Israel, spoke of a newly established relationship with Palestinian President Mahmoud Abbas, a relationship in which they were discovering the value of dialectic as precursor to persuasion. They each held political conditions that needed to be met by their adversary. Yet they approached their task, the task of persuading one another, through dialectic. Clearly, the final chapter has not yet been scripted in any Arab-Israeli peace process, but as Olmert pointed out,

> You have supporters. You have opponents. You have opposition. You have coalition. You have to be able to sort your way amongst all these different elements. My conviction is that, when it comes down to these fundamental issues of historical proportions for the life of my country, you have to look beyond the political difficulties and to look at the ultimate goal of what is really good for your country and what is really constructive for the relations that you want to have with your neighbors. And if you do that, you'll find also the political solutions necessary in order to advance it.[15]

Through the process of preparing a persuasive speech—researching facts, coming to understand an audience, and presenting the best possible case for the soundest position—the goal of persuasion becomes, as argumentation scholar Josina Makau claims, a goal we *share* with our audience.[16]

Likewise, contemporary rhetorician Michael Osborn observed that "the nature of [political and social] communication is profoundly cooperative."[17] Osborn envisions persuasive messages as bridges that "join people who otherwise would be quite separate." Imagine times of great crisis, as at the attack on the World Trade Center in New York City, September 11, 2001. The community perspective articulated by leaders at such times becomes a source of national unity; it becomes each person's *own* expression.

This is true as well in times of great celebration, as when the United States inaugurated its first African-American President. That day in January, 2009, was characterized by joyous and peaceful crowds, by a state of general euphoria, a word used repeatedly in news reports afterward. Into this moment stepped the master of ceremonies for the inauguration, California Senator Dianne Feinstein, who was to introduce President-elect Barack Obama to the two million people shuddering in sub-freezing cold but, yes, *euphoric* to be part of history. Her task was to capture their mood, to elevate and share it with the people, and to uphold this democracy as a model. The persuasive intent of her address, then, was to inspire satisfaction and pride in a milestone for racial equality in the United States.

Senator Dianne Feinstein's Welcoming Remarks Inauguration Day, January 20, 2009

Ladies and Gentlemen, welcome to the Inauguration of the 44th President of the United States of America. The world is watching today as our great democracy engages in this peaceful transition of power. Here on the national mall, where we remember the founders of our nation and those who fought to make it free, we gather to etch another line in the solid stone of history.

The freedom of a people to choose its leaders is the root of liberty. In a world where political strife is too often settled with violence, we come here every four years to bestow the power of the presidency upon our democratically elected leader. Those who doubt the supremacy of the ballot over the bullet can never diminish the power engendered by nonviolent struggles for justice and equality, like the one that made this day possible. No triumph tainted by brutality could ever match the sweet victory of this hour and what it means to those who marched and died to make it a reality.

Our work is not yet finished, but future generations will mark this morning as the turning point for real and necessary change in our nation. They will look back and remember that this was the moment when the dream that once echoed across history, from the steps of the Lincoln Memorial finally reached the walls of the White House.

In that spirit, we today not only inaugurate a new administration, we pledge ourselves to the hope, the vision, the unity and the renewed call to greatness inspired by the 44th president of the United States, Barack Obama. Thank you, and God bless America.[18]

Figure 1.2 Inauguration crowds testify to the significance of this event in American life.
© Paul Hakimata Photography/Shutterstock.com

As in moments of celebration, times of crisis elicit exhortations from leaders, who can, in the best of worlds, inspire unity and reject divisive malice. On Thanksgiving Day, 1963, six days after the assassination of President John F. Kennedy, newly inaugurated President Lyndon Johnson, spoke these words that capture a timeless conflict and aspiration characteristic of the United States of America.

> Since last Friday[19], Americans have turned to the good, to the decent values of our life. These have served us. Yes, these have saved us. The service of our public institution and our [people] is the salvation of us all from the Supreme Court to the States.
>
> And how much better would it be, how much more sane it would be, how much more decent and American it would be if all Americans could spend their fortunes and could give their time and spend their energies helping our system and its servants to solve your problems instead of pouring out the venom and the hate that stalemate us in progress.
>
> I have served in Washington 32 years—32 years yesterday. I have seen five Presidents fill this awesome office . . . In each administration, the greatest burden that the President had to bear had been the burden of his own [people]'s unthinking and unreasoning hate and division. So, in these days, the fate of this office is the fate of us all. I would ask all Americans on this day of prayer and reverence to think on these things.[20]

It may be that some readers of these words can recall the time of President Kennedy's assassination, or were in New York City on September 11, 2001, or attended the inauguration of a President, or were witness to a mass shooting or other brutality. Whether remembering these events with joy or with horror, these readers were not alone. Humans as social animals share their common anguish and elation with others and together are moved by the words they hear. Speeches can animate our lives, calm our fears, and motivate our actions. Our presumption in this book is that we speak not only *to* people but *with* and *for* people, by discovering the concerns of diverse stakeholders so as to develop a unifying perspective. This defines the merit of a dialectical approach to persuasive speech.

So What *Is* Persuasion?

When we use the term **persuasion** in this book, we are referring to *the intentional verbal act that seeks to influence the beliefs, attitudes, or actions of its listeners.* Each of these characteristics is significant in the study of persuasive speaking.

First, we are looking at persuasion as *intentional*, meaning that the person doing the persuading *wants* to affect the hearers in some way. People can be persuaded, of course, without someone intending to persuade them. If I go to see a new film because I overheard you telling a friend about it, you have unintentionally persuaded me. But this book is not so concerned with *unintentional* influence.

Second, we are looking at persuasion that is substantially *verbal*. We know that nonverbal behavior influences others, as when the sight of a homeless family living on the street prompts you to slip them some cash. Even as we speak, our nonverbal speaking presence—facial expression, posture, or distance from the audience, for instance—can exert influence on people. We will discuss such nonverbal elements in Chapter Ten, but the primary focus of this book is on crafting ideas and their verbal expression when we speak to persuade.

Third, a persuasive speech is a particular *act* rather than an ongoing interaction or social movement. We are considering speeches as they occur within a finite time. Naturally, many elements of the communication process affect the speech's outcome—the time of day, the place where the speech is delivered, the pre-speech experience of audience members, and so on. But our focus is on the speech itself.

Finally, persuasion seeks to influence beliefs, attitudes, and actions.[21] There are some, like modern behavioral psychologist B.F. Skinner, who contend that persuaders do not change minds but only behavior or actions.[22] Nevertheless, modern communication theorists describe a three-part scheme of influence. **Beliefs** are ideas that are central to our worldview. Martin Fishbein, who developed a significant body of theory on the subject of attitudes, says that "a belief in a thing means that one contends that the thing exists."[23] Thus one may *believe* that the world is round, that there is a God, that labor unions are fundamental elements in a free market economy, and so on.

Persuasion often seeks to change attitudes.[24] **Attitudes** are predispositions or inclinations to act in one way or another. Once we accumulate information about a person, idea, or situation, we establish a positive or negative attitude toward it. Our attitude indicates how we will *probably act* in one way rather than another, or how we will *respond*:[25] Trusting that the world is round, I would like to sail all the way around it. Or because I believe in God, I want to do good on earth so that I will go to Heaven when I die. And since I believe in the appropriateness of labor unions, I support the picket outside the Sav-U-Mart.

Actions, of course, are when we behave according to the way we think: finally taking that Carnival cruise, putting together a food box for the local mission, or shifting my shopping allegiance to the nearby Foods Plus. Look at these statements schematically. As Figure 1.3 below illustrates, our actions are most often an outgrowth of our beliefs and attitudes.

DISTINGUISHING BELIEFS, ATTITUDES, AND ACTIONS

BELIEFS	ATTITUDES	ACTIONS
The world *is* round.	I *would like* to sail around the world.	I *am going to* take that Carnival cruise.
There *is* a God.	I *want* to please God by doing good in this world so that I may get to heaven.	I *will help* put together food boxes for the local mission.
Labor unions *are* essential to a free market economy.	I *support* the picket outside the Sav-U-Mart.	I *will shop* instead at Foods Plus.

Figure 1.3 The persuasive targets—beliefs, attitudes, and actions—are interconnected. Actions derive from one's beliefs and attitudes.

Yet, as Leon Festinger posited in his Theory of Cognitive Dissonance,[26] people strive to keep their beliefs, attitudes, and actions consistent with one another. In fact, at times, in order to reconcile behavior (or actions) with underlying attitudes, a person may alter either beliefs, attitudes, or actions. Humans either ignore the internal conflict they experience through denial or adjust a behavior, attitude, or belief. For example, Jack is a cigarette smoker. He believes that smoking is hazardous to his health, but he continues to smoke. His mind is in a state of conflict or imbalance; this is **cognitive dissonance**. According to Festinger, Jack will experience significant cognitive/emotional tension if he continues to smoke believing what he believes.

What does Jack do in order to resolve the cognitive imbalance and reduce tension? He begins to discredit studies that demonstrate the health hazards of smoking; that is, he modifies his beliefs. He becomes involved with the issue of smokers' rights, submerging the attitude that smoking is dangerous under a stronger attitude that smokers deserve equal rights and equal access to public space. Jack's behavior (the result of his addiction to cigarettes) has motivated him to modify his attitude in order to preserve cognitive balance and reduce tension.

In the same way, people may think they never want to have children, until they do, at which time they might wonder why they opposed the idea. The conflicting behavior (the presence of a child they have conceived) causes them to modify their attitudes and beliefs.

Of the three primary persuasive targets—beliefs, attitudes, and actions—the most common is attitudes.[27] Generally people's attitudes follow their beliefs and their actions follow their attitudes, but the reverse may occur. Actions may affect attitudes and beliefs. You might persuade me to vote for Jennifer Clark for mayor, and I vote for her. On the other hand, I might capriciously vote for Clark and after doing so convince myself that she is a good mayor. I justify my action by altering my attitude.

This tendency explains for some how religious instincts develop; the *practice* of religion (that is, a person's religious actions, such as prayer and church attendance) may call up a positive *attitude* toward religion.[28] Likewise, even begrudging acts of charity may intensify our charitable attitudes toward the needy. When we persuade someone, we reinforce or change both minds and behavior.

TARGETS OF PERSUASION

Figure 1.4 As the diagram illustrates, our actions or behaviors have their origins first in beliefs and then attitudes. Our actions, then, are a physical outgrowth of our mental processes.
Courtesy of Barbara Breaden

Does Persuasion Infringe on Others' Rights?
How Persuasion Differs from Force

In 2002, a *Wall Street Journal* writer was abducted in Pakistan, four months after the World Trade Center attacks of September 11, 2001. Political commentators concluded that Daniel Pearl, a high-profile United States citizen and a Jew, was an ideal prospect for a terrorist act that would gain international attention. In hostage situations such as that of Daniel Pearl, victims are held in isolation, their diet, daily regime, and access to information strictly controlled. It would not be atypical nor unforgivable for hostages to disavow their country or negotiate with their captors. When Daniel Pearl refused to do so, he was beheaded by his captors.

Not all captives prove so resilient. Kept in captivity and under-nourished, their value systems may crumble under the pressure of their captors' political indoctrination. British psychiatrist J.A.C. Brown in his fascinating study of **brainwashing** delineates the stages of this process:[29]

1. *assault upon identity*, where the captive is addressed as a number and captors deny the captive's occupation—as pilot, cook, teacher, doctor, and so on. In this stage, captives are "reduced to a state of infantile dependency" from loss of sleep, poor food, inability to attend to excretory needs, and irregular, disorienting interrogation.

2. *establishment of guilt*, where the captive must learn to feel responsible, to remove the blame from one's captors and place it upon oneself.

3. *self-betrayal*, where the captive isolates himself or herself by denouncing friends, family, colleagues, organizations, and all the society and standards of his or her former life.

4. *total conflict and basic fear*, where the captive experiences the terror of being annihilated as a person.

5. *leniency*, where small remission of this pressure causes the captive to grasp at the captors as saviors.

6. *final confession and resolution*, where the captive admits to real or invented acts against the captors and their system.

Brown points out, however, that once the captor relaxes repressive tactics, the captive reverts to a former identity and belief system. (See Chapter Seven for more on brainwashing.)

Take the 2002 case of Elizabeth Smart, abducted at age 14 from her home in Salt Lake City. Her retrospective recalls life as hostage. "Over the next nine months, Brian David Mitchell would rape me every day, sometimes multiple times a day, he would torture and brutalize me in ways that are impossible to imagine, starve, and manipulate me, like I was an animal,"[30] she wrote. She went on to explain that she would cope with her plight by thinking of her family and by drawing on her religious faith. Eventually she went into survival mode, doing what she was told to do, so that her captor unchained her, she was recognized in public, and her captors taken into custody. Although she obeyed her captors, Elizabeth Smart withstood attempted brainwashing. As J.A.C. Brown contended, *victims are not persuaded by brainwashing*; brainwashing is not an effective means of persuasion.

Considering Propaganda and False Information

If brainwashing is not an effective means of persuasion, what about propaganda? Rhetoric professors Garth Jowett and Victoria O'Donnell recognize that we associate propaganda with manipulation and disregard for truth or societal well being.[31] Historically, the term propaganda referred to propagation of the faith (*propaganda fide*), methodically spreading information to promote a cause or idea. But today propaganda is linked to concealing information and deliberately spreading disinformation to promote a political outcome.[32]

This dark side of propaganda emerged under the heading of *fake news* in the political climate of the United States 2016 election of President Donald Trump. Fake news was not a new phenomenon, but the label captured public attention in the lead-up to the election and beyond. What was meant by fake news? Because some people adopted the term to refer to any information contrary to their viewpoint, what was called "fake news" was not really false, but rejected information. According to *Merriam-Webster*, the concept of false news has existed since the dawn of journalism, and the precise words *fake news* can be found in US newspapers from the mid- to late nineteenth century.[33] For information that is false, as opposed to information that runs contrary to one's opinion, the University of Michigan Library proposes as a definition for fake news "those news stories that are false: the story itself is fabricated, with no verifiable facts, sources or quotes."[34]

That false stories spread in cyberspace with ever increasing speed has surely magnified the problem of false news. In fact, an MIT study on *Twitter* data between 2006 and 2017 found that while the top 1% of false news stories reached from 1,000 to 100,000 people, true information rarely diffused to more than 1,000 people.[35] That is, false news "spread farther, faster, deeper, and more broadly than the truth in all categories of information."[36] Moreover, "false news spreads . . . more broadly than the truth because humans, not robots, are more likely to spread it."[37]

Thus, even though the internet proliferates false information, we humans are not held harmless. It is human intervention that transforms information into **misinformation** (inadvertent falsehood without intent to mislead) or **disinformation** (deliberate spreading of false information to mislead or influence others), infusing it with propagandistic intent.[38] As MIT discovered with *Twitter*, so did *Facebook* users during the 2016 election cycle find rampant, shocking, often scurrilous stories masquerading as fact threaded throughout their daily news feeds. With a click, any user could choose to spread suspicious, blatantly false, or propagandistic information to millions of people. The prospect of easily swaying millions of voters doubtless encouraged the phenomenon as the election neared.

If false or misleading information is a type of propaganda, is it successful? Did the 2016 tidal wave of false and misleading information shape election results? Even those who deplored the election outcome recognized that such stories tended to further entrench voters in their already established political positions.[39] As an early 2017 Stanford study showed, US media consumers in 2016 tended to believe "ideologically aligned" stories (stories that they *wanted* to believe) including false information.[40] And the average US adult read and remembered an average of one or perhaps several "fake news" articles in the election period, with an impact of 0.02% points, far smaller than Donald Trump's margin of victory.[41] In the end, false information was not altogether persuasive.

Authentic Persuasion and Free Will

This brings us to a question: Is propaganda authentic persuasion? If by **propaganda** we mean distorting and manipulating facts to achieve a set outcome, the listener is not free to accept or reject the message on the basis of genuine information. Authentic persuasion allows the audience to make an informed and reasoned decision. Persuasion respects the listeners' choice, or free will, whereas propaganda does not.

Coercion, on the other hand, refers to force, restraint, pressure, or compulsion. Here the listener senses a veiled (or not so veiled) threat that prevents freely determined attitude change. In 2009, former Connecticut Senator Joseph Lieberman analyzed the political tactics of native Taliban rulers in Afghanistan. Rule under the Taliban brought insecurity, repudiation of human rights, and degraded physical and mental health to the Afghan people. Consequently, the public would not freely support their regime, and the Taliban resorted "to self-defeating tactics of cruelty and coercion."[42]

Notice the pattern: in the face of opposition, when persuasion doesn't work, try force. This reasoning presumes that force, coercion, will quell opposition, that people will accept the outcome. The fact is that they may be cowed into silence, but intellectual assent is another matter. As Steven Littlejohn and David Jabusch observe, "If someone pulls a gun on you and you hand over your money, your compliance is probably not a result of

In late 2017, President Donald Trump fulfilled a campaign pledge to recognize Jerusalem as the capital of Israel. The move angered many United Nations countries who supported Palestine's partial claim to the city, and 128 countries voted for a resolution to reject the US action.

Consequently, The US Ambassador to the United Nations, Nikki Haley, announced to those countries in opposition that "The United States . . . will remember it when we are called upon to once again make the world's largest contribution to the United Nations."[43]

Haley's move enraged the opposition still more. The Palestinian ambassador referred to the US pledge, to withhold money from countries it had previously aided, as blackmail. The Turkish Foreign Minister called it "intimidation," and asserted that "No honourable, dignified, country would bow down to this pressure."[44]

So . . .

1. Is it reasonable for the United States to withhold financial aid from countries who oppose them?

2. Would you suppose that countries supporting the US Jerusalem measure agree with the United States position?

3. Does the US policy announced by Haley—to hold opponents accountable for their votes—help to persuade United Nations member countries to support Jerusalem as Israel's capital?

persuasion."[45] Coercion is short-term and requires continual enforcement, whereas persuasion is durable. Later we will consider persuasive strategies and a speaker's ethical responsibilities, but for now we want to define what authentic persuasion is not. It is not an act of control, manipulation, violence, or force to curtail another's views. It is, rather, the invitation that another join our way of seeing things. But it is essential that the other be free to come along or to choose another route.

Is Persuasion Common to All Societies?

One of the earliest societies immersed in the practice of persuasion was the society of ancient Greece. Persuasion was particularly important to this democracy because in the Greek legal system, when accused of a crime and brought to court, a citizen would be expected to speak in his own defense. As Greek society matured, people were trained in public speaking and the art of *rhetoric* (or persuasive speech) so that they could be hired out as advocates for the accused. Speech schools sprang up as a sort of vocational training ground for these early trial lawyers.

On the other side of the globe, the Classical Chinese culture (c. 500–200 BCE) developed a tradition of persuasive discourse separate from but not unlike the emerging Western tradition. In ancient Chinese texts, the term *shui* referred to ingratiating discourse, a receiver-oriented rhetorical strategy used to lobby the current ruler. With *shui* as the overarching goal, the speaker sought to establish a relationship of trust and likeability with the listener.[46] Rhetorical scholars Sonja Foss and Cindy Griffin point out that since these ancient periods, Western theories of rhetoric often have stressed "the intent to change others,"[47] invoking superiority or dominance. In contrast, Eastern rhetoric, emphasizes mutuality and respect between communicators. As essayist Andrew Gilmore points out, for China and the rest of Asia, it is important that each party to persuasive communication "save face." For this reason, Asian speakers are likely to frame their preferred outcomes so that both speaker and listener are able to keep their "dignity and honor intact."[48]

In the societies of both Greek and Chinese rhetorical practice, *people* have agency; they are able to *act* within the society to bring about a result. This appears to be a prerequisite to the function of persuasion. That is, persuasive speech thrives in an environment of relative freedom, where speaking is not only possible, but it has its rewards.

 Since You Asked...

Question: Shouldn't I avoid rather than practice rhetoric? Isn't rhetoric simply emotional rubbish?

Answer: Partly in response to Protagoras, who claimed that he could make the weaker argument appear the stronger, the fourth-century BCE philosopher Plato attacked rhetoric's focus on opinion rather than absolute scientific knowledge.[49] When Plato's student, Aristotle, defined rhetoric as "the faculty of discovering the possible means of persuasion in reference to any subject whatever,"[50] he declared rhetoric ethically neutral. Its good or bad effects depend upon the speaker, not on the nature of the art.

Other scholars, such as Kenneth Burke, have added their own unique emphases. To Burke, rhetoric is the process by which groups transcend their differences and identify with one another. Burke considers rhetoric the process of bringing people into cooperation with one another through discourse.[51]

Contemporary rhetorician Sonja Foss defined rhetoric as "the use of human symbols to communicate." Rhetoric can persuade, but it also functions as an invitation to understanding.[52] Speaker and audience alike "contribute to the thinking about an issue so that everyone gains a greater understanding" of its subtlety and complexity. Both communicators offer ideas and compare diverse

(Continued)

perspectives.[53] Persuasion results from a transformation within each party consequent to this interaction.

At a 2012 conference at Oxford University, rhetorical scholar Sir Brian Vickers explored the status of rhetoric in the twenty-first century and defined rhetoric today as (1) a tool for analyzing persuasive works, (2) a body of theory for explaining social phenomena, and (3) a set of strategies for understanding political activity.[54] Vickers considers rhetoric an intellectual process, a way to *think about* persuasive messages rather than a tool for *creating* persuasive messages.

While the definitions of rhetoric diverge, often political figures dismiss rhetoric as showy, florid, or empty talk. The late *New York Times* columnist William Safire attributed this shift in meaning to anti-politician sentiments. The word rhetoric, "once a definition of rational argument . . . [developed] a newer sense of artificial eloquence—mere words."[55] Consequently, politicians have found they can gain favor with the public if they engage in "anti-rhetoric rhetoric."

Real estate magnate Donald Trump, as Republican presidential candidate in 2016, embarked on his own version of anti-rhetoric in asserting "I want to be myself." *New York Times* columnist Mark Thompson pointed out that this "tell it like it is," straight-talk violates "conventional wisdom about political speechifying." Donald Trump's blunt, erratic, and impromptu style reflected his rhetorical objective—authenticity.[56] Thompson observes that such anti-rhetoric is not new. "Authenticism" has resurfaced throughout history. Often it emerges in an antihero who pits "the experts" against "the people," stirring audiences to heated factionalism rather than rational acceptance, to fire up voter commitment.

However we define it, we can see that the study of rhetoric has come full circle. Just as Plato had his suspicions of rhetoric, so do people today. As in Aristotle's day, people influence people. Today when we study rhetoric, we continue to speak and to listen. We share information, analyze events, consider human motivations, and generate both understanding and argument, as a way to participate in issues that shape our lives.

The abolition of slavery in the United States was a reward for the abolitionists, like Frederick Douglass, who argued the cause for more than half a century. If American society had never protested slavery, what might have become of the slave system in the United States? Would the term *civil rights* have had any meaning? If freedom of speech were not built into the US system of government, and if speaking out earned only arrest, would its citizens want to perfect persuasive techniques? No, nor would this book have much practical value in a society without freedom of speech. As Jowett and O'Donnell observe in their compelling *Propaganda and Persuasion*,

"No major rhetorical theories have come from nations whose governments have been totalitarian."[57] Rhetorical scholar Edward Corbett adds

> One fact that emerges from a study of the history of rhetoric is that there is usually a resurgence of rhetoric during periods of social and political upheaval. Whenever the old order is passing away and the new order is marching—or stumbling—in, a loud, clear call goes up for the services of the person skilled in the use of spoken or written words.[58]

Jowett and O'Donnell point out that "Persuasion seeks voluntary change,"[59] and according to Kenneth Burke, we can persuade a person only insofar as that person is free.[60] As we move through this book we need to be mindful of the nature of persuasion as an act of communication dependent on and grounded in individual freedom.

The Canons of Rhetoric: Stages of Persuasive Speaking

We know that persuasion is a valuable, reasonable, and often necessary form of communication. We know that it both protects and depends upon the freedom of its listeners. So when and how do we *begin* speaking to persuade?

As ancient Greek and Roman rhetoricians developed their methods for teaching persuasive speechmaking, they devised five areas of focus, which became five speech preparation stages—the **canons**, or guiding precepts, of rhetoric. Figure 1.5 shows these five stages. The first canon of rhetoric, *invention*, looks at the grounds for persuasion: *controversies*. Here is where the speaker *thinks* about what is important, finds out more about issues surrounding a controversy, and considers the people—the audience—to be addressed. What approach will spark their attention, concern, and agreement? How can we anticipate and respond to their arguments against our position?

Once we have thought about the controversy and our audience, we turn to the second canon, *organization*, where we structure our thoughts into a coherent order and form. Once the structure of the speech makes sense, we can polish its *style*, refining word choice and creating verbal images that will engage the audience.

THE CANONS OF RHETORIC

Figure 1.5 The Stages of Persuasive Speaking. The five *canons* leading up to the speech include invention (thinking), organization, style (wording), memory, and delivery.
Courtesy of Barbara Breaden

To complete our preparation, while we continue to reflect on what we will say and rehearse it mentally to confirm both content and form in our minds, we draw on the canon of *memory*. Finally, we rehearse our message aloud to enhance fluency and experiment with adaptations to possible audience reactions during the speech *delivery*.

We will guide you through these canons in the pages to come, digressing at points along the way to consider other concerns. Can I adapt a basic speech for different settings and purposes? What do I have to do to critique a speaker intelligently? As we branch off, these canons will provide our basic persuasive toolkit.

In Summary

Persuasive speaking happens, and it is valuable to our own and other free societies. When we learn to persuade, we are empowered to act positively in our personal lives and cooperatively in the society we inhabit. We also become better able to defend ourselves against negative influence from others.

We consider persuasion the verbal act of attempting to influence others' beliefs, attitudes, and actions. To bring about positive change through persuasion, we must respect the free will of those who hear us speak. In so doing, we become responsible participants in local, national, and global communities.

Endnotes

[1] Bret Stephens, "The Dying Art of Disagreement," *New York Times*, 24 Sept. 2017, https://www.nytimes.com/2017/09/24/opinion/dying-art-of-disagreement.html?_r=0. Accessed 11 Nov. 2017.

[2] "Political Polarization in the American Public," *Pew Research Center*, 12 June 2014, http://www.people-press.org/2014/06/12/political-polarization-in-the-american-public/. Accessed 13 Nov. 2017.

[3] Joshua Greene. *Moral Tribes* Penguin Press, 2013, p. 67.

[4] Alexander Hamilton. "From Alexander Hamilton to Theodore Sedgwick, 10 July 1804," *Founders Online, National Archives*, 1 Feb. 2018, https://founders.archives.gov/documents/Hamilton/01-26-02-0001-0264. Accessed 2 Feb. 2018.

[5] Jason Willick. "Polarization is an Old American Story." *The Wall Street Journal*, 3 Feb. 2018, https://www.wsj.com/articles/polarization-is-an-old-american-story-1517613751. Accessed 3 Feb. 2018.

[6] Citizen Resource Center, U.S. Citizenship and Immigrations Services. "Citizenship Rights and Responsibilities," *Department of Homeland Security*, 8 Feb. 2018, https://www.uscis.gov/citizenship/learners/citizenship-rights-and-responsibilities.

⁷ Richard Goldstein, "Bill Bowerman, 88, Nike Co-Founder Dies," *New York Times*, December 27, 1999, 19 August 2014 <http://www.nytimes.com/1999/12/27/sports/bill-bowerman-88-nike-co-founder-dies.html>.

⁸ Jim Walsh, "Non-Proliferation, Persuasion, and Peace," *Philadelphia Enquirer*, reprinted by Belfer Center for Science and International Affairs, Kennedy School of Government, Harvard University, December 12, 2003, 19 August 2014 <http://belfercenter.ksg.harvard.edu/publication/1287/nonproliferation_persuasion_and_peace.html>.

⁹ Bower Aly, "The Contemporary Rhetoric of Politics and Statecraft," in *The Rhetoric of the People*, ed. Harold Barrett (Amsterdam: Editions Rodopi NV, 1974), 23.

¹⁰ H. E. Butler, trans. *The Insitutio Oratoria of Quintilian, vol. 1* (Cambridge, MA: Harvard University Press, 1980), 319.

¹¹ Ibid., 323.

¹² W. Lance Bennett, "Communication and Social Responsibility," *Quarterly Journal of Speech* 71 (1985): 259–88.

¹³ See Aristotle, *The Art of Rhetoric*, trans. John Henry Freese (Cambridge: Harvard, 1975), 3. As Aristotle begins his treatise, "Rhetoric is a counterpart of Dialectic."

¹⁴ George Packer, "The New Liberalism," *The New Yorker*, November 17, 2008, 87.

¹⁵ MacNeil/Lehrer Productions, *The Online NewsHour*, "Israeli PM: Tough Choices Ahead in Mideast Peace Process," November 27, 2007, 19 August 2014 <http://www.pbs.org/newshour/bb/middle_east/july-dec07/olmert_11-27.html>.

¹⁶ Josina M. Makau, *Reasoning and Communication: Thinking Critically About Arguments* (Belmont, CA: Wadsworth, 1990), 48.

¹⁷ Michael Osborn, "Communication Studies and the World Community," (Presentation at Linfield College, November 15, 1990), 2.

¹⁸ Senator Dianne Feinstein, "Welcoming Remarks," Inauguration Day, 2009, CNN, January 20, 2009.

¹⁹ John F. Kennedy was assassinated on Friday, 22 Nov. 1963.

²⁰ Lyndon B. Johnson. "The President's Thanksgiving Day Address to the Nation," 28 Nov. 1963. Gerhard Peters and John T. Woolley, *The American Presidency Project,* 1999–2017, 27 Nov. 2017, http://www.presidency.ucsb.edu/ws/?pid=25999.

²¹ For a solid discussion of these three factors, see Steven W. Littlejohn and David M. Jabusch, *Persuasive Transactions* (Glenview, IL: Scott-Foresman, 1987), 7. Some theorists will divide cognitions into beliefs, attitudes, and values. Our perspective accepts Fishbein's characterization of attitudes as evaluative.

²² B. F. Skinner, *Beyond Freedom and Dignity* (New York: Alfred A. Knopf, 1971), 92.

²³ Steven W. Littlejohn and Karen A. Foss, *Theories of Human Communication*, 9th ed. (Belmont, CA: Thomson-Wadsworth, 2008), 76.

²⁴ Garth S. Jowett and Victoria O'Donnell, *Propaganda and Persuasion*, 4th ed. (Thousand Oaks, CA: Sage, 2006), 32.

[25] Littlejohn, *Theories of Human Communication*, 75.

[26] Ibid., 79.

[27] Daniel J. O'Keefe, *Persuasion: Theory and Research*, 2nd ed. (Thousand Oaks, CA: Sage, 2002), 19.

[28] This is a complex subject and research is not conclusive on the precise relationship between attitudes and actions. A good discussion can be found in O'Keefe.

[29] J. A. C. Brown, *Techniques of Persuasion from Propaganda to Brainwashing* (Harmondsworth, Middlesex: Penguin, 1967), 279–82.

[30] Elizabeth Smart, *My Story* (New York: St. Martin's Press, 2013), 46.

[31] Jowett, 4–5.

[32] See, for example, *Cambridge Dictionaries Online*, "The Cambridge Dictionary of American English," (Cambridge University Press, 2008), 19 August 2014 <http://dictionary.cambridge.org/us/dictionary/american-english/propaganda?q=propaganda>; or *Dictionary.com, 2014*, 19 August 2014 <http://dictionary.reference.com/browse/propaganda>.

[33] "The Real Story of Fake News," Words We're Watching, *Merriam-Webster,* 4 Jan. 2018, https://www.merriam-webster.com/words-at-play/the-real-story-of-fake-news.

[34] "'Fake News,' Lies and Propaganda: How to Sort Fact from Fiction." *Research Guides, University of Michigan Library,* 21 Nov. 2017, http://guides.lib.umich.edu/fakenews. Accessed 4 Jan. 2018.

[35] Vosoghi, Soroush, et al. "The Spread of True and False News Online." *Science,* vol. 359, no. 6380, 2018, pp. 1146–51, http://science.sciencemag.org/content/359/6380/1146.full.

[36] Ibid.

[37] Ibid.

[38] University of Michigan Library, *op.cit.*

[39] See, for example, Matthew Yglesias. "Fake News is a Convenient Scapegoat, but the Big 2016 Problem was the Real News." *Vox Media*, 15 Dec. 2016, https://www.vox.com/policy-and-politics/2016/12/15/13955108/fake-news-2016. Accessed 4 Jan. 2018.

[40] Hunt Allcott and Matthew Gentzkow. "Social Media and Fake News in the 2016 Election." *Journal of Economic Perspectives*, vol. 31, no. 2, Spring 2017, p. 230, https://web.stanford.edu/~gentzkow/research/fakenews.pdf.

[41] Ibid, 232.

[42] Joseph Lieberman, "Afghanistan will be a Quagmire for Al Qaeda," *The Wall Street Journal*, February 6, 2009, A13.

[43] Colin Dwyer. "U.N. Votes Overwhelmingly to Condemn U.S. Decision on Jerusalem." *NPR*, 21 Dec. 2017, https://www.npr.org/sections/thetwo-way/2017/12/21/572565091/u-n-votes-overwhelmingly-to-condemn-trumps-jerusalem-decision.

[44] "U.N. Jerusalem Vote: U.S. Will Be Taking Names." *BBC News*, 20 Dec. 2017, http://www.bbc.com/news/world-middle-east-42424666. Accessed 4 Jan. 2018.

[45] Littlejohn, *Persuasive Transaction*, 7.

[46] Mary M. Garrett. "Classical Chinese Conceptions of Argumentation and Persuasion." *Argumentation and Advocacy*, vol. 29, Winter 1993, pp. 105–15.

[47] Sonja K. Foss and Cindy L. Griffin. "Beyond Persuasion: A Proposal for an Invitational Rhetoric." *Communication Monographs*, no. 62, March 1995, p. 3, http://www.sonjafoss.com/html/Foss21.pdf.

[48] Andrew Gilmore. "Romancing the Chinese Identity: Rhetorical Strategies Used to Facilitate Identification in the Handover of Hong Kong," reprinted in Sonja K. Foss, *Rhetorical Criticism: Exploration and Practice*. 5th ed., Waveland Press, 2017, 479.

[49] See, for instance, Plato, *Phaedrus*, trans. W. C. Helmbold and W. G. Rabinowitz (Indianapolis: Library of Liberal Arts, 1956).

[50] Aristotle, 15.

[51] Kenneth Burke, A *Rhetoric of Motives* (Berkeley: University of California Press, 1969), 22–23.

[52] Foss, 3–5.

[53] Foss and Griffin, 6.

[54] David A. Frank and Nicholas J. Crowe. "A Revival of Rhetoric at Oxford: A Report from the 2012 Oxford Medieval and Renaissance Studies Interactive Seminar." *Rhetoric Review*, vol. 33, no. 3, 10 July 2014, pp. 285–6, doi:10.1080/0735 0198.2014.917516.

[55] William Safire, "Ringing Rhetoric: The Return of Political Oratory," *The New York Times Magazine*, 19 August 1984, 25.

[56] Mark Thompson. "Trump and the Dark History of Straight Talk." *The New York Times*, 27 Aug. 2016, https://www.nytimes.com/2016/08/28/opinion/sunday/trump-and-the-dark-history-of-straight-talk.html. Accessed 13 Feb. 2018.

[57] Jowett, 42.

[58] Edward P. J. Corbett and Robert J. Connors, *Classical Rhetoric for the Modern Student*, 4th ed. (New York: Oxford University Press, 1999), 16.

[59] Jowett, 38.

[60] Kenneth Burke, *The Philosophy of Literary Form* (New York: Random House, 1957), 307 ff.

Theory into Practice

1. Consider the different occasions for persuasion you have had in your life over the past month. Which are your most common settings for persuasion?

2. Why does a democratic society depend on differences of opinion? Where in our cities and communities are such clashes desirable?

3. Using the definitions given in Chapter One, select a belief you or another person you know well holds to be true. Consider what attitudes derive from this belief. Does the belief ever result in action?

4. Pinpoint one belief you *think* is held by several members of your social group or academic peer group. Imagine three actions you might be able to persuade them to take based on their beliefs.

   EXAMPLE: Several co-workers believe that speech is a valuable skill for your company's employees. You might be able to persuade those in charge to schedule a speech workshop series at your job site.

Oral Practice

Locate an opinion piece in a blog or news source. In a brief presentation (two to three minutes), summarize its content for an appropriate audience, pinpointing the primary beliefs and attitudes expressed by the author.

Subject: _____

Summary of author's main points:

a. _____

b. _____

c. _____

Author's beliefs:

a. _____

b. _____

c. _____

Author's attitudes:

a. _____

b. _____

c. _____

Part Two

Invention: Preparing to Persuade

Chapter
2   Thinking about Controversies

To Make a Long Story Short...

One cannot speak well without knowledge and a clear sense of purpose.

Key Concepts

- Persuasive speeches are most effective when they address timely, significant, public controversies.
- Once the subject is fixed, the speaker should determine the speech's purpose.
- After the purpose, the speaker's task is to articulate a proposition: of fact, value, or policy.
- The proposition should be a single, literal, declarative sentence.
- Evidence is essential to a convincing persuasive speech, and primary evidence is better than secondary.
- Useful evidence is timely, sufficient, relevant, credible, and consistent with what we know to be true.

Key Terms

controversy	propositions of fact, value, and policy
purpose	evidence
proposition	primary source/secondary source

Considering Controversies and Issues
What Is Worth Arguing?

Often it is easier to avoid confrontation. You ignore antagonistic remarks, unjust criticisms, and narrow points of view. Argument aggravates stress, and stress can be fatiguing, if not hazardous to your health. Yet there are times when you cannot be silent. Maybe you are outraged over a racist remark. Socially, your exasperation with a friend's troublesome relationship unleashes a flood of warnings. Publicly you may hold a corrupt city councilor accountable. You decide, however reluctantly, to question what has been done or said and to propose an alternate view. So goes persuasion.

In interpersonal conversation, of course, you may persuade people about informal issues, such as where to go for the best pizza or which grocery chain has the lowest prices. Persuasive speeches are public in nature. You develop persuasive *speeches* when you want to confront *significant* problems. Most of us know the gut-level tension that accompanies a decision on whether or not to speak out. It's wise at this point to take a moment to consider whether a problem *needs* airing, whether it is *significant*. What makes a problem significant? It is one that has substantial consequences to you and to others.

In a persuasive speech, significance exists when a problem goes beyond personal concern. Significant problems are public, not personal or private. A decision on whether mustard or mayonnaise is better on a turkey sandwich is a personal preference, not a public problem. Parents' decisions to send their children to public or private school are personal, not public concerns.

Personal problems become public when they are cast into a public framework. If the choice between mustard or mayonnaise is a healthier choice for consumers or if private schools threaten the viability of public schools (or vice versa), the problem becomes pertinent for a persuasive speech.

To be worth arguing, a persuasive speech should address what are durable (or *timely*) and *relevant* issues, which is to say the problem should not be passé or fleeting. The question of whether to see the most recent Coen[1] film is neither a public nor a durable problem; whether the Coens' films show great artistry is both more public and more durable, since it considers an evaluation over time. The question of whether the people of Springfield should vote for Ballot Measure 8 is clearly public, but it is not timely or relevant if the election is past.

Finally, persuasion deals with the *controversial*. A **controversy**, a subject on which people disagree, is *the* catalyst for persuasion. If no one questions the truth or falsity of an issue, why argue it? Not many rational people would question that child abuse is wrong or that the judicial system is an essential branch of the United States government. If an audience concurs on a proposition, there is no need to persuade them to accept it. Move on.

When We Must Choose a Subject

You may be asked to speak on a subject of your own choosing. The first hurdle is to uncover a noteworthy controversy, applying the tests above: is it public, significant, timely, relevant, and controversial? Next, you could ask yourself the following questions:

1. *What subjects do I faithfully follow?* If you find you consistently read articles and editorials or take notice when a certain subject is discussed—be it smokers' rights, victims' rights, parenting, sustainable energy—that subject may suit you well for a speech.

2. *About which subjects do I always have something to say?* If you find you *cannot* be silent on certain issues, these may be worth considering in a speech.

3. *What controversies exist within my profession, area of study, or interests?* Educators may favor subjects dealing with educational reform, nurses with medical procedures, lawyers with mandatory sentencing, union members with wages, athletes and sports fans with sport topics, and students with education costs. Your speech subjects need simply be important to you and to the people you address.

> **Landing Your Subject**
>
> If you are an invited speaker or a student, try the *Speech Subject Brainstorm*, a worksheet on page 65, to help generate topic ideas for your speech.

The list below demonstrates the diversity of speech subjects across our public landscape at this writing:

Merit pay for teachers	Government health care
Pay equity between genders	Genetically modified foods
Sexual harassment	Gender identity
Children's screen time	Driving and cell phones
Steroids and athletes	Speed limits
Air traffic safety	Body image and eating disorders
Childhood obesity	The vegan diet

Marriage	Urban planning
Voting rights	College costs (including textbooks)
The two-party political system	School testing and failing schools
Chemotherapy	Automobile emissions standards
Art in education	Race and capital punishment
Wealth redistribution	Second-language study in early grades
Corruption (or unionized) college athletics	Climate change
Tax vouchers for private schools	Arts education
Physical education	Off-shore oil-drilling
Sanctuary cities	Sending jobs overseas
Solar energy	Human rights
Electric vehicles	Plastic surgery
Immigration reform	Campus speech codes
Identity theft	

New controversies emerge daily in every public arena, whether local, national, or global. By the time you read this, the topics above may have lost their relevance. You will need to look at *your* community and audience to determine what issues make a difference to *them*. By scanning your job or career goals, your social or political interests and family life, you will recognize controversies that you and your audiences care about. Most promising may be a speech that flows naturally from a story, perhaps from your own experience, that speaks to a salient controversy.

Focus on **Political Persuasion**

To Tip O'Neill, a United States Congressman from 1952 to 1987 and longtime Speaker of the House, all politics was local. But for twenty-first century audiences, all politics may be online, through wireless messaging, social media, and video posts, such as YouTube. As of May, 2017, the Pew Research Center found that 73% of urban dwellers and 63% or rural dwellers in the United States had access to wireless technology for public information,[2] suggesting that the American public's increased exposure to national and global issues may extend their interests beyond their personal—or local—lives.

Defining the Purpose

Every persuasive speech has at its root some particular purpose. As noted in Chapter One, the purpose may be to change audience beliefs, attitudes, or actions. The **purpose** or goal of the speech is the reason for the speech: it answers the question "Why am I giving this speech?" Another way to view the purpose is to ask, "What do I want from my audience?" Do I want them to be convinced? excited? angry? indignant? elated? determined? The speech goal can specify the state of mind or emotion the speaker wants to evoke in the audience. This becomes important when you deliver your speech as well.

Any subject may have a number of disparate purposes. If you want to question the policies of a school board on how they plan to teach human sexuality, your goal may be to have them consider alternatives to the current program, to resist modifying the program under pressure from certain groups, or to change the program's emphasis and approach altogether. In most cases, the more precisely you define your purpose or goal, the more clearly you will convey your message.

Look at three different subjects and see how each could be developed into very different speeches:

SUBJECT	PURPOSE
Legalizing marijuana initiative	To get people to vote for it
	To get people to vote against it
	To generate sympathy for it
Diversity quotas in higher education admission	To provoke skepticism
	To promote the value of diversity on campus
	To stimulate campus protests over affirmative action
Automobile emissions standards	To downplay the danger of emissions
	To urge more stringent standards
	To inspire people to buy hybrid and electric cars

By clarifying your purpose, you are making the speech more focused, hence more specific and vivid. You can more easily connect the speech to tangible audience concerns and values, so that you engage them. In the same way, a clear purpose can make you more confident by limiting what you need to cover in the speech. Your search for evidence becomes more direct, and your recall of speech content more secure. In short, with a clear purpose, you streamline your preparation as you amplify the speech's significance and impact.

Framing the Proposition

Whatever the setting or purpose, the most fundamental requirement of a meaningful act of persuasion is that it make sense. Presumably the speaker has a point to make. What is that point? In persuasion we call this central point the proposition. And no matter what the persuasive setting, no matter how formal or informal, the speaker will have a proposition, whether conscious or subconscious. The **proposition** is *the thesis statement of a persuasive speech*. We call it a proposition because with it we are *proposing* that the audience adopt a particular point of view or action. Just as the thesis of a speech or essay is the central idea, or the core point to be communicated, so the proposition distills into a single declarative statement what the persuader wants to tell the audience. You may reflect here that we often engage in informal persuasion without writing or even imagining a proposition. Agreed. But in a public persuasive speech, the speaker's and the audience's focus depends on the speaker taking pains to clearly, consciously articulate a proposition.

For the proposition to do its job (the job being to keep the purpose clear), it helps to follow a few guidelines:[3]

> *State the proposition as a sentence.* You learned early in your educational experience that a sentence is a complete thought. As the controlling idea for the speech, so should the proposition be a complete thought. Notice how the following statements do not express complete thoughts. We can test them by imagining walking up to someone on the street and making the statement. If it makes no sense as a stand-alone statement, chances are it is not a complete thought, as in the following examples.

> Taking action on climate change

> Punishment for substance-impaired drivers

> Marijuana legalization

> *Make sure the proposition is a single sentence.* See how the following propositions, because they contain more than one sentence, confuse the issues we want to discuss. With more than one main idea, the focus is obscured and diluted.

> American citizens should reduce their dependence on cars. They should recycle paper products, too.

> Drunk drivers should be more severely punished. We need to make our streets safe and protect our children.

> Marijuana will benefit cancer patients and it helps the economy.

Make the proposition a declarative statement. The proposition should not pose a question. As a persuader, you take a stand on the issue; you do not force the audience to speculate on where you stand. You can see how the following questions do not make clear the position of the speaker or what the speaker expects from the audience.

Does climate change endanger our quality of life?

Are substance-impaired drivers being punished too much or not enough?

Why is marijuana illegal?

State the proposition directly and literally rather than in figures of speech, slang, or emotional terms. In the following statements the language does not promote a rational analysis of the problem. The proposition does not need to be exciting or profound; the rest of the speech can accomplish that. The proposition needs simply to be clear.

The slothful and greedy energy hogs that depend exclusively on their cars for transportation are ravaging the environment by fanning the flames of global warming.

Drunk drivers are society's most treacherous thugs and should all be doing hard time.

The thugs who crucify potheads for victimless crimes are torching our judicial system.

Now see how these propositions might be reworded for clarity.

American drivers can reduce climate change by gradually reducing their automobâile dependence.

State legislators should enact stricter mandatory penalties for substance-impaired drivers.

By legalizing and taxing marijuana, we can restore declining funding for law enforcement.

A well stated proposition is no small hurdle for the persuasive speaker. It is the focus of the entire speech. It is this idea that the speaker wants the audience to remember if it remembers nothing else. This statement is the litmus test for speech content. Whatever supports the proposition stays in; the rest is tossed. The proposition keeps the audience and the speaker centered on a single point, and its proof (or not) determines whether audience conviction is won or lost.

Types of Propositions

As each offensive pattern in football calls for a particular line-up on the field, so does each kind of proposition call for an organization that fits its intent. Thus once you have worded the proposition, you need to determine what *kind* of proposition you have: a proposition of *fact*, *value*, or *policy*.

A **proposition of fact** is a statement asserting that something has existed (or happened), does exist, or will exist. It claims (*proposes*) a fact about the past, present, or future. The formula for a proposition of fact is *X is (was/ will be) so*. Look at some examples:

Republicans will win the next presidential election.

Homeowners' use of chemical weed killers pollutes the city water system.

Nuclear disarmament was the most important international issue of the twentieth century.

You may notice that we are not calling any of these statements indisputable facts or truths because we do not know for sure whether Republicans will win, that chemical weed killers enter the city water supply, and so on. This is what makes the statements *propositions* of fact rather than absolute facts. Depending on your level of knowledge, a proposition of fact is not immediately acceptable as a factual statement. If listeners know for certain the truth about each of these propositions, then the statements are not controversial. You would not need to persuade audiences about them, since a persuasive speech has as its subject a controversial issue. Rather, there is a degree of uncertainty about the statements in that they *are* controversial. *Propositions of fact, then, are disputable assertions of the existence or non-existence of something in the past, present, or future.*

A **proposition of value** states that a thing is good or bad, though it may not always use the terms *good* and *bad*. *A proposition of value offers an evaluation of an idea, policy, person, or thing.* This sort of proposition claims that something is beneficial or harmful, moral or immoral, effective or ineffective, right or wrong, just or unjust. The formula for a proposition of value is *X is good/ bad*. Here are some sample propositions of value:

The American Civil Liberties Union benefits American citizens.

The U.S. government is ineffective as a world police force.

The Electoral College is an unjust way to elect a president.

In each of these propositions you can find a value term: *benefit, ineffective, unjust*. The value term is inherently positive or negative, as you would not consider *ineffectiveness* a positive; it is a term that is itself negative. Likewise a *benefit* is inherently positive. Thus, when the proposition contains value terms, or terms that are inherently positive or negative, the proposition is a proposition of value.

When speakers propose value statements, they are attempting to persuade you that a value term genuinely applies. Value statements can seem biased or unreasonable to you, but this is their nature. The value speech claims, and attempts to prove, that in light of evidence, the stated evaluation is accurate.

The **proposition of policy** is really the easiest type of proposition to recognize. *The proposition of policy states that something should or should not be done or that a policy is necessary or unnecessary.* The formula for a proposition of policy is X *should/should not be done*. Consider these sample propositions of policy:

College and university annual tuition rate increases should be controlled by the states.

States should be required to comply with national immigration regulations.

The city of Riverside should build a rapid-transit system.

While a speech of fact or value seeks the audience's agreement, with a proposition of policy, the persuader is appealing to the audience to act or to support action.

Speeches of fact, also known as *forensic rhetoric*, are often found in the courtroom, where a judge or jury is persuaded to determine whether a crime occurred or, if it did, to rule on what the crime was and who committed it. Values speeches, or *epideictic rhetoric*, are speeches of praise and blame. Most often they exhort an audience to acknowledge and accept a common value framework, as you might hear at a graduation ceremony, where a speaker urges graduates to aspire to a moral and conscientious life. Eulogies are other common value speeches, where the dead are evaluated as having led praiseworthy lives. Abraham Lincoln's epideictic Gettysburg Address goes beyond evaluating lost lives. Lincoln mourns the fallen soldiers while upholding the United States' foundational values of liberty and equality as what the soldiers sought to preserve.

Fourscore and seven years ago, our fathers brought forth on this continent a new nation conceived in liberty and dedicated to the proposition that all men are created equal. Now we are engaged in a great Civil War, testing whether that nation, or any nation so conceived and so dedicated, can long endure.

One finds persuasion about policy, *deliberative rhetoric*, in legislative bodies, such as British Parliament, the United Nations, or the United States Congress. We will see in Chapter Six how each kind of proposition calls for a different kind of speech structure.

You can streamline your speech preparation by nailing down early a proposition that reflects accurately the *content* and *intent* of your persuasive speech. Once your proposition is set, the rest of your speech content will more easily fall into place.

Looking for and Using Evidence
Why Evidence?

Is there anyone who has not said of a speaker at one time or another, "He doesn't know what he's talking about?" And haven't we each spoken from ignorance once or twice in our life?

Evidence makes a difference to an audience. Aristotle, the Greek philosopher who first formalized systematic speech training,[4] pointed out that the speech *exists* for the audience. In essence *the audience is the end and object of the speech*. The audience is "the end" and "the object" because the speech is not for ourselves, but for the audience's enlightenment. If an audience finds itself ill informed because the speaker is *un*informed, its reaction may be disillusionment or worse: anger, outrage, or contempt for the speaker who deceived them. When you approach persuasion from a dialectical perspective (see Chapter One), your goal is not to browbeat your audience into a limited point of view but to apply good judgment.

Earlier we pointed out that persuasion depends on the free choice of its listeners. Disinformation or absence of information does not promote free choice. It thwarts the audience's ability to make a rational decision. The speaker becomes a barrier rather than a conduit for sound decision-making.

The human condition in the 21st century is to be perpetually flooded with information. A responsible speaker is expected more than ever to provide an audience with the tools for reaching an accurately informed conclusion on a controversy. The fundamental tool for establishing the validity of any position is **evidence**. *Evidence is any support offered to draw a conclusion or to substantiate that what we say is believable.* Debate scholar Austin Freeley calls evidence "the raw material of argumentation;" it consists of facts, opinions, and objects used to prove one's position.[5]

Where does a speaker find evidence? The easiest way to begin is to look at what you already know to be true. If, for instance, you have some *experience* with the subject, sharing that experience with the audience constitutes evidence. Suppose you have been playing for the past four years with a city softball league. During last summer's playoffs, it occurred to you that the teams had been improperly matched. Now at the next season's opening, you bring your observation before the Parks and Recreation District. You address their board meeting, and though no one on the board has played in the league, you have. You use your experience to support your point of view.

Just as experience adds believability to your views, so does the *knowledge* you already possess. In speaking to the Parks and Recreation board, you could refer to a league in a nearby community where a friend of yours plays softball. You consider their system fairer. Again you call upon evidence you already have—your own knowledge through your informed connections.

In the same way, you can consult with friends or relatives for their input on the subject. Whatever access you have to *informed opinions* or direct experience can serve as evidence for your speech.

Experience, prior knowledge, and informed opinions may suffice for evidence, but there may be times when an audience expects a higher quality of evidence. Listeners may demand information from a recognized authority on the subject. They may ask, for example, what the team sponsors thought of the tournament matching and why they had not complained. What of the coaches and umpires? Why had the board heard nothing about this inequity before your appearance? In this case, the audience is questioning your authority and requesting evidence to supplement your experience and knowledge. Where can you go for further support?

Primary versus Secondary Sources

Your most credible information will come from **primary sources**, *the evidence most directly or closely connected to the subject*. Primary sources include firsthand descriptions and records on the subject. For example, to analyze a bill being debated in Congress, a primary source would be the *Congressional Record*.[6] On the other hand, a **secondary source** might be an article in *The Washington Post* describing the debates or a *PBS NewsHour* interview with a congressional representative. The primary source is the actual record of the debates while the secondary source is a secondhand account of what was said, like the difference between friends' actual words and what someone said they said. The primary source gets closer to what actually took place. *The further removed our source is from the subject matter, the less valuable it is* *as evidence.* Look at some examples of primary and secondary evidence in the following table. It is true that in each of these cases, the source listed as "secondary" may have accurate information, but this is true only if that source has access to primary information in the first place.

PRIMARY	SECONDARY
An interview with the District Attorney	A local newspaper story on the operations of the District Attorney's office
The *Journal of the American Medical Association* on heart disease	An article in *Time* magazine about heart disease
The direct testimony of an earthquake victim	Hearsay about the condition of earthquake victims
The warden on local jail conditions	A city councilor on jail conditions

Sources of Evidence

The Foundational Value of Online Information

Thanks to the Internet, whatever your speech subject, as long as you have online access, you will have plentiful information. Online research has never been easier. If you're not convinced, let's consider a few reasons why:

1. *Online resources save time.* It is faster to scan internet source lists than to search for print materials.

2. *Online resources are often more up-to-date than hard copy sources.* Print sources take time to compose, print, and distribute. Online resources can be updated minute by minute.

3. *Online resources are comprehensive and precise.* One can search for information over thousands of sites or may limit the search to certain terms or time periods. At this writing, a Google search of *communication apprehension* returns about 11.4 million results in 0.33 seconds. If I specify the period between 2016 to 2018, I get 261,000 results in 0.51 seconds. Finally, by using Google Scholar, I can locate 4,440 results in 0.12 seconds. In less than one minute and only three searches, I have accessed thousands of primary sources.

There are drawbacks, of course, to online research. You may wind up with thousands of sites that are only tangentially related or not at all. The sites you locate may contain only recent information, thus overlooking a complete view of the controversy, or they may cost the user, such as with investment and financial research through Bloomberg Professional Services, where an individual or institution must pay a hefty fee for access.

Focus on **Evidence Selection**

While all people like to find information that supports their beliefs and attitudes, in 2004, the Pew Research Center found that in the United States people used the Internet not only to find information that bolstered their views, but people also researched candidates and issues that challenged their own positions.[7] More than a decade later, that inclination to explore both sides appeared threatened by the public's mistrust of the information they access.

In 2017, the Pew Center found that 38% of the US adult population were engaged, interested, and trusted sources of information, 13% wavered in their engagement and trust, and a full 49% were leery of information sources and likely to distrust them. The sources people trusted most were (1) local libraries and librarians, (2) healthcare providers, and (3) family and friends. National news organizations came in close to the bottom, and dead last were social media sites.[8]

Distrust of social media may be a sign of good judgment, but the Pew Center also found that the further removed information-seekers were from the source of information, the more dubious they became. For example, local and known sources were favored over national or institutional findings. This tendency varied among age groups and levels of education, though a lesson emerges. While primary sources are indeed the most objectively reliable, audiences often trust more the evidence grounded in personal connections and experts close to home or to their immediate realm of experience. The need for evidence does not disappear, but trust factors take center stage in persuasive evidence.

Online Resources: *Academic* Searches

If you are a student, your college or university will probably require a login with your student identification number to access specific fee-based databases in such research areas as government, law, medicine, science, and social science.

If you are not a student but live in a city with a college or university research library, you can probably acquire a user card that will give you access. One of the best-known and broader databases is *EBSCO Host Research Databases*. *EBSCO* is a Massachusetts-based reference source for academic research (spanning virtually every academic discipline), hospitals and medical institutions, businesses, and government institutions. Through *EBSCO*, you can read full text articles online through a subject or database search.

If you have a public library card, you may be able to find *EBSCO* services in your library, but the database available to you probably will include only the library's holdings. Such restrictions may limit your access to academic research, as well as government and institution-based search engines.

Aside from *EBSCO*, there are countless other databases particular to the school, business, or institution for which you are conducting research. The library or research department director will likely provide rudimentary information about where to begin.

General search engines, such as Google, have made inroads into academic searches with such search programs as Google Scholar, that can link you to databases like *EBSCO*, streamlining the process for locating academic research. However, you still need to have a database subscription to use this service. Google Scholar does publish federal and Supreme Court opinions and provide access to abstracts (summaries) of academic papers, while full articles may require an additional fee.[9]

Online Resources: *General* Searches

When we leave the world of academic research to rely on general search engines, we encounter two major hurdles. First, any person with internet access can easily suffer from information overload through any subject search. Second, because most internet findings are not scrutinized for accuracy, we bear the responsibility for their accuracy ourselves.

The trick to overcoming information overload is to structure your search to maximize results while limiting irrelevant sources. How do each of these search engines compare in meeting our need for evidence?

According to NetMarketShare, in December, 2017, the top four search engines (the only ones with whole-number percentages rather than fractions of percentages of users), include Google, Baidu, Bing, and Yahoo. Google outstrips its nearest competitor, Baidu, about 80% to 8%. Bing stands around 6% and Yahoo at 4% market share.[10] These rankings are continuously updated, but the trend is clear. Google reigns.

> **Google** (www.google.com) When it premiered in 1998, Google trumpeted itself as the world's largest search engine. Today, no one would dispute the claim. Google responses are listed in order of relevance according to the terms entered and most popular sites or page rank, but that is not the whole story.
>
> To improve the quality of search results, Google says it limits potential links to reduce spam. Further, they provide webmasters with website development tips that will produce more hits from you, the researcher. At this writing, Google has been called out for questionable nonneutral search practices. In one case, Yelp (a popular travel search site) complained to the Federal Trade

Commission (FTC) that Google was stealing its content. Eventually, "Google promised to make it easier for websites to opt out of automatic copying" according to Pulitzer Prize winning journalist, Charles Duhigg.[11] He went on to point out in a 2018 analysis of Google, that "almost 90 percent of the company's revenues derive from advertisements." Thus Google search results demote or refuse to display links to economic competitors, sites that use different, often more productive, search strategies. In 2012, the FTC found "instances in which Google seemed purposely to be privileging less useful information, substandard search results and suboptimal links," especially when the search included an economic component. Such findings suggest that researchers have good reason to try search engines other than Google.

Baidu (www.baidu.com) According to its company overview, Baidu serves the world's largest Internet population—731 million in 2016—and it is the highest ranked search engine in China. Awarded Silicon Valley funding in 2000, Baidu was the first Internet search engine to support advertising. The company touts as its distinctive feature their deep understanding of Chinese language and culture, which allows them "to tailor . . . search technology for . . . users' needs."[12] Since search results are predominately in Chinese, the site is most useful to those who live in China, do business with China, or speak Chinese. Although a first-rate search engine, Baidu's value is limited for non-Chinese language users.

Bing (www.bing.com) Microsoft's search engine, since 2009, has developed some appealing features aimed toward enhancing the visual experience in the search process. For example, their home page presents an image of the day and thumbprint media previews of newsworthy items. Yet as a search engine, it will produce a fraction of the results you would get from Google. The communication apprehension search we performed with Google returned more than six million results. Bing provides 32,800. Yet this resource touts the difference as an advantage. It does not call itself a search engine but a "decision engine." Bing questions what we would do with six million search results anyway. As Josh Briggs points out in *How Stuff Works*, Bing is designed to minimize the amount of junk you pull up when you perform a search and to help simplify tasks so you can make the most informed decision.[13] The Microsoft theory is that you want relevant and high-quality search results. Google results, they might say, are overwhelming. Bing search results are productive.

Figure 2.1 In 21st-century research, the computer is preeminent, print sources optional.

© CristinaMuraca/Shutterstock, Inc.

Yahoo! (www.yahoo.com) Yahoo! pre-dated Google (1994) in its development as a search engine.

Primary YAHOO! Shortcuts
Mail
News
Sports
Finance
Politics
Entertainment
Lifestyle

A distinctive Yahoo! feature is its search shortcuts. Across the horizontal navigation menu of the Yahoo! home page are a list of search subheadings. You can click on a subheading, such as *Finance*, and narrow your search to the next level of subheadings, such as *My Portfolio* or *Personal Finance*. If I click on *Personal Finance*, I can get to the next level, for instance, to *Fix my Finances*. By narrowing your search through shortcuts, you can reduce information overload and increase relevance in your results.

Keep in mind as you begin to research your subject that different search engines use different algorithms, yielding different results. Try to run a brief check of results by search engines against one another to discover the tool that leads you to your strongest evidence.

About *Wikipedia*

Wikipedia is in a different world altogether from the world of search engines. Who has not turned to *Wikipedia* to check the biography of a previously unknown political figure or entertainer? What's not to like? First of all, it's free and at this writing has versions in at least 299 different languages. Second, *Wikipedia* provides diverse perspectives on any entry, often including those of experts in the subject matter. Third, it provides a general disclaimer on what it is and is not,[14] the overarching disclaimer being that *Wikipedia* does not guarantee the validity of any of its information, the advantage of this being that at least they are telling the world the truth about content reliability on their site.

Since *Wikipedia* is straightforward about its shortcomings, you need to be aware of just how it works so you know what you have when you draw information from its pages. "The Five Pillars of *Wikipedia*"[15] outline its fundamental principles and *Wikipedia's* limitations as a resource:

- *Wikipedia* is an encyclopedia, intended to be reference-based as opposed to an open forum for personal opinion.

- *Wikipedia* strives to present a neutral point of view rather than advocating a single perspective.

- *Wikipedia* is free content, open to contributions from anyone, though not to copyrighted material.

- *Wikipedia* subscribes to a code of conduct that urges civility, consensus, and freedom from personal attacks.

- *Wikipedia* has no firm rules (aside from these pillars). Users are urged to be bold in submitting, editing and moving information.

Consequently, the content you uncover in *Wikipedia* may be useful for general background on a subject, but it is not entirely dependable. *Wikipedia* administrators urge users to rely for research purposes on articles that have been subject to substantial updating and revision and to be somewhat cautious of newer material that may contain significant misinformation not yet corrected.

Because posting information on the Internet is free and unregulated at this writing, the researcher needs to develop a critical eye in using any and all internet information, as illustrated in the guidelines on page 49.

First-Hand Sources

Getting information from people directly connected with an issue is a valuable and efficient strategy. When you think of sifting through reams of secondary source material for hours online or in the library, you may be stunned to find that you could have accomplished as much or more through a five-minute email or telephone call or a fifteen-minute interview.

Where should you begin to make contact: online, by telephone, by direct personal contact, or by handwritten communication? If *Wall Street Journal* writer Sarah Needleman is onto something, you should make a professional contact professionally. According to Needleman, youthful job hunters in the twenty-first century overuse the informal contact of e-mail or text-messaging by sending communiqués "hastily from their mobile phones," a move that "suggests an on-the-fly mentality" and infringes on the recipient's personal space.[16] According to one company president, job candidates should compose a thoughtful email rather than firing off a hurried message.

The same advice holds for those seeking information from experts. If a contact is made online, it should be through a thoughtful and professional e-mail. If you find there is a local or nearby agency specializing in some aspect of your subject (which can be found in a local newspaper, if one exists, or an online search for local resources), you can either call directly to question a person affiliated with the issue or arrange a time to interview the expert first-hand. If the contact is direct, proceed through formal telephone channels or through an appointment with a receptionist, requesting as brief a time frame as possible. Remember that many, if not most, people prefer to schedule a telephone interview, a video chat, or an email correspondence to a physical meet-up. In setting an interview time, it is customary to offer options.

The advantage of the interview, as opposed to spontaneous questioning, is that the authority will set aside time for the interviewer and may be more carefully prepared with supporting and helpful materials. You may be permitted to record the information, which naturally makes recall easier. You may be reluctant to attempt an interview, humbly assuming the interviewer is too busy to talk to you. This is rarely the case, however. Most experts love the chance to promote their cause in the form of an interview. You should offer to supply experts with a transcript of any quotations used for the speech, which will increase their confidence that they have been represented accurately.

Regardless of how interviewers acquire information, they must be prepared with a set of questions. These ought to be simple, direct, and well considered to elicit information of substance. The interviewer wants to learn from the interview; the better prepared the questions, the more useful the responses. Many textbooks in business and professional communication can assist the interviewer in setting the goal, structuring the interview, framing questions, and providing feedback within the interview.[17] When you do seek first-hand information for a persuasive speech, you will find it lends substance to the speech while bolstering your credibility.

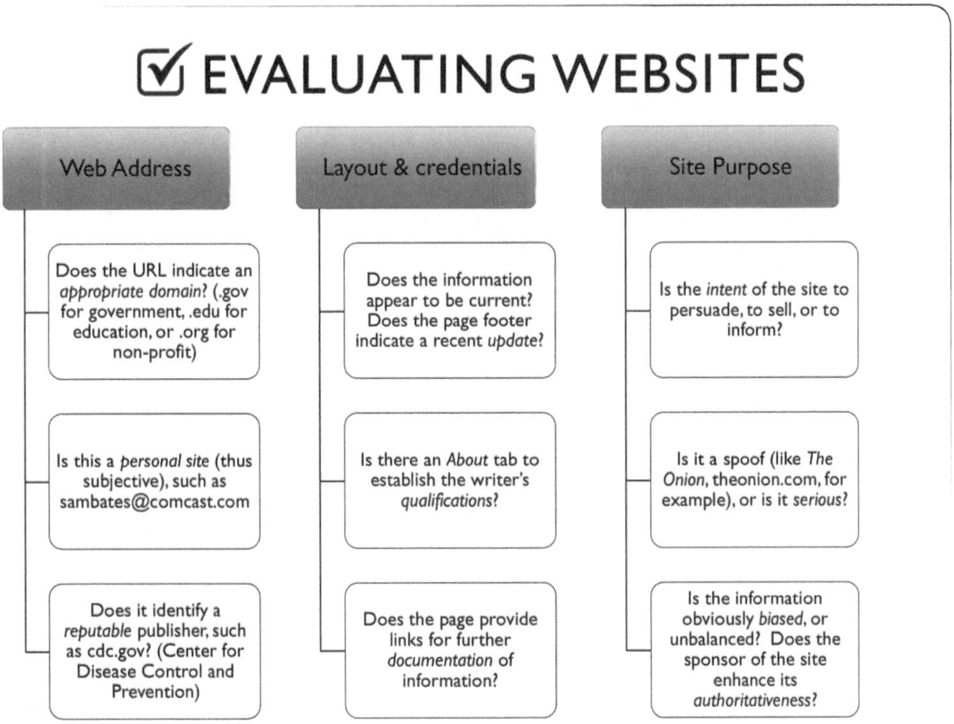

☑ EVALUATING WEBSITES

Web Address	Layout & credentials	Site Purpose
Does the URL indicate an *appropriate domain*? (.gov for government, .edu for education, or .org for non-profit)	Does the information appear to be current? Does the page footer indicate a recent *update*?	Is the *intent* of the site to persuade, to sell, or to inform?
Is this a *personal site* (thus subjective), such as sambates@comcast.com	Is there an *About* tab to establish the writer's *qualifications*?	Is it a spoof (like *The Onion*, theonion.com, for example), or is it *serious*?
Does it identify a *reputable* publisher, such as cdc.gov? (Center for Disease Control and Prevention)	Does the page provide links for further *documentation* of information?	Is the information obviously *biased*, or unbalanced? Does the sponsor of the site enhance its *authoritativeness*?

Figure 2.2

Diagram courtesy of Barbara Breaden. Checkmark © Standard Studio/Shutterstock.com

Types of Evidence

If a co-worker tells you your boss plans to quit in 30 days, do you respond as a critical thinker by asking, "How do you know?" We must assume that our audiences are just as critical. No matter what your claims, audience members wonder, "How do I know that what you say is true?" The sources you gather are a beginning, but what do you glean from them? As you sift through your sources, try to look for a variety of "proofs" for your claims.

Testimony

For a start, notice how effective speakers draw on experts to defend their positions, as did General Douglas MacArthur when he defended his conduct of the 1950s Korean War:

> Of the nations of the world, Korea alone, up to now, is the sole one which has risked its all against communism. The magnificence of the courage and fortitude of the Korean people defies description. They have chosen to risk death rather than slavery. Their last words to me were, "Don't scuttle the Pacific."

With this statement MacArthur supplies the evidence of the Koreans' own words to fortify his claims.

Another use of testimony can be seen in the comic strategy of *The Daily Show* on Comedy Central, when they use video montages to show politicians contradicting themselves. This artful use of testimony to criticize political figures, *The New York Times* observed, has been "widely imitated by 'real' news shows."[18]

Examples

Both real personal and hypothetical examples can help prove the plausibility of your claims. Classical rhetoric scholar Edward Corbett says, "The more facts or instances that are observed, the narrower will be the gap of the unknown that has to be leaped."[19] An argument for handgun control laws could cite the stretch of school shootings from Columbine High School in Colorado to Sandy Hook Elementary in Newtown, Connecticut to prove that handgun violence is out of control.

A hypothetical example could be used in place of a real example, although its impact might not be as dramatic:

> Suppose you are a thirteen-year-old in a stable and happy family. One night as you are all seated around the kitchen table playing Scrabble, a mentally deranged man climbs in through a bathroom window and shoots your parents as you dive for the telephone. Your parents die before emergency crews arrive, but you survive to battle for handgun control, maybe not for yourself, but for other adolescents who may by your efforts save their families.

This example does not pretend to be factual, but it is meant to stir audience belief in your cause. One caution: a speech that relies solely on hypothetical examples and no other substantial evidence will be dismissed as unbelievable, so choose your examples broadly but your hypotheticals sparingly.

Facts and Data
Considering "Facts" and Disinformation

After the January, 2017, inauguration of President Donald Trump, his press secretary disputed media reports of the inauguration crowd size. The media universally observed the crowds as significantly smaller for the Trump inauguration than for President Obama's 2009 inauguration. Kelly Anne Conway, a senior counselor on President Trump's staff, revisited the dispute with media personality, Chuck Todd, on *Meet the Press* the next day. Conway defended the press secretary, who, she said, used "alternative facts" in his observations. Todd jumped on her claim to assert that alternative facts are not facts, but falsehoods.

Our societies revolve around what we consider to be factual. Take, for example, the following claims.

> The homeless population in my city has tripled over four years.

> Digital technology has reduced our consumption of paper.

> My recycling service will not accept wet cardboard or plastic bags.

For practical purposes, we can accept these statements as true, or at least not egregiously incorrect. Nevertheless, we know that people of good will find a way to dispute statements such as these, just as they might differ on a defendant's guilt or innocence.

Most of us believe that facts do exist—wood comes from trees, the Earth revolves around the sun, and the universe changes. Audiences base their beliefs and disbeliefs on what they consider the "facts" of a case. However, as American philosopher Rebecca Newberger Goldstein observes, when audiences align with particular ideologies, they may assert or deny "facts" as "a pledge of allegiance to [their] political tribe." They accept or reject facts so as to defend their political identity, or "tribal banner."[20] This tribal loyalty often resists counterevidence. Objective fact as truth becomes suspect.[21]

With some issues, as with the issue of climate change—while the National Aeronautical and Space Administration (NASA), American Association for the Advancement of Science, the US National Academy of Science, a joint statement of international science academies and hundreds of additional science academies assert that greenhouse gases from human activity constitute the gravest threat to the Earth's climate[22]—there are people, including a small number of scientists, who do not subscribe to that conclusion. In the end, it is up to each individual's integrity to recognize when their assertions or denials are tribal banners, detached from reality. If our tribal loyalties consign us to promote political ends beyond what is true or factual, we are abandoning the common ground of facts as a basis for meaningful communication and civic action.

Just as we pointed out in Chapter 1 that ideologically aligned false information *is not persuasive* (see page 16) so if we want to persuade, we must seek for our evidence balanced and tested information, whether or not it conforms to our political identity. Let us consider facts not absolutes but information that is widely agreed upon—and not widely disputed—both in the realm of public and expert discourse. "Facts" can be found in many sources, particularly in those that strive to be objective, such as reputable encyclopedias, technical reports, professional journals, and public records, such as census data, court dockets, criminal records, or the *Congressional Record*.

Some facts are statistics. As useful as data can be in proving a speaker's point, statistics are notorious for their ability to be manipulated and distorted. Mark Twain once said "Facts are stubborn, but statistics are more pliable," and 18th-century British statesman George Canning was known to have said "I can prove anything by statistics, except the truth." A history professor once demonstrated with his data that Germany was victorious over Allied forces at the conclusion of World War II. Now his claim could be a matter of historical interpretation, but the professor was trying to show how easily you can disprove accepted conclusions through statistics.

Because public belief and opinion change according to new understanding and discoveries, what is fact for one audience may no longer be factual for another. As a persuasive speaker, then, you should *eliminate unsupported "facts" and offer additional, balanced support for what you consider factual.* This means, of course, that you may have to adjust or admit to what conflicts with your political leanings.

 Since You Asked...

> **Question:** I've been salmon fishing since I was six years old. With this much experience, why do I need to provide evidence for a speech about the Department of Fish and Wildlife's handling of salmon habitat?

Answer: This is an interesting question echoing Aristotle's own biases. He referred to *artistic proof* as the proof that comes from within oneself and one's reasoning, as opposed to *inartistic proof*, which comes from other sources—from education or evidence.[23] Even so, Aristotle and his followers (such as the Roman rhetoricians Cicero and Quintilian) encouraged *inartistic* proofs drawn from the orator's strong liberal education. And even though reference books were not available in ancient Greece and Rome, these writers recommended the use of written materials, such as contracts, for persuasive support.[24]

A persuader's prior experience and knowledge do provide a springboard for a persuasive case. The more credibility a speaker has (see Chapter Four), the less need for external evidence.[25] But for a number of reasons, experience and knowledge, like your knowledge of salmon fishing, are seldom enough. The believability of evidence depends on who is in the audience. A neutral or uninformed audience may be the most receptive; unformed opinions are the most malleable. But if the audience, too, has prior knowledge and experience on the subject, then the speaker's own evidence and personal experience will carry less weight, especially if they conflict with audience experience. On the other hand, if the speaker's credibility is moderate or unimpressive, evidence will boost it.

The catch is that the audience will accept only the evidence it believes and trusts. This sounds like circular reasoning, but the bottom line is that speakers should not choose sources indiscreetly; they should select sources believable to the audience.[26]

Once you have selected evidence, your task becomes to link that evidence with your persuasive intent. If you want to critique the Department of Fish and Wildlife in front of listeners sympathetic to the department, select sources *they* trust who agree with you on some point. This way you link what they favor with what you favor.

In the final analysis, you can risk omitting evidence if you want, but since it is difficult to know your audience's attitudes, knowledge, and experience, you probably will be more persuasive backing up what you know.

Facts and data drawn from your research can enhance the believability of a speech, but they need to be used with caution and integrity—taking care that they are representative and accurate—and subjected to the tests of evidence mentioned in the next section.

Finally, for your evidence to matter in your speech, you must cite it. Avoid the insolence of presenting others' findings as your own. Rather, attribute information to its source. By rightfully citing or attributing information, you build credibility as one who is well informed, and you sidestep the risk of later being found a plagiarist.

Evaluating Evidence

No doubt social media and our vast array of Internet sources have hardened the hearts of readers and listeners about what they can believe. In the world of instant research, we have come to respect the need to check facts. Consequently, since the Internet was in its infancy, we have seen a proliferation of fact-checking sources, beginning with *Snopes*,[27] a rumor-checking site founded in 1994. Decades later, fact-checking resources abound on the Internet, from the Tampa Bay Times' *PolitiFact*[28] to virtually every major newspaper and news outlet in the United States. Media distrust among

US Presidents is not a new phenomenon, but the election of President Donald Trump raised media skepticism to a new level, with the President regularly and aggressively denouncing certain reports as "fake news" (see Chapter 1). Pervading skepticism can serve as a caution that as speakers we need to demand high quality information.

It is important to recognize that we might be contributing to the existence of distorted and outright false information when we clamor for scandalous and shock-worthy stories. Because we are eager to disprove what displeases us and to accept what we agree with, we face perpetual temptation toward lax evidence evaluation. If we share reports for their shock value over their veracity, we promote disinformation and send the message that intentional inaccuracy is an acceptable media strategy. Moreover, our participation in disinformation intensifies rather than defusing polarization, that trend we consider destructive to democratic processes. The era in which we live is no time to indulge this temptation. Our most useful practice in evidence-seeking, then, is to take on the role of our staunchest critics when we evaluate information.

Questioning Your Evidence

Beginning with the five questions to ask of your evidence (see Figure 2.3) can guide you in assessing the information you find. Once you gain experience in the ways of research, these fundamental questions become ingrained; as a seasoned researcher, you develop a healthy skepticism.

Is the evidence relevant to the controversy? It is tempting to use every good story or impressive statistic that you uncover. The problem is that sometimes the information adds interest (at best) but nothing to help prove the proposition. Suppose you are giving a speech about colleges controlling corruption in their athletic programs. In your research you run across a story about a coach convicted of a misdemeanor unrelated to his coaching position. Tempting as it is to use the story for its shock value, the story has no direct bearing on your issue. In the long run, the evidence will make you out a scandal-bearer while it does nothing to help your case.

Is the evidence timely? Take a look at a cookbook from the 1940s or 1950s. What one considered wholesome in that time period was meat and potatoes, liberally doused with butter and gravy, with canned vegetables warmed to a slimy mass. You would not use one of these cookbooks today to represent a healthy diet. What we currently know about heart disease, cholesterol, and fat would render 1940s nutrition standards out-of-date. You need to determine if the time frame in which your evidence was recorded makes it inapplicable to the point you want to prove now. Any story, study, or statistic should be current enough for today's audience.

What is "current enough"? If we find that subsequent studies have disproved, contradicted, or raised serious questions about the validity of earlier information, we are better off without it. For instance, we cannot cite test scores from 1998 to show that the educational system of our country is failing in 2024. If current studies produce the same results, we must use the new, not the older ones.

On the other hand, sometimes older information is not only acceptable; it is also essential. A speaker who chronicles the history of archaic contraceptive methods (to prove that humankind will go through uncommon extremes to avoid having children) will not want to restrict research to the most current. Information from the past is necessary for proving the proposition. In short, the date of your evidence should be contemporary with the time frame it references.

Is the evidence sufficient? One study does not make a proof. This idea was vividly illustrated when in 1989 scientists at the University of Utah claimed they had found how to produce nuclear fusion in cold water, a discovery that would have provided a new and inexpensive source of abundant energy. When other scientists tried to replicate the first cold-water fusion test, they found that they could not; the first study was seriously flawed—not a breakthrough.[29]

Figure 2.3 A small but significant step in your preparation is to subject any piece of evidence you acquire to these five tests.
Courtesy of Barbara Breaden

Whether the speech deals with cold-water fusion, climate change, or the institution of marriage, you cannot substantiate your position by quoting two close friends. Likewise, any poll requires representative sampling from an adequately sized group. Although we mostly deplore the word "never," the speaker must be prudent in *never* relying on a single source. To be believed as a speaker, you need to test your information by holding it up to the light of comparative evidence.

Is the evidence accurate or consistent with what we know to be true? If you test your evidence for sufficiency, you will likely be testing it for accuracy or consistency as well. Inconsistent evidence might be a statistic indicating that the majority of adults show symptoms from Alzheimer's disease by the age of 40. We know that the phenomenon of Alzheimer's has reached alarming proportions in the elderly, but our experience tells us that Alzheimer's is not a widespread occurrence in forty-year-old adults.

Partisan politicians often question the consistency of their opponent's claims. An opponent opposed new taxes during the campaign but swiftly *imposed* new taxes once elected, for example. If evidence claims that the dangers of climate change are overstated, but goes on to say the dangers are well founded, the evidence is fundamentally inconsistent. If you find that evidence is insufficient to prove a point and is also inconsistent with what you know, certainly it will not augment the persuasiveness of your speech.

Is the source of evidence credible? We will address credibility later in this book, but for now let's say that credibility refers to a person's *believability*. Our evidence comes from one source or another; whatever the source, it must be perceived by the audience as believable.

Credibility depends on the *subject matter* addressed. Oprah Winfrey built her credibility over twenty-five years (1986–2011) as a talk show host. In 2018, she became the first black woman to receive the Golden Globe Cecil B. DeMille award, and accepted the award with a riveting speech about her improbable ascension from a childhood of poverty in Milwaukee, Wisconsin. In 1964, seeing a black man (the elegant actor Sidney Poitier) receive the DeMille award, fueled her confidence and inspiration to achieve success. She would surmount childhood abuse to become one of the wealthiest self-made women in America.[30] Her story after that speech stirred talk of Oprah as a potential US presidential candidate,[31] largely because she had spoken of what she knew. If Oprah had sounded off on subject she had not known so intimately, would the speech have resonated so loudly and far? Not likely. *The source of information, then, is more credible in the source's area of competence.*

Credibility is also *audience-related*. The pope, for instance, makes regular statements concerning faith and morals to the Roman Catholic faithful and pronouncements on other matters, such as economic injustice, to the world at large. There are some who will follow his words closely and seriously, others who will disregard the pope's statements, and still others who will despise his remarks as presumptuous impositions on independent thought. *The source's credibility depends on the audience being addressed.*

These examples refer to live sources. What of the printed word? Are some written sources more believable than others? The same rules hold for these. Some periodicals are believable on some subjects but not on others. *Wine Spectator* may provide useful information on wines of the world, but it will

---

ETHICS WATCH

It may happen that the more a persuader wants to attain an objective, the more she or he is willing to stretch the facts to obtain it. During the hard fought Democratic primaries leading up to the 2008 presidential election, Hillary Clinton and Barack Obama battled for their party's nomination. Clinton's lead in the campaign slipped away gradually throughout the spring of 2008. To establish with voters what she considered her superior experience in foreign affairs, Clinton delivered a speech depicting her experience as First Lady (in the presidency of Bill Clinton), when she and her daughter Chelsea landed in Bosnia, a political hotspot, dodging sniper fire when they exited their aircraft.

The problem with Hillary Clinton's story was that CBS examined and corrected her account on its news program, showing its inaccuracies frame by frame. Their report subsequently ran on *YouTube*, showing Clinton and her daughter descending calmly from the aircraft, greeting a small child who had brought them flowers, neither of the Clintons ducking, dodging, or running.[32]

Some commentators maintained that Clinton's faulty report, an example of evidence that is inconsistent with what we know, was a significant contributing factor in her eventual loss to Obama for the Democratic party nomination.[33]

The harsher lesson here is in the reputation that followed Hillary Clinton, (although not from just this episode) as untrustworthy when she ran as Democratic party candidate for President again in 2016. At this point she had had abundant foreign policy experience as Secretary of State, but the question of truthfulness re-emerged.

So consider . . .

1. Do audiences forgive a candidate's "creative" reporting of his or her history?

2. How might Clinton have used the Bosnia episode more credibly as foreign policy experience?

3. Is public scrutiny of political figures by journalists reasonable and necessary?

---

not enlighten us much on the subject of psychology. While *The National Review*, a conservative political magazine, is accepted by conservative readers, a more liberal audience will dismiss or ridicule its content. Likewise, some are captivated by an obscure but entertaining blog while others would never bother to read it much less lend it any credence.

Beyond the five questions to ask of your evidence, you will find that you need to investigate particular clues in your sources to detect false information, or what is sometimes popularly referred to as "fake news." Some of the evidence we have selected may not be simply less authoritative than other evidence; it may be spurious. There are sources that do not *fail* at being careful and thorough; they deliberately distort information. This is what we have called disinformation. Such material may contain untruths, invented stories, pieced together images, quotes, and news tidbits to create a false narrative. Your task as speaker is to subject suspicious information to careful examination of its elements, as shown in Figure 2.4.

Evidence, for all its usefulness, is best taken skeptically. If we fail to question evidence as we encounter it, we can be sure that our audience will hold us accountable.

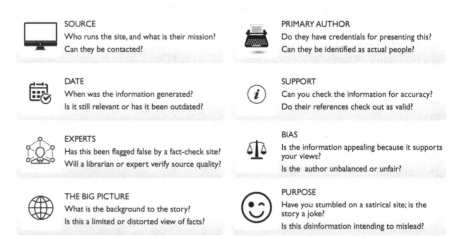

DETECTING FAKE NEWS

SOURCE
Who runs the site, and what is their mission?
Can they be contacted?

PRIMARY AUTHOR
Do they have credentials for presenting this?
Can they be identified as actual people?

DATE
When was the information generated?
Is it still relevant or has it been outdated?

SUPPORT
Can you check the information for accuracy?
Do their references check out as valid?

EXPERTS
Has this been flagged false by a fact-check site?
Will a librarian or expert verify source quality?

BIAS
Is the information appealing because it supports your views?
Is the author unbalanced or unfair?

THE BIG PICTURE
What is the background to the story?
Is this a limited or distorted view of facts?

PURPOSE
Have you stumbled on a satirical site; is the story a joke?
Is this *disinformation* intending to mislead?

Figure 2.4 This graphic applies to information that may not be web-based. To avoid disinformation, we need to make rigorous scrutiny of *all* evidence habitual—whether print, broadcast, *or* online.

Left images (top to bottom): © StockAppeal/Shutterstock.com, ©T. Lesia/Shutterstock.com, © MD. Delwar hossain/Shutterstock.com, © howcolour/Shutterstock.com, © M-O Vector/Shutterstock.com. Right images (top to bottom): © AZVector/Shutterstock.com, © CB studio/Shutterstock.com, © Magic Pasta/Shutterstock.com, © keksik97/Shutterstock.com

In Summary

The persuasive speech begins with ideas: ideas about what you want to say and ideas that you gather from sources outside yourself. Once you have located a public controversy that is both significant and durable, you must establish your focus—in the form of a purpose and a proposition. The proposition may be one of fact (asserting the plausibility that a thing is factual), value (evaluating a thing), or policy (proposing a plan of action).

From this point in your preparation, you gather evidence that teaches you about the controversy. Your evidence may be drawn from your own knowledge and experience, as well as from online and print references or other people. Whatever evidence you discover, you need to subject it to analysis, determining whether it is relevant, sufficient, timely, credible, and accurate. As a researcher, adopting the attitude of skeptic will lead you to more reliable, believable, and responsible information that serves your purpose and your audience, while it appeals to their better instincts.

Endnotes

[1] Joel and Ethan Coen, independent filmmakers known for their films *Fargo, No Country for Old Men, Inside Llewyn Davis, Unbroken,* and *Bridge of Spies,* to name a few, and winning Best Picture and Best Director Academy Awards in 2007.

[2] Andrew Perrin, "Digital gap between rural and nonrural America persists," FactTank, *Pew Research Center,* 19 May 2017, 15 January 2018 <http://www. pewresearch.org/fact-tank/2017/05/19/digital-gap-between-rural-and-nonrural-america-persists/> .

[3] There are many possible criteria for the proposition in persuasive speaking and debate. The ones listed here are generally agreed upon as fundamental to a useful proposition. See, for example, Austin J. Freeley, *Argumentation and Debate,* 12th ed. (Boston: Wadsworth Cengage Learning, 2009), 55–58.

[4] Aristotle, *The Art of Rhetoric,* trans. John Henry Freese (Cambridge: Harvard University Press, 1975), xxii. "The creator of a systematic and scientific 'Art of Rhetoric' is Aristotle."

[5] Freeley, 105.

[6] Congressional Record, GPO: U.S. Government Printing Office, 13 April 2014 < http://www.gpo.gov/fdsys/browse/collection.action?collectionCode=CREC>. This is a rich online primary source with links to official documents in all three branches of the United States government.

[7] John Horrigan. "The Internet and Democratic Debate." *Pew Internet and American Life Project,* 27 Oct. 2004, 3.

[8] John B. Horrigan. "How People Approach Facts and Information." Pew Research Center, 11 Sept. 2011, http://www.pewinternet.org/2017/09/11/how-people-approach-facts-and-information/. Accessed 27 Jan. 2018.

[9] "Search Tips." *Google Scholar*, 30 Jan. 2018, https://scholar.google.com/intl/en/scholar/help.html#coverage.

[10] Search Engine Market Share, *NetMarketShare*, Dec. 2017, https://netmarketshare.com/search-engine-market-share.aspx?options=%7B%22fil
ter%22%3A%7B%7D%2C%22dateLabel%22%3A%22Trend%22%2C%22attri
butes%22%3A%22share%22%2C%22group%22%3A%22searchEngine%22%
2C%22sort%22%3A%7B%22share%22%3A-1%7D%2C%22id%22%3A%22se
archEnginesDesktop%22%2C%22dateInterval%22%3A%22Monthly%22%2
C%22dateStart%22%3A%222017-01%22%2C%22dateEnd%22%3A%222017-
12%22%2C%22segments%22%3A%22-1000%22%7D. Accessed 28 Jan. 2018.

[11] Charles Duhigg. "The Case Against Google." *The New York Times Magazine*, 20 Feb. 2018, https://www.nytimes.com/2018/02/20/magazine/the-case-against-google.html.

[12] "Baidu's History." *Baidu*, 28 Jan. 2018, http://ir.baidu.com/phoenix.zhtml?c=188488&p=irol-homeprofile.

[13] Josh Briggs. "How Microsoft Bing Works." *How Stuff Works*, 3 Sept. 2009, https://computer.howstuffworks.com/internet/basics/microsoft-bing.htm. Accessed 28 Jan. 2018.

[14] "Wikipedia: General Disclaimer," *Wikipedia, The Free Encyclopedia*, 17 December 2015, 30 January 2018 <https://en.wikipedia.org/wiki/Wikipedia:General_disclaimer >.

[15] "Wikipedia: Five Pillars," *Wikipedia: The Free Encyclopedia*, 13 December 2017, 30 January 2018 <https://en.wikipedia.org/wiki/Wikipedia:Five_pillars >.

[16] Sarah E. Needleman, "Thx for the IView! I Wud ♥ to Work 4 U!!" *The Wall Street Journal Digital Network*, August 4, 2008, 19 August 2014 <http://online.wsj.com/news/articles/SB121729233758791783>.

[17] See, for example, Dan O'Hair, Gustav W. Friedrich, and Lynda D. Dixon, *Strategic Communication in Business and the Professions*, 6th ed. (Boston: Allyn & Bacon, 2007).

[18] Michiko Kakutani, "Is Jon Stewart the Most Trusted Man in America?" *New York Times*, August 17, 2008, 19 August 2014 <http://www.nytimes.com/2008/08/17/arts/television/17kaku.html?pagewanted=all&_r=0>.

[19] Edward P. J. Corbett and Robert J. Connors, *Classical Rhetoric for the Modern Student*, 4th ed. (New York: Oxford University Press, 1999), 61.

[20] Rebecca Newberger Goldstein. "Our Moment of Truth." *The Wall Street Journal*, C2. 17–18 Mar. 2018.

[21] Ibid.

[22] Susan Callery, editor, Earth Science Communications Team. "Scientific consensus: Earth's climate is warming." Global Climate Change, *NASA*, 19 Mar. 2018, https://climate.nasa.gov/scientific-consensus/. Accessed 19 Mar. 2018. This report includes the following caveat to the term *consensus*: "Technically, a 'consensus' is a general agreement of opinion, but the scientific method steers us away from this to an objective framework. In science, facts or observations are explained by a hypothesis (a statement of a possible explanation for some natural phenomenon), which can then be tested and retested until it is refuted (or disproved).

As scientists gather more observations, they will build off one explanation and add details to complete the picture. Eventually, a group of hypotheses might be integrated and generalized into a scientific theory, a scientifically acceptable general principle or body of principles offered to explain phenomena."

[23] Aristotle, 15. The Freese translation *uses artificial and inartificial* rather than *artistic* and *inartistic*, although these latter are more frequent in modern translations.

[24] Ibid.

[25] Gordon L. Dahnke and Glen W. Clatterbuck, eds. *Human Communication: Theory and Research* (Belmont, CA: Wadsworth, 1990), 245. These editors summarize nicely the classic studies by James McCroskey on the interaction of source credibility and evidence.

[26] Ibid.

[27] "About Snopes.com." *Snopes*, 8 Feb. 2018, https://www.snopes.com/about-snopes/.

[28] See http://www.politifact.com/.

[29] M. Browne, "Physicists Debunk Claim of a New Kind of Fusion," *New York Times*, May 3, 1989, 19 August 2014 <http://partners.nytimes.com/library/national/science/050399sci-cold-fusion.html>.

[30] Alix Langone. "Oprah Winfrey is Worth Nearly $3 Billion. Here's How She Made Her Money." *Money*, 9 Mar. 2018, http://time.com/money/5092809/oprah-winfrey-net-worth-billionaire/. Accessed 19 May 2018.

[31] "Read the full transcript of Oprah Winfrey's speech that fired Up the Golden Globes." *Los Angeles Times*, 7 Jan. 2018, http://www.latimes.com/entertainment/la-et-golden-globes-2018-live-updates-here-s-the-full-transcript-of-oprah-s-1515383639-htmlstory.html. Accessed 8 Feb. 2018.

[32] kitchenfloorconflict, "CBS Exposes Hillary Clinton Bosnia Trip," *YouTube*, March 24, 2008, 19 August 2014 <http://www.youtube.com/watch?v=8BfNqhV5hg4>.

[33] See, for example, Beth Fouhy, "Thirst for Change Trumped Clinton's Experience," *Fox News Digital Network*, June 4, 2008, 19 August 2014 <http://www.foxnews.com/wires/2008Jun04/0,4670,HowClintonLost,00.html>. After the 2008 election cycle, Hillary Clinton served as President Barack Obama's Secretary of State, logging nearly a million miles in her travel to more than one hundred countries in 306 days served, handily defusing further arguments concerning her lack of foreign affairs experience. Glenn Kessler, "Hillary Clinton's Overseas Diplomacy Versus Other Secretaries of State," *The Washington Post*, January 9, 2013, 14 April 2014 <http://www.washingtonpost.com/blogs/fact-checker/post/hillary-clintons-overseas-diplomacy-versus-other-secretaries-of-state/2013/01/08/742f46b2-59f3-11e2-9fa9-5fbdc9530eb9_blog.html>.

Theory into Practice

1. For practice in selecting appropriate speech subjects, critique the following speech subjects according to the criteria given in Chapter Two.
   a. whether to attend the Bach Festival this weekend
   b. whether Bounty or Viva paper towels are superior
   c. whether Steve Colbert should run for President
   d. whether the United States is spending appropriate amounts of money on national defense
   e. whether this year's consumer price index is higher or lower than last year's

2. With another person or group, brainstorm for potential speech purposes for the subjects listed on pages 33–34.

3. Critique the following propositions according to the criteria given in Chapter Two.
   a. Providing for our national defense
   b. How should the city increase downtown development?
   c. To care for the homeless in our community
   d. The U.S. Fish and Wildlife Service should rescind protection for the gray wolf.
   e. Our police department stinks and is letting our citizens rot to pamper local criminals.

4. Label which sort of proposition each of the following is:
   a. The Chicago Cubs are the best team in baseball's National League.
   b. The city should offer free parking to promote downtown businesses.
   c. Senator Elizabeth Warren is the only viable Democratic candidate for President in the next general election.
   d. The university should divert more of the athletic budget to general education programs.
   e. Reducing your driving speed will save fossil fuel consumption.

5. Suggest two likely sources of information for each of the propositions in number 3 above.

Speech Subject Brainstorm

If you have been asked to present a speech, and you are finding it difficult to land on a subject, try generating ideas with this worksheet. The idea is to list, for example, what jobs, books, sports issues, etc., interest you, then after reflection, enter a possible speech topic on the "Potential subject" line. You need not fill in the entire worksheet to locate a workable subject.

JOBS	BOOKS	STUDIES
_____	_____	_____
_____	_____	_____
_____	_____	_____
_____	_____	_____
Potential subject:	Potential subject:	Potential subject:
_____	_____	_____
CAREER/GOAL	**ORGANIZATIONS**	**SPORTS/HOBBIES**
_____	_____	_____
_____	_____	_____
_____	_____	_____
_____	_____	_____
Potential subject:	Potential subject:	Potential subject:
_____	_____	_____
ADMIRABLE PEOPLE	**POLITICAL ISSUES**	**TRAVEL**
_____	_____	_____
_____	_____	_____
_____	_____	_____
_____	_____	_____
Potential subject:	Potential subject:	Potential subject:
_____	_____	_____

Chapter 3
Discovering Arguments: Using the Common Topics

To Make a Long Story Short...

Beyond having information about a controversy, you need to discern pivotal issues within that controversy.

Key Concepts

- The process of invention helps the speaker identify issues and arguments to address in the speech.
- Critical thinking is essential to developing a convincing speech.
- The common topics are aids to critical thinking.
- The common topics help speakers find the central issues in the speech subject.
- The topics of definition, comparison, size, cause and effect, possible and impossible, and testimony and authority can be applied to any subject to uncover persuasive angles.
- The common topics assist memory and reveal counterarguments to a speaker's position.

Key Terms

invention
common topics
critical thinking

The Search for Ideas

As one sage has noted, "The human mind is an amazing organism. It starts working the minute we're born and never stops until we get up to speak in public." Rare are those among us who have never embarrassed themselves in speaking before a group. More often than not our embarrassment comes from failing to think before speaking.

Cicero, who lived in the first century BCE observed that first-rate speakers were rare because the speaker needs "knowledge of very many matters." Yes, you do have to know something to be able to speak well, but as rhetorical scholar Edward Corbett points out, the speaker "must either *have* something to say or *find* something to say."[1] Sometimes you have only a general interest in a subject. Sometimes you have ideas about the subject, but the ideas are vague or confused. You must somehow move from vagueness and confusion to clarity and certainty, to find worthy thoughts and merge them with well-chosen words. This requires venturing into the stage of **invention**, the process by which you discover ideas and arguments to support your position.

Once you have evidence, your question becomes what to do with it. The answer is that you develop (or *invent*) good reasons for your views. By *invention*, we do not mean that you "make up" speech material. Your ideas and reasons will come from what you know, from what others know, and from your own critical thinking powers. Research is helpful, but *thought* is essential to persuasive speech.

Critical Thinking and Persuasion

After more than twelve years of schooling, it would seem that you know how to think. But the problem of thinking has been a popular subject among educators at least since the 1983 publication of *A Nation at Risk*,[2] which threw light on the importance of "higher order thinking skills" in education. Even as early as 1906, William Sumner, a Yale professor of sociology, had defined critical thinking as

> The examination and test of propositions of any kind which are offered for acceptance, in order to find out whether they correspond to reality or not.[3]

By 1980, Dr. Richard Paul at Sonoma State University had established a Center for Critical Thinking, designed to resurrect the ancient Socratic tradition that may have launched Western critical thinking 2500 years ago. A fundamental component of Greek philosophy, Socrates' method consisted in asking probing questions before accepting any idea. As the Center for Critical Thinking describes it,

[Socrates] established the importance of seeking evidence, closely examining reasoning and assumptions, analyzing basic concepts, and tracing out implications not only of what is said but of what is done as well.[4]

The Center points out that in analyzing thinking, we need to identify the purpose of an assertion, the question at issue, and its point of view.

We could fast forward to the 21st century and to the Association of American Colleges and Universities' call for Essential Learning Outcomes, including intellectual and practical skills, such as critical and creative thinking,[5] but let's pull out a few of the Critical Thinking Center's terms. Critical thinking focuses on

- identifying the question at issue

- examining reasoning

- recognizing points of view

These factors are essential to the invention process in persuasive speech. As a critical thinker you ask questions of yourself; you recognize and examine issues and their supporting reasons without fearing what you might find. You are not enslaved by a particular point of view but seek to understand and compare all points of view. As you gain skill in analysis, you clarify your subject by choosing from a broad range of issues those aspects on which you want to focus, or more specifically on those issues central to the controversy. By thinking critically you begin to see the controversy clearly.

The Function of the Common Topics

Luckily we need not reinvent the wheel. The ancient speech teachers of Greece and Rome lay the groundwork for discovering issues when they developed the *common topics*. The **common topics** or *topoi* point out opposing perspectives or suggest questions we can address about any controversy to analyze it. Edward Corbett says that we can understand the topics better if we

think of the topics as 'suggesters,' or 'prompters,' or 'initiators,' as a 'checklist,' of ideas on some subject. . . by suggesting general strategies of development, they help to overcome inertia.[6]

The common topics are tailor-made for those who have, as Corbett observes, "(1) no ideas at all on a subject, (2) only a few ideas or not enough ideas to develop a subject adequately, or (3) a mass of vague, jumbled, inaccurate, or untenable ideas."[7] The common topics are *angles* on a subject—ways of looking at a subject.

To visualize the way the topics work, imagine that one clear summer night you are on a lonely country road, far from city lights. As you look into the deep, broad sky, your eyes take in an expanse of millions of stars. If you are fortunate to have a basic knowledge of astronomy, you are able to give your view of the universe some coherent form. You notice the many constellations and planets, the Big Dipper, Orion, and Mars. Your perspective gives the sky some sense and shape. If you had a telescope with which to explore the heavens, again you would no longer be quite general in your observations because your attention would be framed and focused.

In the Willamette National Forest in Oregon, there is an observatory at the mile-high McKenzie Pass. When you stand at the foot of the observatory, you see the sweep of the Cascade Mountain range, with a string of snow-capped peaks emerging from the thinly wooded volcanic rock. But when you climb up into the observatory, you enter a shelter with several pane-less windows. Looking through any one of these windows, your eyes land on a single peak: The North Sister or Black Butte, or Mount Jefferson. The observatory is constructed to focus your perspective on particular mountains. It provides a way of looking at the mountains.

Figure 3.1 Dee Wright Observatory, McKenzie Pass, Oregon. The viewing window frames various mountain peaks in the Cascade Range, providing a way of looking at the range, as common topics provide a way of looking at controversy.
©Natalia Bratslavsky/Shutterstock, Inc.

Applying the Common Topics	
Definition	What is the meaning of the subject? For example, what is the meaning of abortion? Is it taking innocent life or is it a right? of *drug testing*? of *stem cell research*? How would each of two different sides of the controversy define the subject?
Comparison	How does the situation disputed in our controversy compare to other similar (or dissimilar) situations? For example, is abortion like or unlike ethnic cleansing? Can drug testing be compared to Jews being required to wear self-identifying stars during the Holocaust? Note that those who favor a position will compare it to a positive; the opposed will compare it to a negative.
Size	Is the controversy large or small? of little or great concern? affecting few or many people? For example, how many people in the country have little or no health care? Is this an acceptable number?
Cause and Effect	What is the cause of the problem? or what are/will be the effects? For example, does abortion access reduce child abuse? Does stem cell research lead to solutions for presently "incurable" diseases?
Possible and Impossible	Is it possible to impose certain solutions? Is the current plan feasible? Is a solution affordable? (Is it possible to enforce laws against obscenity? Can we legislate morality?)
Testimony and Authority	What is the opinion of experts in the subject? (What do major research hospitals or the Congressional Budget Office say about the cost of health care, its affordability for the public at large?

This is precisely the way the common topics help us, though to look at controversies rather than at stars or mountains. When you apply the common topics, it is as if you are looking at a controversy through a telescope, an observatory window, or a camera. You are framing an aspect of the subject to make it understandable and approachable. You clarify what issues are important to you and which are most worth persuading an audience about.

If you already have a well-formed sense of what you want to say, or if you already know a good deal about the subject, the topical analysis may be less useful, though it may firm up your speech structure. Look over the following common topics with your own controversy in mind, considering if one or more topics focus on issues essential to your speech subject. Remember that the following topics[8] are potential issues or angles to be used in analyzing the subject of *any* persuasive speech.

Putting the Topics to Use

Example 1 Suppose you want to speak about a controversy that has been heating up in your workplace, a retail outlet for a store in a large grocery chain: whether to unionize. As a member of the negotiating team for the store, you are opposed to the union. How do you begin? What are some ways of looking at the subject? Let's try a few of the common topics to get you started.

Definition—What is a labor union? Since I oppose the union, I might want to define it in such a way that reveals the downside of a union. I could define a union as an organization to protect workers' rights *or* as an organization for undermining management goals in favor of employee demands. Which definition will serve my speech purpose best?

Comparison—To what can I compare a union shop? A perpetual battleground, with fixed animosity between managers and employees, a work scene of endless confrontation and "casualty"? Now if I favored the union, I might compare it to a security system in the home, a system that monitors and protects my daily existence.

Size—How many people are affected by the problem? How many employees are involved in the decision? What is the current breakdown of pro- and anti-union sentiment? What will be the impact on prices? Will the change affect the public at large?

Cause and Effect—What conditions have brought about the move to unionize? What will be the effect? Will it generate better working conditions or concessions on current working conditions? Is the cause of a union proposal disgruntled employees or agitation from other retail outlets? Do employees stand to benefit or lose by the change?

Possible and Impossible—Can the store generate enough votes to unionize? Will it be possible to preserve positive manager-employee relationships in a union shop?

Testimony and Authority—What do employees from unionized stores say about the quality of their work life after voting the union in? Has the move increased store productivity? Has it enhanced their benefits?

You can see that as we move through the common topics, we no longer have a formless and aimless jumble of thoughts on the subject. Suddenly our speech begins to take on direction and substance.

Example 2 Suppose you are concerned about a proposed bilingual education program—English and Spanish—throughout your school district. As a member of the school board, you want to speak in favor of the proposal. You have determined a proposition for what you want to say: "Our school district should adopt the proposed bilingual education program." How will the common topics help shape what you want to say?

Definition—What is *bilingual education*? Does it mean that all subjects will be taught in two languages all the time? Does it mean that some subjects would be taught in English and some in Spanish— or some in English part of the time and Spanish part of the time? You could address the purpose of bilingual education as well as its limitations. In this way the definition might say something about leveling the playing field for all students in the community, along with enriching diversity of perspectives and improving speaking and writing skills across both languages.

Comparison—You could compare your proposal to what has been done in other schools and how those programs have fared. You could compare bilingual education today to what early immigrants to the United States experienced in the education system, the appropriateness or inadequacy of public education in those times.

Size—How many students in our school district come from non-English linguistic backgrounds? How many speak Spanish at home? How many are native speakers of English? How much will the program cost? Can the school district afford it?

Possible and Impossible—Is it possible for students to learn in two different languages? Is it feasible to administer this program with a sufficient number of qualified teachers? Is it ethical or legal to require students to study in a language different from their native language?

Testimony and Authority—What do education experts have to say about this program? What do those who have studied in a bilingual school think of the program? What do authorities in the school offer as a justification for their proposal? Have the superintendants, principals, and teachers been polled for their opinions?

With this analysis you have gone from a general subject to a wealth of ideas for speech content. You begin to see that you will need certain kinds of evidence. Now you might return to your research, looking in particular for examples of bilingual programs, educators' opinions of bilingual education, and so on. The questions prompted by the topics give your research concrete direction. When you have established an appropriate organizational scheme for your speech (see Chapter Six), you will have arguments to plug into the content.

Example 3 How will a topical analysis proceed for a proposition of fact or value, a type of proposition often required by lawyers or engineers, for example? (Did X commit the crime? Will the bridge withstand certain stresses?) Let's say you are a lawyer and were attempting to establish

Since You Asked...

Question: Question: I already know what I want to say about my subject, so why would I need to go through an analysis involving the common topics?

Answer: Research in speech and communication studies indicates that the common topics *(topoi)* help speakers in ways other than in developing a speech's substance. First, speakers who use a topical system or are able to categorize information into common topics improve their memory of the issues.[9] Speakers who can remember the common topics (definition, comparison, and so on), will more easily recall arguments associated with each of the topics.

Besides improving memory, using the common topics provides more ideas on a subject than does generating ideas without using the common topics.[10] While our government and private agencies make use of think tanks, task forces, and brainstorming to solve problems, it is reasonable to conclude that by using the common topics, they would generate more ideas and more creative thought than by looking inward individually for ideas.

Another related finding shows that speakers are able to perceive counterarguments more readily when trained in using the topics.[11] The common topics, then, bring to light others' points of view and opposing positions.

You may know what you want to say, but effective speakers welcome rather than resist alternative explanations and approaches. The common topics will improve your memory, generate creative ideas, and recognize diverse perspectives—all useful social and professional skills.

that Sam Lewis did not murder Tony Mandrell (The proposition of fact would be that Sam did not murder Tony). You could draw on the following common topics:

> *Definition*—What is murder? Was the death a homicide, manslaughter, or an act of self-defense?
>
> *Testimony and Authority*—What did witnesses have to say? What were police findings at the scene of the crime?
>
> *Possible and Impossible*—Where was Lewis on the night in question? Would it have been possible for him to commit the murder?
>
> *Cause and Effect*—Did Lewis have any motive for killing Tony Mandrell? What was the nature of their relationship?

Example 4 As for a proposition of value, one might try to argue that chemical weed killers for the home lawn are harmful to our local water supply.

Definition—What are chemical weed killers? What is their composition? How do they work?

Comparison—How does the potency of chemical weed killers compare to other hazardous substances?

Possible and Impossible—Is it possible to control weeds without these products? Do organic weed control products produce satisfactory results? Can these chemicals be diverted from the water table?

Cause and Effect—What factors encourage weed growth? Why are we led to believe that chemical weed control is our only option? What is the effect of these products on the water table? other plants? insects? animals? humans?

Not every subject will lend itself to each of the common topics. Sometimes, for instance, the topic of definition will not help much in analyzing the controversy. If in Example 3 we had used the issue of *size* and asked "How large is Sam Lewis?" we might find that common topic useless. On the other hand, if we asked about Lewis' size relative to Mandrell's—or about the size of a weapon—the size issue does become relevant.

In your analysis, do not worry that you are using the topics incorrectly if a question seems silly or does not make sense for your subject. This happens. Still, if you experiment with each of the common topics, you will discover ways to word questions to enhance your analysis of the controversy.

Finally, as mentioned in Chapter Two, every subject has the potential to produce a multitude of different purposes and speeches. This illustrates the fact that most speech subjects—climate change, human rights, health care, and so on—are broad. To say all there is to say about a subject can take days, but a single speech occurs in a limited time frame, generally from a few minutes up to an hour. You can simplify the speech task by limiting your subject in the invention stage, and the common topics help to limit it. Focusing on three of the common topics would make for a substantial speech. Thus, the common topics help you discover what you want to say and limit your task by limiting your focus.

Speech Preparation Checklist

The topics, or *topoi*, take a formless subject and give it shape. This is not the form of the final speech, but a preliminary set of issues surrounding the controversy. Once you have a grip on these, you can fit them into an organizational scheme appropriate to your proposition (see Chapter Six).

All this preparation and still no speech! What does this tell us? That good speaking—persuasive speaking—takes more mental preparation than we think. At this point in your preparation, you can complete the worksheet at the end of Chapter Three to ensure your grasp of the following persuasive speech essentials:

Subject Have you found a subject that is controversial, public, significant, and durable? Write down your subject on the worksheet at the end of the chapter.

Proposition Do you have a proposition of fact, value, or policy that is a single declarative statement? Write out your proposition on the worksheet, and check to see that it meets the requirements of a sound proposition.

Evidence Have you found some information to support your position, evidence that is relevant, timely, sufficient, credible, and consistent with what is known? List at least five good sources of information on the worksheet, and begin to pinpoint examples, quotes, and other information you think you can use in your speech.

Issues (*common topics*) Have you narrowed your approach to the subject by zeroing in on at least three areas of argument? List on the worksheet three common topics you would like to cover in your speech. Write a question for each, following the examples in this chapter.

From this point on, you will move on in your preparation to discover

- how to enhance your *credibility* as a speaker;.
- the attitudes of your *audience*.
- *counterarguments* to your position and how to *refute* them.
- how to *organize* (or structure) the speech.
- ways to refine your *language* choices.
- techniques for an effective speech *delivery*.

In Summary

When you speak in public, you need to have something substantial to say. However, ideas do not always flow naturally. In fact they often come slowly, so that you come up short on content when called upon to speak. The common topics provide a way to discover core issues contained within your subject. By applying the topics of definition, comparison, size, cause and effect, possibility, and testimony to your speech subject, you will find an abundance of ideas worth exploring and airing.

Endnotes

[1] Edward P. J. Corbett and Robert J. Connors, *Classical Rhetoric for the Modern Student*, 4th ed. (New York: Oxford University Press, 1999), 85.

[2] National Commission on Excellence in Education, *A Nation at Risk: An Imperative for Educational Reform* (Washington, D.C.: U.S.Government Printing Office, 1983), 9.

[3] William Graham Sumner. *Folkways: A Study of the Sociological Importance of Usages, Manners, Customs, Mores, and Morals*. Ginn and Co., 1940, pp. 632–3.

[4] Richard Paul, "California Teacher Preparation for Instruction in Critical Thinking: Research Findings and Policy Recommendations: State of California, California Commission on Teacher Credentialing." Sacramento, CA, Mar. 1997. "A Brief History of Critical Thinking." *The Foundation for Critical Thinking*, 9 Feb. 2018, http://www.criticalthinking.org/pages/a-brief-history-of-the-idea-of-critical-thinking/408.

[5] "Liberal Education and America's Promise (LEAP)," *Association of American Colleges and Universities*, 2014, 14 April 2014 <http://www.aacu.org/leap/vision.cfm>.

[6] Corbett, 86.

[7] Ibid., 85.

[8] There are *many* more possible topics than these few, and Corbett includes an extensive selection in his study. These are easy for any prospective persuasive speaker both to understand and to apply. The common topics should not be confused with the traditional stock issues, which serve as organizational points for a debate. Here we are using the common topics as a means of analysis prior to a speech, as a way to break into a subject from many angles.

[9] W. F. Nelson, "Topoi: Functional in Human Recall," *Speech Monographs* 37 (1970): 121–26.

[10] W.F. Nelson, "Topoi: Evidence of Human Conceptual Behavior," *Philosophy and Rhetoric* 2 (1969): 1–11.

[11] J. L. Petelle and R. Maybee, "Items of Information Retrieved as a Function of Cue System and Topical Area," *Central States Speech Journal* 25 (1974): 190–97.

Theory into Practice

1. Generate a series of questions about the following or your own subjects using the common topics, such as definition, cause and effect, or size:
   a. illegal immigration
   b. fertility treatments
   c. emotional support animals on flights
   d. sign language for infants

2. Select an opinion piece from a news source. Generate a series of arguments for and against the position of the writer by using one of the common topics.

Speech Preparation Worksheet

Subject: _____

Proposition: _____

_____

Potential sources of evidence

1. _____

2. _____

3. _____

4. _____

5. _____

Potential Common Topics: Here write in selected common topics on each top line and provide a specific question prompted by each topic below.

1. *[Example: Definition]*_____

Question: _____

_____

2. *[Example: Possible or impossible]*_____

Question: _____

_____

3. *[Example: Testimony or authority]*_____

Question: _____

_____

Chapter 4

Discovering Arguments: Analyzing and Repairing Your Credibility

To Make a Long Story Short...

The foundation of persuasive effectiveness is a speaker's believability.

Key Concepts

- Credibility or *ethos* is a form of persuasive proof—that is, a way of proving your proposition.
- Audiences determine whether a speaker is credible; thus components of credibility are as variable as audiences.
- Credibility can be established, protected, and repaired over time.
- Identifying with the audience boosts a speaker's credibility.
- Ethical persuasion depends on establishing a climate of trust with the audience.
- Trust is grounded in a speaker's fundamental honesty.

Key Terms

ethos   invitational rhetoric
credibility   ethics
identification

Finding Arguments in *Ethos*
The Ancient View

Most of us strive for self-improvement sometime in our lives. This is a valuable impulse for a public speaker. As a speaker, you want to look acceptable, but you also want to impart an image that goes beyond the physical. If there were a single quality that you would like to possess as a speaker, what would it be?

You would be wise if the quality you chose were ***ethos***, the Greek term once commonly used to refer to the composite of a person's image and character. We hear more often today of the speaker's *credibility*.

Most of us do not think of credibility as a kind of argument or proof. Yet this chapter's heading suggests that the proof of your proposition resides within your credibility. Your credibility is evidence that what you say is believable. Likewise, those who disagree with your views may oppose them by questioning your credibility.

Aristotle, the Greek philosopher of 400 BCE who wrote of *ethos* in his *Rhetoric*, viewed *ethos* as a kind of tacit argument: the speaker "persuades by moral character when his speech is delivered in such a way as to render him worthy of confidence."[1] This ability of the speaker to communicate worthy character to the audience is, said the philosopher, *the most effective means of persuasive proof*. Think of it. One's credibility is more persuasive than a wealth of statistics, striking visual aids, or a quick tongue.

Modern studies of speech and communication bear Aristotle out—that *ethos*, or credibility, is the most reliable predictor of persuasive success.[2] Most often, contemporary scholars identify competence and trustworthiness (or character) as key traits in a speaker's credibility. Less frequently cited traits include dynamism (or charisma) and good will (or caring).[3]

Current events illustrate the validity of these findings. At the retirement of General Colin Powell, the popular Chairman of the Joint Chiefs of Staff under two presidents, it was said that "he won over many critics if not by persuasion, then by principles and charisma."[4]

The inverse of *ethos* as a predictor of persuasive success also holds true. Without *ethos*, persuasion falters. For example, in 2018, the widely acclaimed film producer, Harvey Weinstein, fell dramatically from the pinnacle of achievement and power in the film industry after a surge of accusations and lawsuits against him for sexual assault.[5] Whether or not he had lost effectiveness in his professional skill set, he had lost the trust of the industry that fueled it. As with credibility, so fell the man.

A Contemporary Perspective

Contemporary speech and communication theorists do not dispute Aristotle's conclusions, but they do present different angles on the nature of credibility. For instance, Steven Littlejohn and David Jabusch argue that credibility emerges not from speaker traits, but from the speaker's *relationship* with the audience.[6] It is easy to recognize the existence of speaker–audience relationships when you consider how persuasion works in judicial settings. Attorneys win cases on the basis of courtroom relationships—not their relationships with judges, who will be skeptical in any case, but their relationships with jury members, who view attorneys as personalities that reflect the legitimacy or fraudulence of the people they represent.[7]

Consider also the speaker's "story" as a way to establish credibility. The value of a story framework for a persuasive message supports the relational view of credibility. Through stories, presenters show their human side to audiences, establishing a relationship between speaker and listener. Presentation guru Nancy Duarte points out that the story "creates a bond between you and them, and opens them up to hear your ideas for change."[8]

This relational perspective on credibility is based on four speaker-audience bonds (see Figure 4.1):

- **Trust** Does the audience trust the speaker's words and reputation?

- **Identification** Do audience members perceive similarity between themselves and the speaker?

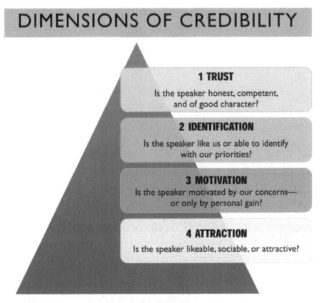

DIMENSIONS OF CREDIBILITY

1 TRUST
Is the speaker honest, competent, and of good character?

2 IDENTIFICATION
Is the speaker like us or able to identify with our priorities?

3 MOTIVATION
Is the speaker motivated by our concerns— or only by personal gain?

4 ATTRACTION
Is the speaker likeable, sociable, or attractive?

Figure 4.1 A relational view of speaker credibility.
Courtesy of Barbara Breaden

- **Motivation** Does the audience believe the speaker has worthy reasons, or motives, for speaking?

- **Attraction** Do audience members find the speaker attractive, friendly, or likeable?

You can predict greater credibility and persuasive success when the audience 1) trusts your competence and character, 2) feels you resemble them in some way, 3) accepts or admires your motives, and 4) finds your looks or personality appealing.

Credibility and Leadership

These credibility factors apply to persuasive situations beyond formal speeches. They are critical to organizational leadership, to business relationships, and to an institution's public relations. Often the driving force behind a young business's growth is a credible and even inspirational leader who motivates employees by the force of personality, competence, and integrity.

Apple, founded in 1976, was far from new when Steve Jobs returned to the helm in 1997 after a twelve-year absence. The company recognized Apple had lost its way without Jobs' vision and creativity.

On Jobs' return, Apple developed a new line of sleeker, more colorful computers. The company introduced the revolutionary iPod personal music player in 2001, eclipsed in 2007 by the iPhone, streamlining the features of a telephone, camera, music player, handheld computer, and more. Within ten years, Apple had sold 1.2 billion iPhones since its inception,[9] in spite of Steve Jobs' death in 2011 to pancreatic cancer, which put at risk Apple's seeming invincibility. Although profits soon wobbled, by 2017, Apple had more than regained its value, from generating $108 billion in 2011 to $224 billion in 2017,[10] and becoming the first company ever to be valued at more than one trillion dollars in August, 2018.

Since Jobs had been long gone by 2018, does this *disprove* the theory that a successful company requires a charismatic leader? Not exactly. As it turns out, Apple continues to invoke the persona of Steve Jobs long after his death. Jena McGregor reported in *The Washington Post* that at the 10-year anniversary of the iPhone launch, CEO Tim Cook kicked off Apple's dedication of a smashing new auditorium to Jobs' memory. But for his speech, Cook stood under a towering projected image of Steve Jobs, and the audience heard from the outset not Cook's, but *Jobs'* voice. When interviewed later about whether Cook felt overshadowed in this context, he brushed off the characterization.

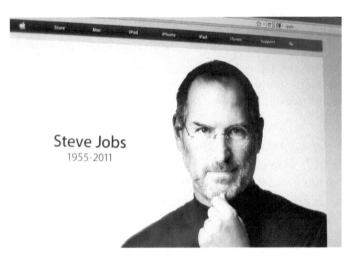

Figure 4.2 As this posting on Apple's home page suggests, Jobs became a symbol for Apple's credibility as expressed in his relentless pursuit of innovation, simplicity, and quality. With Jobs' death, the survival of those attributes was, for a time, uncertain.
© Annette Shaff/Shutterstock, Inc.

"I love hearing [Steve's] voice and his inspiring message, and it was only fitting that Steve should open his theater," Cook said, appearing emotional in the tribute. "Steve's spirit and timeless philosophy on life will always be the DNA of Apple."[11]

In essence, an extraordinarily credible leader can become legendary and a source of inspiration for generations, as we have witnessed in the durable reputations of past cultural heroes, such as First Lady Eleanor Roosevelt after her husband's death in 1945 or Martin Luther King after his assassination in 1968.

If personality can have a profound impact on credibility, what about similarity? We could use gender as an example. Are men more inclined to believe men and women to believe women? Or is one gender more trustworthy than another? Not so fast. Similarity as a credibility factor is more complex than one element. In fact, audiences evaluate both male and female speakers depending on the context of the communication as well as on the speaker's occupation, success, and power.[12]

Credibility and Power

Power can be tricky, certainly extending beyond any influence of gender on credibility. The meaning of power can range from energy to force. Consider Figure 4.3, the continuum of power, as shown on page 88.

You might say that power begins with energy or enthusiasm from a speaker. We can engage an audience with energetic power, whereas

Energy ▸ Ability ▸ Strength ▸ Authority ▸ Control ▸ Force

Figure 4.3 Power Continuum. As the perception of a speaker's power moves from energy to force, credibility recedes.

Courtesy of Barbara Breaden

moving to the right end of the continuum, perception of a speaker's forceful power can nullify the advantage of similarity between speaker and audience. If power is expressed as force against or over another, it separates speaker and audience in fundamental inequality. Because power emerges inadvertently in nonverbal factors, a *dominant* speaking style, can reflect forceful power, as in a loud, angry voice, aggressive gestures such as pointing, and unyielding eye contact. These characteristics tend to be less persuasive than a *social* style that reveals energetic power in a friendly look, open posture and lower-key, natural gestures.[13]

A speaker's high-power profile can undermine both credibility and persuasion. Through the lens of invitational rhetoric, Western rhetorical style reflects strategies that emphasize controlling or dominating listeners. When our ultimate aim appears to be the exercise of inordinate or forceful power, our words can impact listeners in the same way coercion does (see Chapter 1). Listener attitudes do not budge. That is, when audiences perceive that the speaker's intent is to control or manipulate them, they remain unmoved.

Speakers who apply the precepts of **invitational rhetoric** focus on understanding and appreciating the views of listeners, as an alternative to viewing credibility as power-centric. An invitational approach displays energy toward the message and a nonverbal demeanor of openness and respect rather than confrontation and control.[14] In all, an invitational speaking style aligns with three of Littlejohn and Jabusch's credibility factors. First, if a speaker exudes forceful or coercive power, the *motivation* factor suffers. Why? If a speaker wants to "win over" an audience while imposing a fixed viewpoint, the speaker's motives appear to be self-centered rather than other-oriented. Second, invitational rhetorical style enhances the *identification* factor, since with identification speakers and listeners reflect openness and mutual respect toward one another. Finally, this style optimizes the *attraction* factor, achieving likeability in its nonthreatening approach that recognizes equality between communicators.

We should remember that these principal dimensions of credibility—trust, identification, motivation, and attraction—are interrelated. For example, the adage of "When in Rome, do as the Romans do" demonstrates that if you want to be *trusted*, you must *identify* with people who differ from you. If you are a North American in Italy and insist on eating dinner at five o'clock in the evening, that fact that you do not fit in with cultural norms extends beyond the dinner table. Even within one's own cultural context, we trust and believe those who are like us in mundane ways. Consider the track record of Presidential food preferences in the United States.

President Ronald Reagan was known to love black jelly beans. George H. W. Bush hated broccoli but loved pork rinds, while both Bill Clinton and Donald Trump admitted a weakness for Big Macs. In the 2008 Presidential election, *The Boston Globe* published a voters' gastronomic guide to Republican candidate John McCain and Democratic candidate Barack Obama;[15] McCain favored pulled pork and Obama Mexican cuisine, especially guacamole, mole, and margaritas. You could call that a draw. According to credibility researchers, candidates' food preferences help to shape their public image.[16] In some cases, political handlers reveal food preferences to transfer connotations about foods to the political figure.[17] The strategy of associating specific foods with candidates, then, is to promote voter *identification* with the candidates, as if to say "Obama drinks margaritas; he can't be all bad."

The Variability of Credibility

We must remember, though, that credibility does not remain constant but reflects the variable mind of the audience. No speaker is all things to all people in all subjects. Who do you consider the most credible or believable public figures—Pope Francis? Tom Hanks? Oprah Winfrey? Melinda Gates? Jeff Bezos? Steve Colbert? Ellen DeGeneres? Matt Drudge? Of course, not all audiences would consider your favorite credible. Likewise, whatever you do to establish credibility with one audience, you cannot assume the credibility will be there the next time you speak. Credibility must be built speech after speech.

Credibility can be won by a single speech, as was Barack Obama's, at that time a virtual unknown, with his 2004 keynote address[18] to the Democratic National Convention. Credibility can be lost in a single stroke, as was Vice-President Dan Quayle's in the 1980s when, visiting an elementary school, he "corrected" a child's spelling of *potato* with *potatoe*, turning a correct spelling into an incorrect one. Credibility can be nearly irretrievable, as President Richard Nixon's seemed to be when he was forced to resign from the presidency in the wake of the Watergate Scandal in 1974. Even though Nixon would salvage some of his credibility as elder statesman before his death,[19] the association with scandal is the one that persists in public memory. George W. Bush left the presidency in 2009 with record low popularity. By 2013, with the opening of his presidential library and art collection (he had taken up painting after returning to his Texas ranch), he rebounded. From a low point of 23% in 2008, Bush's approval rating had jumped to 47%. Five months after the inauguration of President Donald Trump, Bush's approval ratings surged once more, up to 59%,[20] proving there is life after public disgrace.

Politicians seem to be more prone than others to suffering long-term damage to their credibility from simple mistakes. Social gaffes provoke one's social "degradation."[21] Degradation occurs when a public figure violates a social norm and fails to repair the breach of confidence. This is what occurred when an affair with Monica Lewinsky undermined President Bill Clinton's second-term popularity. As degradation occurs, the public reassess the offender's character. If the person does not attempt to address the breach, credibility plummets. Repeated efforts to replace the degradation with new evidence of better behavior (as in Bill Clinton's stalwart support for his wife, Hillary's, political life) in time can restore credibility, but the stain of degradation often remains.

The unpredictability of credibility is a frustrating lesson for anyone to learn. Teachers, for instance, after many years of practical experience and lively, successful classes, must never take for granted their students' responsiveness. Credibility is always critical to persuasiveness, but it can never be assumed. You are responsible both for building and maintaining it.

What Can We Do about Our *Ethos*?

We can summarize the findings of both modern and ancient writers by applying their advice to the speech preparation process. Here are some practical suggestions:

1. *You can be more persuasive if you make clear your good intentions.* As you prepare to speak, reflect on your motives as a check against self-seeking and the *appearance* of ulterior motives. If, as a nurse, you tried to persuade an audience of physicians that nurses are ill-treated and underpaid, you would surely be suspected of ulterior motives, no matter how justifiable your cause. If you suggested instead that a certain group of nurses is underpaid—and that that group does not include you—you can hardly be accused of selfish intentions. Even when you do have to persuade an audience on an issue you are involved in, if you can detach yourself from the outcome, can keep your credibility intact.

   Second, recall the continuum of power. Review your use of language to ensure you demonstrate competence rather than dominance. If an audience perceives that you are asserting coercive power, your credibility will suffer. Language that is intense, concise, and clear boosts credibility, while hedging, hesitancy and repeated qualifiers convey evasion or incompetence. In favoring the language of competence, as opposed to power or aggression, you can limit audience uneasiness about your motives for speaking. What if a speaker has legitimate power, as in a position of authority over others? The same credibility issues arise. While an audience may respect competence borne of authority, that same audience may be put off when a speaker asserts manipulative or coercive power over them. On the other hand, if a speaker with legitimate power urges an audience to favor a direction that will benefit them and others, the speaker's credibility can be enhanced rather than diminished.[22]

Whether a speaker has expert, legitimate, or coercive influence, rhetorical or political power can become addictive.[23] Consider those political figures who run for re-election over several decades. Those with power seek to extend their power.[24] In a cycle of tyranny, perpetual power grabs lead to resentment among the powerless. The perilous inebriation of power is a shortcut to credibility degradation from which speakers seldom recover. It is perhaps the most dangerous trap for a speaker, for it reveals the speaker's opportunistic motives and suspicious trustworthiness.

2. *You can be more persuasive if you are trustworthy and your character is beyond reproach.* This sounds a little like the Scout Law, but there is some sense in the observation that we will have less to excuse ourselves for if we try in our words and actions to be trustworthy, loyal, helpful, courteous, and brave. The people of the United States take honesty seriously, whether they live up to this ideal or not. When one lies about important information in an interpersonal relationship, the relationship is more likely to be terminated.[25] Not surprisingly, then,

Figure 4.4 Into his second decade of the Russian Presidency, Vladimir Putin has adopted a more open and invitational style of gestures, in contrast with Moscow Mayor Yuri Luzhkov's high-power style of control and dominance.

Left: © Frederic Legrand - COMEO/Shutterstock.com; right: © De Visu/Shutterstock.com

audiences typically seek nonverbal evidence, such as eye contact, as a means of verifying a speaker's competence and honesty.[26]

We sometimes make the mistake of trying to conceal bad behavior (such as sexual harrassment), while continuing to engage in it, on the assumption that no one will notice. Public figures who bat away charges of unethical—or illegal—conduct eventually face the voters once again, or an ethics panel, or jail. If we want to *appear* "clean," we are safest if we *remain* clean, or as St. Teresa of Avila, founder of the order of Discalced Carmelite nuns, wrote, "However enclosed you are, never think that the good you do or evil you endure will remain a secret."[27]

Naturally, a critical aspect of trust is belief in a speaker's competence on the subject. We build competence first by being informed about the subject, second in being prepared to speak, and third by providing reliable and authoritative information within our speech.

3. *You will be more persuasive if you are friendly and respectful with your audience.* You don't have to act unnaturally gregarious, but you should try to learn about the hopes and fears of your audience before trying to change their minds. This is not formal audience analysis; it is instead a genuine desire to understand the inner workings of the people you address—to develop a true and lively sympathy for their concerns. You can imagine their lives, their problems and their dreams. When you can put yourself in their shoes, your respect and concern for them cannot help but surface in the speech.

Another way you can treat the audience with respect is in your speech preparation; you can prepare thoroughly and dress as you would for an important event, like a job interview or an appointment with an important client. Negligence in your physical presence can translate into indifference toward the audience. Yet your appearance and dress must be true to our own best style. Peggy Noonan, President Ronald Reagan's speechwriter tried to encourage the President to take off his coat and roll up his sleeves for an address to the nation, but Reagan's Communications Director Richard Darman protested that when Reagan was *relaxed* he was sitting at his desk, his tie neatly knotted, his collar unloosened, his sleeves never rolled. "He is fastidious," Darman told Noonan. "Your directions are not pertinent to his style."[28]

For some, a professional appearance comes naturally; for some, it takes more forethought. There is no need to put off the audience with overdone dress, and you will want both apparel and appearance to correspond with the occasion. Ordinarily, dress is an easy matter to attend to, so it makes no sense to risk low credibility with careless or contextually inappropriate physical appearance.

4. *You can be more persuasive if you can demonstrate your similarity to the audience.* One of the United States' founders, Gouverneur Morris, told a story about how once in France at the time of the French Revolution, he was accosted as an aristocrat. In self-defense Morris removed his peg leg and, waving it in the air, shouted that he, too, had fought for independence in America. The French revolutionaries cheered him and let him go.[29] The well-bred Morris had played down his differences and demonstrated his likeness to them.

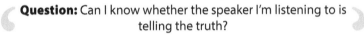

Since You Asked...

> **Question:** Can I know whether the speaker I'm listening to is telling the truth?

Answer: Your best defense against the unscrupulous is to be informed. If you are not, you can become so by asking questions, doing some research on your own, and thinking critically about the speaker's proposals. (See Chapter Twelve.)

You also can examine the speaker's nonverbal behavior. Nonverbal cues to deception reside in the speaker's leg and foot movement (perhaps one source of the term *shifty*), facial adjustments, changes in posture, and message length.[30] The more movement, the more likely your perception that you are being deceived. Moreover, liars demonstrate greater vocal nervousness, more non-fluencies (such as "um, uh" and stammering) and a more rapid speaking rate.[31] You will probably take these non-fluencies as indicators that you are not getting the whole truth. Naturally your perceptions can be inaccurate; a speaker may shift because of a bad back, stammer from apprehension about speaking, and talk fast just because that comes naturally. Still your perceptions will be stubborn.

The trouble is that the better the liar, the more adept at concealing nonverbal cues to deception. Good liars exhibit fewer gestural cues, although vocal nervousness remains.[32] But if the speaker *is* lying, know that deception is easier for speakers to maintain over a short time than over lengthy periods.[33] Nonverbal control wears thin. In any case, do not be reluctant to submit the speaker to extended questioning, just as in the courtroom cross-examiners will wear down a witness through repeated questioning until the truth comes out.

While you do want to establish yourself as competent, you don't want to appear so distant that you alienate your audience by seeming too remote. As contemporary rhetorician Kenneth Burke has pointed out, persuasion depends largely on your ability to achieve **identification** with your audience—that is, to demonstrate to them that you and they have similar interests at heart. Burke explains,

You persuade a man only insofar as you talk his language by speech, gesture, tonality, order, image, attitude, idea, *identifying* your ways with his.[34]

As a speaker, you can point out experiences you have had in common with your audience, or you can indicate your own similar fears and hopes, thus *identifying* with them. Senator Joe Biden as 2008 Democratic nominee for Vice-President of the United States accomplished this in his speech before the 2008 Democratic National Convention, when he told his national audience of "regular" people,

> When I was not as well-dressed as the other kids, [my mother would] look at me and say, "Joey, oh, you're so handsome, honey, you're so handsome." And when I got—when I got knocked down by guys bigger than me—and this is the God's truth—she sent me back out and said, "Bloody their nose so you can walk down the street the next day." And that's what I did.[35]

Former New York City Mayor Rudy Giuliani in a stirring address to the United Nations following the 2001 destruction of the World Trade Center in New York City, expressed identification with representatives of the many countries present:

> The response of many of your nations—your leaders and people— spontaneously demonstrating in the days after the attack your support for New York and America, and your understanding of what needs to be done to remove the threat of terrorism, gives us great, great hope that we will prevail. The strength of America's response, please understand, flows from the principles upon which we stand.
>
> Americans are not a single ethnic group.
>
> Americans are not of one race or one religion.
>
> Americans emerge from all your nations. . . .
>
> There is no nation, and no city, in the history of the world that has seen more immigrants, in less time, than America. People continue to come here in large numbers to seek freedom, opportunity, decency, and civility.
>
> Each of your nations—I am certain—has contributed citizens to the United States and to New York. I believe I can take every one of you someplace in New York City, where you can find someone from your country, someone from your village or town, that speaks your language and practices your religion. In each of your lands there are

many who are Americans in spirit, by virtue of their commitment to our shared principles.[36]

Audiences love the speaker who understands them not only in words but in experience. But you must go beyond thinking or feeling this identification; you must *express* identification for it to be known.

Ethical Considerations for the Persuasive Speaker

You can be pro-active in revealing your most credible self to your audience or you can *act* credible to craft an image that improves upon reality, which is, of course, a falsification, hence unethical. *Ethical* persuaders, however, prefer what they ought over what they want, according to communication ethicists James Jaksa and Michael Pritchard.[37] The U.S. Congress frequently investigates ethics breaches of its members. Often those who are reprimanded will argue that what they did was *legal.* But ethical and legal concerns are not the same. It is not legal to cheat on your income taxes, but some citizens refuse to pay taxes to protest tax dollars being spent unethically. Ethics go beyond law. If it is legal to pollute the air with toxic emissions, is it ethical? Jaksa and Pritchard outline several "reasonable" audience expectations or standards for ethical communication:[38]

1. *Truthful, relevant information that allows an audience to make a rational choice.* You should not cloud the audience's judgment with distorted information. Recall that *mis*information (unintended inaccuracy) is unfortunate and needs to be corrected, but *dis*information (purposely faulty or misleading) is unethical, deserving of censure.

2. *A range of alternative actions.* You should not present the audience with false dilemmas or act as if there is only one solution possible.

3. *Time to reflect before responding.* You should not force an immediate irrational response.

4. *Respect for the audience's ability to make a rational decision.* You should not assume that you know what is best for your audience. You can suggest a course of action but should demonstrate respect for people's judgment and right to self-determination by allowing them to choose their course.

Jaksa and Pritchard point out that ethical speakers create a *climate* of trust, a consequence of considering the impact of their suggestions on the audience. If a climate of trust disposes audiences to support the speaker's position, mistrust inclines them to turn away from the speaker.

As a case in point, consider the 2015 primary campaign for the US Presidency, when Republican candidate Donald Trump began tapping into anti-immigrant sentiment among likely Republican voters. He continued to ride this wave of support right into the White House, promising to deport more than 11 million undocumented immigrants. When the first ripple of deportations hit in the first year of Trump's administration, community members found they were losing pleasant neighbors, the college sophomore across the aisle in economics class, the Mexican family their church had helped to settle, the landscaping business that cared for their lawns, and the energetic grocery employee who worked twice as fast as the rest of the crew.

Trump the candidate had kindled fears, but post election support for the new President dropped off on anti-immigration issues, when the public began to experience the loss of real people who produce real value to communities. While Trump had promised more jobs for citizens through deportations, the jobs left behind were not much coveted nor even mildly desirable. Even an informal cost-benefit analysis of this policy direction revealed a net loss to the country.[39]

Did President Trump commit an ethical breach by distorting or withholding information? Measured against the four ethical standards above, Donald Trump's persuasive approach could be considered ethically flawed. As a lifelong employer of immigrants, he most likely was aware that the simple equation of them versus us was not the whole story. Was he rewarded for his hard-core position? According to the Pew Research Center, a year into President Trump's administration, the US public began to adopt a nuanced view on the issue of undocumented immigrants, most opposing deportation of children brought to the United States illegally.[40] In the long run, then, President Trump's immigration stance ran counter to public opinion. It did not in itself appear likely to boost his prospects for political longevity.[41]

Jaksa and Pritchard also cite the observations of Sissela Bok on lying: that lying has unanticipated negative consequences, including loss of credibility and trust. What's more, with outright falsehoods, the liar must perpetually lie to conceal the primary lie.[42] It is *intentional* deceit that is most deplorable, says Richard Johannesen, another communication ethicist; without a base of truth, how can authentic persuasion on important issues proceed?[43]

A Pulitzer Prize winning fact-checker for the *Tampa Bay Times* first appeared in 2007. Within six years, *Politifact's* "Truth-o-Meter" and "pants-on-fire" ratings had an established place in U.S. political controversy. It was then that *Politifact* declared then President Barack Obama's pledge concerning the Affordable Care Act, "If you like your health care plan, you can keep it," the "Lie of the Year." Although President Obama had held to this claim in 2009 and 2012 and the administration tried to justify it, they were running up against those implementing the Act, who maintained that some insurance plans would go

CREDO FOR ETHICAL COMMUNICATION[44]

Approved by the NCA Legislative Council, 1999; Reaffirmed by the Legislative Assembly passing the report and recommendations of the Taskforce on the Public Policy Platform, 2011. Reaffirmed by the Legislative Assembly with edits, 2017.

Questions of right and wrong arise whenever people communicate. Ethical communication is fundamental to responsible thinking, decision-making, and the development of relationships and communities within and across contexts, cultures, channels, and media. Moreover, ethical communication enhances human worth and dignity by fostering truthfulness, fairness, responsibility, personal integrity, and respect for self and others. We believe that unethical communication threatens the quality of all communication and consequently the well-being of individuals and the society in which we live. Therefore we, the members of the National Communication Association, endorse and are committed to practicing the following principles of ethical communication:

- We advocate truthfulness, accuracy, honesty, and reason as essential to the integrity of communication.

- We endorse freedom of expression, diversity of perspective, and tolerance of dissent to achieve the informed and responsible decision making fundamental to a civil society.

- We strive to understand and respect other communicators before evaluating and responding to their messages.

- We promote access to communication resources and opportunities as necessary to fulfill human potential and contribute to the well-being of families, communities, and society.

- We promote communication climates of caring and mutual understanding that respect the unique needs and characteristics of individual communicators.

- We condemn communication that degrades individuals and humanity through distortion, intimidation, coercion, and violence, and through the expression of intolerance and hatred.

- We are committed to the courageous expression of personal convictions in pursuit of fairness and justice.

- We advocate sharing information, opinions, and feelings when facing significant choices while also respecting privacy and confidentiality.

- We accept responsibility for the short- and long-term consequences for our own communication and expect the same of others.

away. *Chicago Tribune* columnist Clarence Page, an ardent supporter of the President, admitted that Obama "would have to be delusional to think he was telling the truth." Eventually President Obama apologized for being insufficiently clear on this issue. A month later, a *Pew Research/USA Today* poll found that Obama's untrustworthy rating had shot up 15% in the fallout from this issue.[45]

Other news organizations have contributed their efforts toward holding political figures accountable, notably *The Washington Post* Fact-Checker, added to the newspaper as a permanent feature in 2011. Instead of "pants-on fire" designations, the *Post* measures the grievousness of a lie by "Pinocchios," from one (mostly true) to four (a whopper). If a statement expresses "the truth, the whole truth, and nothing but the truth," it receives the highest honor, the "Gepetto Checkmark."[46]

In early 2018, the *Post* announced a fact-checking milestone. President Donald Trump had exceeded 2,000 lies since his inauguration one year earlier.[47] One of the President's violations charged that President Obama's Affordable Care Act was dying or dead while the Congressional Budget Office countered that the Act's enrollment was increasing and its functioning stable. Trump also asserted that the tax cut crafted and approved during his tenure was the largest in history, while the Treasury Department stated it was only the ninth largest. In all, the Post awarded President Trump only four Pinocchios because he repeated the same false information as many as sixty times, making the lies less numerous.

Although these fact-checking sites claim that they are being balanced and transparent, some do question their ratings. Whether or not you agree with the speakers or the fact-checkers, we can recognize that political leaders often are not truthful. Voters need to hold their leaders accountable. Being aware of their truthfulness track record can assist you in knowing just how far you can trust them. It also can remind you that the truth will out. When we remember that *persuasive speakers are ethically bound to provide their listeners with sufficient accurate information, thereby establishing a climate of trust and truthfulness from which authentic persuasion can proceed*, we begin to take seriously our roles as speakers in a democracy. And when we conform to ethical standards, we preserve our integrity, in fact our whole credibility, as the foundation for meaningful social engagement.

In Summary

Issues do not present themselves; *we* present them. If you want audiences to believe in your view of the controversy, then the audience must believe you. You can enhance your credibility by purifying your intentions, showing yourself competent and trustworthy, taking a sincere interest in the audience's welfare, and demonstrating identification with your listeners. You can speak ethically by presenting truthful information, giving your audience choices, allowing them time to respond thoughtfully, and entrusting them with their decision. When you fail to live up to basic ethical standards, you risk sacrificing the goal of your efforts: to develop sound reasons for advancing good decisions that will positively impact one or another's quality of life.

Endnotes

[1] Aristotle, *The Art of Rhetoric,* trans. John Henry Freese (Cambridge: Harvard Univ. Press, 1975), 17, 169.

[2] Gordon L. Dahnke and Glen W. Clatterbuck, *Human Communication: Theory and Research* (Belmont, CA: Wadsworth, 1990), 239.

[3] See, for example, James C. McCroskey,. "Toward a General Model of Instructional Communication." *Communication Quarterly*, vol. 52, no. 3, Summer 2004, pp. 202–4.

[4] "Harvey Weinstein timeline: How the scandal unfolded." *BBC News*, 12 Feb. 2018, http://www.bbc.com/news/entertainment-arts-41594672. Accessed 16 Feb. 2018.

[5] Eric Schmitt, "Powell Retires, as Popular with the Public as with His Troops," *New York Times*, October 1, 1993, A8. General Powell went on to become Secretary of State under George W. Bush. During his term as Secretary of State, Powell held reservations concerning President Bush's plan to invade Iraq to unseat its leader, Saddam Hussein. In obedience and loyalty to his Commander-in-Chief, however, Powell spoke before the United Nations Security Council, presenting evidence to establish that Iraq was concealing weapons of mass destruction, thus violating U.N. agreements. On the force of Powell's testimony, the U.S. Congress voted in favor of military action against Iraq. Much of Powell's evidence was later discredited, leaving Secretary Powell the object of derision. See "General Colin L. Powell," *American Academy of Achievement: A Museum of Living History,* February 5, 2008, 23 April 2014 <http://www.achievement.org/autodoc/page/pow0bio-1>.

[6] Steven W. Littlejohn and David M. Jabusch, Persuasive Transactions (Glenview, IL: Scott-Foresman, 1987), 66-68. The dimensions of credibility depicted below are derived from Littlejohn and Jabusch, though their terms (trust, homophily, attribution, and attraction) have been revised here to reflect more common usage.

[7] See Kathryn Stanchi, "What Cognitive Dissonance Tells Us About Tone in Persuasion," *Journal of Law and Policy,* 22, 1 (January, 2013): 93–133.

[8] Nancy Duarte. "Structure Your Presentation Like a Story." *Harvard Business Review,* 31 Oct. 2012, https://hbr.org/2012/10/structure-your-presentation-li. Accessed 22 Feb. 2018.

[9] Niall McCarthy "Apple Has Sold 1.2 Billion iPhones Over the Past 10 Years." *Forbes,* 29 June 2017, http://www.forbes.com/sites/niallmccarthy/2017/06/29/apple-has-sold-1-2-billion-iphones-over-the-past-10-years-infographic/. Accessed 17 Feb. 2018.

10 Evan Niu. "6 Years Later, 6 Charts That Show How Far Apple, Inc. Has Come Since Steve Jobs' Passing." *The Motley Fool*, 5 Oct. 2017, https://www.fool.com/investing/2017/10/05/6-years-later-6-charts-that-show-how-far-apple-inc.aspx. Accessed 17 Feb. 2018.

11 Jena McGregor. "Steve Jobs Still Looms Large at Apple. Tim Cook Seems Just Fine with That." *The Washington Post*, 13 Sept. 2017, https://www.washingtonpost.com/news/on-leadership/wp/2017/09/13/steve-jobs-still-loomed-large-at-apples-big-event-tim-cook-seems-just-fine-with-that/?utm_term=.b2df2e5bfb80. Accessed 17 Feb. 2018.

12 Christopher J. Zahn, "The Bases for Differing Evaluations of Male and Female Speech: Evidence from Ratings of Transcribed Conversations," *Communication Monographs* 56.1 (1989): 59–74.

13 Linda Carli, et al. "Nonverbal Behavior, Gender, and Influence." *Journal of Personality and Social Psychology*, vol. 68, 1995, pp. 1030–41.

14 Sonja K. Foss and Cindy L. Griffin. "Beyond Persuasion: A Proposal for an Invitational Rhetoric." *Communication Monographs*, vol. 62, 1995, pp. 1–6, http://www.sonjafoss.com/html/Foss21.pdf#page=5&zoom=auto,-50,537.

15 Devra First, *Boston.com*, "Palate Initiative," September 10, 2008, 5 September 2014 <http://www.boston.com/news/nation/articles/2008/09/10/palate_initiative/>.

16 Barry Brummett, "Gastronomic Reference, Synecdoche, and Political Images," Quarterly *Journal of Speech* 67.2 (1981): 138.

17 Ibid.

18 Barack Obama Speech at 2004 DNC Convention," C-Span, *YouTube*, 18 August 2008, 22 February 2018 < https://www.youtube.com/watch?v=eWynt87PaJ0 >

19 Chris Cillizza and Sean Sullivan, "George W. Bush's popularity just hit a 7-year high. Here's how." The Washington Post, April 23, 2013, 17 April 2014 <http://www.washingtonpost.com/blogs/the-fix/wp/2013/04/23/george-w-bushs-approval-rating-just-hit-a-7-year-high-heres-how/>.

20 Lydia Saad, "George W. Bush and Barack Obama Both Popular in Retirement," *Gallup*, 19 June 2016, 18 February 2018 <http://news.gallup.com/poll/212633/george-bush-barack-obama-popular-retirement.aspx>.

21 Lance Bennett, "Assessing Presidential Character: Degradation Rituals in Presidential Campaigns," *Quarterly Journal of Speech* 67.3 (1981): 310–21.

22 Edwin P. Bettinghaus and Michael J. Cody. *Persuasive Communication*. 5th ed., Wadsworth/Thomson Learning, 1994, pp. 217–8.

23 As defined by Robert Dahl in "The Concept of Power," cited by Linda K. Stroh et al., *Organizational Behavior: A Management Challenge*, 3rd ed. (Lawrence Erlbaum, 2001), 191 ff.

24 Ibid.

25 Steven A. McCornack and Timothy R. Levine, "When Lies are Uncovered: Emotional and Relational Outcomes of Discovered Deception," *Communication Monographs* 57.2 (1990): 119–38.

26 Steven Beebe, "Eye Contact: A Nonverbal Determinant of Speaker Credibility," *The Speech Teacher* 28.1 (1974): 21–25.

27 Kieran Kavanaugh and Otilio Rodriguez, trans., *The Collected Works of St. Teresa of Avila* (Washington, D.C.: Institute of Carmelite Studies, 1976).

28 Peggy Noonan, *What I Saw at the Revolution: A Political Life in the Reagan Era* (New York: Random House, 1990), 121.

29 In fact, Morris' peg leg was the result of an accident climbing into a carriage. He did "fight" for independence in America, but mostly in the political realm and through the power of the pen, as a framer of the U.S. Constitution.

30 Michael J. Cody and H. Dan O'Hair, "Nonverbal Communication and Deception: Differences in Deception Cues Due to Gender and Communicator Dominance," *Communication Monographs* 50.3 (1983): 175–92.

31 John E. Hocking and Dale G. Leathers, "Nonverbal Indicators of Deception: A New Theoretical Perspective," *Communication Monographs* 47.2 (1980): 130.

32 Ibid.

33 Ibid., 131.

34 Kenneth Burke, *A Rhetoric of Motives* (Berkeley: Univ. of California Press, 1969), 55.

35 "Joseph R. Biden's Convention Speech," *New York Times,* August 27, 2008, 23 April 2014 <http://www.nytimes.com/2008/08/27/us/politics/27text-biden.html>.

36 Rudy Giuliani, "Opening Remarks to the United Nations General Assembly Special Session on Terrorism," *American Rhetoric: Online Speech Bank,* October 21, 2001, 23 April 2014 <http://www.americanrhetoric.com/speeches/rudygiuliani911unitednations.htm>.

37 James A. Jaksa and Michael S. Pritchard, *Communication Ethics: Methods of Analysis* (Belmont, CA: Wadsworth, 1994), 32.

38 Ibid., 33.

39 See, for example, Sean Severe. "Here's What'll Happen to the Country if We Deport Undocumented Immigrants." *Fortune,* 8 Sept. 2017, http://fortune.com/2017/09/08/trump-undocumented-immigrants-daca/. Accessed 8 Mar. 2018.

40 Carroll Doherty. "Americans broadly support legal status for immigrants brought to the U.S. illegally as children." *Pew Research Center*, 18 June 2018, http://www.pewresearch.org/fact-tank/2018/06/18/americans-broadly-support-legal-status-for-immigrants-brought-to-the-u-s-illegally-as-children/. Accessed 18 Aug. 2018. According to this poll, both Republicans and Democrats supported by more than half each legal status for these children.

41 "Shifting Public Views on Legal Immigration into the U.S." *Pew Research Center,* 28 June 2018, http://www.people-press.org/2018/06/28/shifting-public-views-on-legal-immigration-into-the-u-s/. Accessed 18 Aug. 2018. Eighteen months into President Trump's administration, only 24% of the US population thought immigration should be decreased.

42 Jaska and Pritchard, 78–9.

43 Richard L. Johannesen, Kathleen S. Valdee, and Karen S. Whedbee, *Ethics in Human Communication,* 6th ed. (Long Grove, IL: Waveland, 2007). See especially 121 ff.

44 "Credo for Ethical Communication," Public Statements, *National Communication Association,* 2017, 17 August 2018 < https://www.natcom.org/sites/default/files/Public_Statement_Credo_for_Ethical_Communication_2017.pdf>.

[45] Angie Drobnik Holan, "Lie of the Year: If you like your health plan, you can keep it," *Politifact*, December 12, 2013, 23 April 2104 <http://www.politifact.com/truth-o-meter/article/2013/dec/12/lie-year-if-you-like-your-health-care-plan-keep-it/>.

[46] Glenn Kessler. "About the Fact-Checker." *The Washington Post*, 11 Sept. 2013, https://www.washingtonpost.com/news/fact-checker/about-the-fact-checker/?utm_term=.7b3ecec522c3. Accessed 22 Feb. 2018. The *Post's* ratings are based on the story of *Pinocchio*, a wooden puppet made by Gepetto. Pinocchio becomes a real live boy when he learns to tell the truth.

[47] Glenn Kessler and Meg Kelly. "President Trump has made more than 2000 false or misleading claims over 355 days." *The Washington Post*, 10 Jan. 2018, https://www.washingtonpost.com/news/fact-checker/about-the-fact-checker/?utm_term=.7b3ecec522c3. Accessed 22 Feb. 2018.

Theory into Practice

1. Consider what aspects of credibility you perceive in the following people (or which they lack). Feel free to consider the names of people no longer living. Which of their desirable characteristics might you be able to emulate and which negatives could you strive to avoid?
   a. Ruth Bader Ginsburg
   b. Justin Trudeau
   c. Bill Gates
   d. Hillary Clinton
   e. Michelle Obama
   f. Malala Yousafzai
   g. Dalai Lama

2. List some strategies you might use to establish identification with a political action group that opposes a policy you believe in.

3. As a means to raising your consciousness about speaking ethics, evaluate how a recent scandal (such as the actions of a corrupt official, sexual harassment in your work place, or financial crisis) violated the ethical standards discussed in this chapter.

Oral Practice

For speaking practice and to internalize the factors that produce credibility, imagine you are nominating a figure you admire to a Credibility Hall of Fame. This can be someone relevant to your occupation, a political figure, a social reformer, and so on. If you are preparing this in a group setting, when the speakers have concluded, select whose nominee struck you as most credible, and discuss the meaning of the results. For your preparation, complete the following:

1. In what way might your nominee's qualities relate to your audience's values?

   _____

   _____

2. What biographical information about your nominee supports your assessment of him or her?

   _____

   _____

3. What struggles has your nominee overcome, or what accomplishments achieved?

   _____

   _____

4. What are the predominate aspects of credibility your nominee possesses?

   _____

   _____

Chapter

5   Analyzing the Audience

To Make a Long Story Short...

Knowledge about your audience should guide your potential speech content.

Key Concepts

- Audience analysis should target the audience's knowledge, experience, and attitude toward the speech subject.
- Demographic information reveals generalizations about an audience, but attitude questionnaires uncover their true opinions.
- A persuasive speaker should adapt the speech plan to fit the audience.
- When the audience is strongly opposed *or* supportive, the speaker may need to modify the speech's proposition.

Key Terms

demographic information	*pathos*
ego-involvement	social judgment theory
issue-involvement	latitude of acceptance
Likert scale	latitude of rejection
semantic differential	

Uncovering Audience Information
First Steps

It is not difficult to get hooked into giving a speech. Once you know it is going to happen, salvage your composure, and begin to think about your listeners. The preliminary detective work on your audience begins at that moment. You will find information about your audience from diverse sources: a co-worker, an event organizer, or audience members themselves.

President Ronald Reagan's speechwriter, journalist Peggy Noonan, recognized this essential step in speech preparation.

> I thought about the audience. I would think how happy they were to be near the President and how each deserved something special, something personal . . . .[1]

So she would ask the White House staff researchers,

> And in the town where he's speaking, what are people talking about . . . does the local school have a winning team, what's the local department store and are they hiring? Anything to make it seem as if someone thought about this speech and these people . . . . Show them respect and be honest and logical in your approach and they will understand every word you say and hear—and know that you thought of them.[2]

Easiest to acquire may be objective information about the audience: how many will be there, and what external facts about them are evident? These are audience demographics. **Demographic information** profiles groups of people according to measurable known factors, including age, gender, marital and family status, income level, educational level, and so on. You may be able to draw up a form to tally what you learn about your audience:

DEMOGRAPHIC QUESTIONNAIRE	
Age	Employment status
Gender identity	Income level
Years college	Homeowner/renter?
Major/minor studies	Political or other group affiliation

DEMOGRAPHIC QUESTIONNAIRE	
Religious affiliation _____	Marital/family status _____
Primary language _____	Ethnicity _____

Speakers addressing a group they know have an advantage, of course. If you find yourself in this situation, or if you have e-mail contact with your prospective listeners, you can solicit demographic information by circulating an online survey, using a resource like Survey Monkey.[3] In this case, you would input online the questions you want to ask, providing a range of responses, such as:

1. What is your age?

  ○ Under 18   ○ 40-59

  ○ 19-24   ○ 60-74

  ○ 25-39   ○ 75 or older

The survey instrument will tally your responses into an overall profile—either demographic or attitudinal. Naturally, you will want to consider how much effort to exert if audience response is voluntary. However, even beginning to construct such a device forces you to look at and think about the make-up of the group you will address.

Once you have gathered a few facts, consider the pertinent questions that arise from those facts. Would an audience respond differently to your speech about a cultural experience if audience members were familiar with the language of that culture? Would a work group respond differently to a technical speech if their educational background lacked the technical expertise to understand it? For speeches on political controversies, won't audience members support or oppose a position based on their religious inclinations, their group affiliations, or their economic circumstances?

Your knowledge and observations on your audience provide clues (though not certainty) about their attitudes toward you and your subject and about their knowledge and experience with your subject.

Cautions and Considerations

While demographic analysis generates basic statistical information on audience composition, it is surely not a complete audience survey. Consider what demographic information gives us and what it doesn't. Demographic information provides the raw material for *generalizations.* For instance, if you know that the audience members are all over the age of 65, you might assume that they are retired and concerned about financial security issues, health care, and political stability. While these conclusions seem reasonable, you have stereotyped the audience by age. You have assumed that because the audience members belong to a certain group, their opinions are predictable.

Group affiliation does influence audience reactions,[4] but to infer absolute conclusions on the basis of group affiliation is risky. As Carroll Arnold and John Bowers note, "group ideology ultimately forces itself" on the public speaker,[5] but while group members tend to hold "group opinions," they can maintain individual views at the same time.

Let's look at a few exceptions to our age stereotype: older performers—like Morgan Freeman, winner of multiple film awards, including an Academy Award at the age of 67—who cannot be grouped with retired seniors in general. The independently wealthy (at this writing, Microsoft founder, multi-billionaire, and international philanthropist Bill Gates is well into his sixties) and political figures (like some past Presidents, Senators, and Supreme Court justices, who have worked into their 80s or 90s) are unlikely to fret about their financial security in the same way the retired population at large would. If you assume generalizations about your audience, you risk misreading your audience, who they are and what they think.

You can observe what you may in terms of demographic audience characteristics, but draw general conclusions from them with caution. Daniel O'Keefe's summary of demographics and audience persuasibility is enlightening. He points out that the demographic factor of gender, for example, reveals no consistent difference in overall susceptibility to persuasion.[6] In other words, men and women seem to be equally susceptible to persuasion. Another interesting twist is found in the persuasibility of debaters. We might assume that because debaters are politically alert and opinionated, they would resist being persuaded. The reverse is true, as demonstrated by a study[7] showing that highly argumentative people are easier to persuade. Again, if we had assumed such a group to be hostile to attitude change, we would have been mistaken.

You should test conclusions about audiences gradually—by talking with audience members before the speech and listening to their questions during the speech. If you perceive general audience resistance to your assumptions about them, you can back off presumptuous arguments and conclusions until you are able to assess more accurately your audience's views.

Finally, to move toward audiences psychologically, you must first know something of their interests, beliefs, and values.[8] These are not found in demographic analysis, which stops short of your listeners' interior state while revealing only external factors.

The Opportunity for Audience Polling

For quickly developing, informal speaking situations, the audience poll is virtually never possible. But there may be times when you have the luxury of time and audience access before a scheduled speech. With an opportunity such as this, you will be able to assess audience knowledge, experience, and attitudes for a deeper understanding of them than demographic analysis provides. Political candidates benefit from sophisticated audience polling before speaking engagements. Comedians playing to new audiences in new venues will learn enough about a community, its watering holes and political wrangles, to include references to them in their acts, thereby flattering and identifying with the audience. Jerry Seinfeld's one-night-only performance in my home town fell on the night of an enormous snowstorm, unusual for this part of the country. When the curtain opened, to a surprisingly packed house, he expressed disbelief that we all showed up. He had come to know that the city shuts down with as much as an inch of snow, yet there we were, ready to laugh.

Figure 5.1 Comedians like Jerry Seinfeld tend to be expert audience analysts, tapping into local inside jokes pre-performance.
© Featureflash/Shutterstock, Inc.

If you are able to circulate a questionnaire—either online or hard copy—to the prospective audience or representative members, so much the better. If that audience is a representative group of clients, as for example, in the case of an architect trying to get input on diverse needs for an institutional construction project before presenting a proposal, you might have the speech coordinator circulate a questionnaire in advance of your meeting. With this you can uncover some keys to your audience's attitudes, as presented graphically in Figure 5.2.

Attitude toward the speaker The audience may think of you in at least three possible ways. First, they may have no opinion of you as a speaker. Second, they may question your ability to speak credibly about the subject. Or third, they may respect your abilities and find you credible. Finding out what your audience thinks of you is intimidating, to be sure, but it is better to find this out *before* the speech so that you can repair your image if necessary. If you find the audience thinks well of you, your confidence will help you speak with greater enthusiasm and force.

Level of knowledge Sometimes the audience knows little or nothing about a speaker's subject matter. Sometimes they know a good deal and may even consider themselves experts on the subject. Whatever the audience's level of knowledge, try to *anticipate* it. In doing so, you will be sure not to address

WHAT'S ON YOUR AUDIENCE'S MIND?

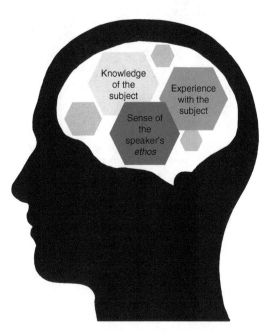

Figure 5.2 The audience's preconceptions comprise attitudes about both subject and speaker. The speaker who can access those attitudes is better able to judge what information is needed to make the speech understandable, relevant, and believable.
Image © KaiMook Studio 99/Shutterstock.com

an uninformed audience as one that is informed. Thus you will avoid both confusing and losing them. It helps to be aware of whether the audience has at least some vague ideas about the subject so that they can be motivated to develop firmer ideas. If the audience is well informed, of course you need to recognize their level of knowledge so that you do not insult them by presenting as new information what they consider common knowledge.

Experience Experience can tempt people into thinking they know it all. Experience can wreak havoc with an audience's ability to listen openly and may cause them to focus on irrelevant factors. Communication theorists refer to two especially pertinent types of audience experience: **ego-involvement** and **issue-involvement**.[9] Audience members who are ego-involved consider the subject important to their well-being. Thus a fisherman will be ego-involved in the issue of state and federal restrictions on commercial fishing; his job is on the line. Those who are issue-involved consider the subject important, even when it does not affect them personally. An example of one who is issue-involved is one who does not have children but advocates children's equal access to organized sports.

When audience members are experienced, knowledgeable, or involved in the subject, they may be more likely to oppose you, to treat your message more critically, or to feel hostile toward the subject altogether, as with the driver who has felt threatened by reckless bike riders hearing about new laws favoring cyclists. The audience's level of involvement may reflect under- or overexposure to the subject, so that they are either apathetic or wearied of hearing about it—in which case they may simply tune you out.

Constructing an Audience Questionnaire

The easiest and sometimes the most accurate audience analysis is informal: the product of interpersonal interaction prior to the speech. As we pointed out in discussing audience demographics, if you have no opportunity to question your audience (or those who know them), it might be possible to obtain audience attitudes formally. The coordinator of the speaking event can email or circulate questionnaires to prospective audience members and feed them back to the speaker. If you are able to obtain such valuable information, take care to seek a range of information and in a number of ways.[10] Even if you have no access to the audience's written comments, considering what you *might* ask if you did will help you think about what your audience's attitudes might be.

The Likert Scale

The **Likert scale**, conceived in 1932, is a form of scale questioning where respondents, given an attitude statement, are asked to indicate their attitudes along a continuum of positions. This popular form of questionnaire may look familiar to you.

Mass transit is not essential to our town.

strongly agree ____ ____ ____ ____ ____ *strongly disagree*

                     5   4   3   2   1

Only poor people ride the bus.

strongly agree ____ ____ ____ ____ ____ *strongly disagree*

                     5   4   3   2   1

As you can see, the questions are parallel; an agreeing response for either of these statements suggests a *negative* attitude toward mass transit. The object of the Likert scale is to compute an overall score for audience agreement or disagreement with the your position. This score helps you gauge how appealing the audience finds your position.

If you use an online survey, your questions might look like this:

1. Mass transit is not essential to Springfield.

strongly agree	agree	not sure/neutral	disagree	strongly disagree
○	○	○	○	○

The Semantic Differential

Like the Likert scale, the **semantic differential** (1957) allows a range of responses, but in this case, audience members depict their attitude toward the subject by selecting a position between contrasting descriptors, as in this example:

Local Mass Transit

necessary ____ ____ ____ ____ ____ ____ ____ unnecessary

beneficial ____ ____ ____ ____ ____ ____ ____ harmful

affordable ____ ____ ____ ____ ____ ____ ____ costly

convenient ____ ____ ____ ____ ____ ____ ____ inconvenient

                 7   6   5   4   3   2   1

In this case, with an online survey you could introduce a device impossible for a paper form—a sliding scale. For the question below, respondents are able to move the slider to a point that they feel accurately represents their positive, neutral, or negative attitude.

2. Local mass transit

necessary 7   not sure/ neutral   unnecessary 1

To assess your own credibility, you could provide a semantic differential where respondents could judge whether you are trustworthy or untrustworthy, competent or incompetent, and so on. Whatever items you seek attitudes on, the semantic differential score can indicate whether you have sufficient evidence, the right kind of evidence, whether the audience is open to your position, what values are important to them, and how they feel about you as a speaker.

Fixed Alternative Questionnaires

As their name suggests, fixed alternative questionnaires present certain *fixed* or *set* responses for audience members. As with other forms of audience analysis, the speaker tries to determine the audience's level of knowledge and experience as well as an attitude toward the speaker. For example:

What is your most frequent form of transportation?	bus _____ bicycle _____	car _____ subway _____
Do you own a car?	Yes _____	No _____
Do you purchase a ridership card for any form of mass transportation?	Yes _____	No _____
Do you consider the speaker informed on the subject of mass transportation?	Yes _____	No _____

The online version for this kind of question will offer simple and appropriate formatting options.

3. What is your most frequent form of transportation?

☐ bus
☐ car
☐ bicycle
☐ subway
☐ other (please specify)

From fixed alternative responses, you can obtain simple and concrete information about your audience. By tallying responses, you can compile a clear picture of how many have had experience with or indirect knowledge of your subject. The drawback to this type of question is that it allows no room for a nuanced response or gradations of opinion; it is most useful when the audience can enter simple and straightforward responses.

Open-Ended Questionnaires

Probably the simplest poll to construct is the one that requests the most thoughtful and extensive comments from the audience. See how the following cannot be answered quickly or simply:

> What do you like/dislike about mass transit?

> Describe the benefits (or drawbacks) of transportation you use for your daily routine.

> What kind of people do you think ride the bus?

The online alternative to the open-ended question often provides an adjustable comment box, so that respondents can submit as complete or terse a response as they wish.

4. What do you like or dislike about mass transit?

The advantage of open-ended questions is obvious: You can acquire a more nuanced and detailed picture of your audience. Often respondents mention their arguments against a speaker's position, so that the speaker can prepare a reasoned rebuttal in advance. But there are disadvantages. You must contend with as many opinions as there are audience members. It is difficult (though not impossible) to draw up an objective and quantified audience profile with an open-ended questionnaire. It is not impossible because you *can* review the questionnaires, tallying audience responses, pros and cons, and summarizing attitudes.

The chance for an audience questionnaire often is unlikely, but by strategically planning, you may be able to seize an opportunity to provide one. If you find such an opportunity, you will be fascinated by the results and will find your speech strengthened by this preparation, since you are no longer going in blind.

What to Do with Audience Information
About Me, the Speaker

Pre-speech audience discovery equips you to maximize audience acceptance. You may want to alter the audience's perception of your credibility, to make up for their lack of knowledge, or to consider how their experience will impact where they stand. In the speaker-audience dialectic, you want to remove obstacles that prevent the audience from seeing issues clearly and accurately.

Consider the audience's attitude toward the speaker. Suppose, as a worst-case scenario, they know me, and they do not like me. They have heard me speak at a city council meeting, and they find me brash and uninformed about the city's budget. They feel I have no qualifications for speaking to a group of business people about personal investments and financial planning. But the fact is that as a Certified Financial Planner and accountant, I do have qualifications for speaking on my subject. Now what can I do about the audience's predisposition against me?

1. *Correct negatives.* First, I can take care not to repeat any previous rudeness. Where I was then overbearing, now I will be restrained. Where I was abrupt, I will be low-key and patient.

2. *Acknowledge misgivings.* Second, I can acknowledge the audience's distrust or hypothesize their misgivings. "I imagine you're wondering just what makes me an expert on financial planning when I can't even see the light on the city's proposed budget levy." This will help to air questions of character and competence as we discussed in Chapter Four.

3. *Present qualifications.* Third, I can state directly my qualifications. So I might say, "It may surprise you, and it surprises me, too, to think of how many years of study I've devoted to the science of investment, but you know time flies when you're having fun."

4. *Demonstrate competence.* Finally, I can present a carefully researched, planned, and rehearsed speech to demonstrate that I care enough about the subject to present it worthily.

Speakers who care about their subjects will not be offended by the suggestion that a speech needs to be modified for greater persuasive impact. After all, there is nothing wrong with patience, reasonableness, and work—the work it takes to strengthen one's controversial position. If you can exhibit self-control and energy in fine-tuning your presence before an audience, you will enhance the outcome. Such interpersonal sensitivity, characterized by eager adaptability and understanding, can overcome division and audience alienation.

About Experience

If an audience is ego-involved or issue-involved in the subject of your speech,[11] you can but should not simply say whatever you feel like saying.

Some speakers do so in trying to be straight-talkers, but they often attract fringe elements to their position while losing the audience at large.

The audience may have no significant experience with your subject, but they feel involved in the issue, which makes for tricky handling. If you are speaking, for instance, about the concussion dangers among young children playing full-contact football, whose experience counts? Parents only? Coaches? Athletic league coordinators? Doctors? Do listeners without direct connections count—and can they care? Here are some guidelines.

1. *Treat audience experience with respect.* The speaker must not threaten the audience's experience by treating it as insignificant or irrelevant. For the avid football fan, no matter the age group, you could point out that children can learn fundamental skills at various ages: six-year olds learning running strategies and ball handling, nine-year olds field positioning, and so on. There are ways that youth football can be regulated without keeping children from acquiring skill in the sport over time. In adopting this approach without denigrating the fan's enthusiasm, you have accommodated it.

2. *Find a connection between the subject and the audience.* The other extreme is the audience member who has no experience with the subject and feels it has no relevance whatsoever. This person is prepared to tune out after the introductory quip. For such listeners, you want to suggest potential connections between your subject and their lives. Your approach might be as follows:

   You are all relatively young and, presumably, want to enjoy the opportunities that life presents you. Your livelihood depends on your efforts and drive, of course, but it also depends on others who may seem not to affect you in the least—our youth.

   How do our youth shape *your* life? If their contributions to society will be curtailed by needless physical problems and insurance costs, it will be you who pay—in retirement benefits these young people would have earned, in your higher insurance premiums to factor in their care needs, and in the lost health and welfare of a society that has put a precious future resource at risk.

Knowing your audience and recognizing the validity of their experience is a gracious act of identification that warms the speaker-audience relationship.

Former President Barack Obama embraced the value of sympathy with his audience early in his 2008 campaign. As his close colleague Cass Sunstein

Since You Asked...

Question: Once I get to know my audience, I imagine I'll discover ways to tap into their emotions. Should I be aware of unforeseen complications in targeting audience emotion?

Answer: Yes, you probably will uncover some emotional underpinnings of audience attitude. As Aristotle pointed out, you can persuade by force of argument (*logos*), by character (*ethos*), and by emotion (*pathos*). He analyzed the play of each emotion on the audience with three questions: 1) What *mental state* elicits the emotion? 2) What *people* provoke the emotion? and 3) What *occasions* elicit the emotion?[12] Thus to arouse audience anger, you can remind the audience of people and circumstances that make them angry. You can craft your survey, then, to reveal what causes your audience to feel angry or happy, to feel pity or grief.

You also are correct in surmising that a speaker's use of emotional appeal is fraught with landmines. For instance, in the pro-life/pro-choice disputes over abortion rights, each side tends to vilify its opposition[13] as disingenuous and evil rather than as good people with faulty ideas. This approach may motivate social activism, but in turn it creates social division, frustrating collaborative approaches to the controversy.

One of the trickiest emotions to deal with is fear. In Daniel O'Keefe's summary of fear appeals research,[14] he points out that graphic descriptions (mangled bodies, gruesome depictions) often induce audiences to tune out the message, to be desensitized by the message, or to respond in unpredictable ways.

This appears to be exactly what happens in the case of speeches issuing dire warnings on climate change. First, in response to severe and shocking projections, listeners perceive the climate-change issue as overwhelming and feel powerless to alter projected conditions.[15] Since the efficacy of fear appeals depends on the audience's sense that they can impact outcomes,[16] they will, in this case, avoid the issue or resort to denial that danger exists. Second, the long-range consequences of climate-change tend to desensitize audiences, who begin to perceive those predictions as hypothetical, or to submerge them as lacking urgency. Finally, as O'Keefe warns, listeners perceive climate change communication as guilt-inducing, and they respond (unpredictably) with anger toward the guilt-tripper.[17]

In short, what climate-change communication studies have found about arousing audience fear pertains to other emotions as well. Emotional appeal can be useful in hooking audience attention, but the speaker's proof must direct emotion purposefully with sound information.

reported, Obama wanted "to pursue large goals in a way that offends the deepest values of as few people as possible."[18] President Obama's view was that "if you take on board people's deepest commitments . . . show respect for them, then you make possible larger steps than would otherwise be imagined."[19] Audience analysis and sympathy for the audience are profoundly pragmatic practices.

About Knowledge

The audience may be uninformed, little informed, or well-informed on your speech subject. Some speakers may think they like best to address uninformed, neutral audiences. Not knowing about the subject, the audience is unaware of arguments against your position and accepts your claims as indisputable, even if you show minimal competence. There is a downside, though, to audience ignorance, in that you must backpedal through background information that consumes time otherwise spent in developing a case. Yet this background is invaluable because it accomplishes a few key functions.

1. *Show good reasons for the audience to modify its views.* With the vaguely informed audience, a little knowledge is a dangerous thing. The problem is that an uninformed audience often does not recognize its deficiency, but the gaps in their knowledge may lead them to resist your message. You can overcome this difficulty by providing evidence showing why the audience should modify its position, but you must do this with great tact. Rather than stating outright, "You people have only half the story," you can assist your cause by crediting the knowledge the audience *does* possess. You might say, "I'm glad to see you have considered this problem, and glad, too, to be able to share with you some of my own findings to round out what we know." Meager knowledge in the audience should not be mocked, but credited and supplemented with solid evidence.

2. *Avoid speaking from ignorance.* The greatest peril you may face may be that informed and intelligent audience members can be more resistant to persuasion to an opposing viewpoint.[20] For instance, a coach in the audience hearing the youth football speech is more likely than a layperson to find fault with an opposing position and to have ready replies. The best way to avoid this awkward situation is to be sure that as a persuader you do not speak from ignorance.

3. *Remain tentative in the presence of superior knowledge.* You should state your opinion humbly, deferring to superior knowledge (if it is evident) in the audience, even to the extent of soliciting explanations or corrections from audience experts present. You will want to present your position more tentatively, as opposed to dogmatically, if an audience expert strongly opposes the position you advance.

You do not need to abandon your position altogether. There is evidence that can overcome the audience expert, particularly the evidence of experience—your own experience or the experience of someone close to you. For instance, in the youth football speech, you mention in the presence of the coach a football injury that seriously hampered the physical well being and future of your son. You admit that you don't have the broad perspective of the coach, but neither does he identify with the trauma of your experience. This combination of humbly acknowledging knowledge and firmly adhering to a viable viewpoint can defuse the competitive dynamic of whose experience matters more.

ETHICS WATCH

The process of audience analysis highlights the potential power of the persuader over the human mind. It suggests that if you know your audience well, you will know how to get the response you desire. This science is most refined in the practice known as brainwashing, not a new phenomenon, as Robert Lifton attested in his study of post World War Two China.[21] Lifton points out that "imposed dogmas, inquisitions, and mass conversion movements have existed in every historical epoch."[22]

Lifton believes that the practice of brainwashing presents a critical ethical dilemma:

"Some people considered [thought reform] a relentless means of undermining the human personality; others saw it as a profoundly 'moral'— even religious—attempt to instill new ethics in a people."

So…

1. Based on our definition of persuasion in Chapter One, is brainwashing an authentic means of persuasion?

2. What are the acceptable limits (if limits exist) of analyzing, adapting to, and shaping audience attitudes?

Audience Attitude and the Proposition

Whatever the audience's attitudes toward the speaker, whatever their knowledge and experience, you still cannot be sure you know their stand on the proposition. If you are able to survey an audience, you should surely give them an opportunity to express their attitude toward your proposition, as in a Likert scale. For example, your survey could include:

Mass transit is essential to our city's economic stability.

strongly agree _____ _____ _____ _____ _____ *strongly disagree*

                  5   4   3   2   1

The city should increase its mass transit subsidy.

strongly agree _____ _____ _____ _____ _____ *strongly disagree*

          5   4   3   2   1

From this information, you can judge how acceptable your position is to the audience. If direct audience feedback is not available, you can project from your other questions (see pages 113–116) where the audience stands, though this projection would be less dependable than a direct response.

How should you interpret responses to your proposition? For help in answering this question, we can turn to one of the more convincing theories of attitude change, social judgment theory, developed by Carolyn Sherif, Muzafer Sherif, and Roger Nebergall.[23] **Social judgment theory** is an attempt to predict and explain the effects of persuasive messages. According to this theory, effectiveness depends on the audience's *perception* of where the speaker stands in relation to them.

Let's look at one proposition as an example:

The university should stop using animals in laboratory testing.

strongly agree _____ _____ _____ _____ _____ *strongly disagree*

          5   4   3   2   1

There are five levels of agreement/disagreement with the proposition. Of course, you would like to move your audience to agree with you fully, but according to social judgment theory, this absolute agreement is not required for a persuasive outcome. Rather there is a *range* of positions with which an audience can agree to be persuaded. This is the audience's **latitude of acceptance**. The audience will accept a number of positions not exactly in line with its own; it will *assimilate* positions that *approximate* its own. That sounds like a productive step in reaching agreement.

The bad news, of course, is that the audience is also capable of rejecting our position. To make matters more difficult, it will not only reject positions extremely different from its own but reject positions that contrast or differ slightly from its latitude of acceptance. This range of positions is the **latitude of rejection**.

Thus the audience will distort messages in order to *assimilate* or *contrast* them with positions they already hold. They may simplify and pigeonhole messages: those positions that approximate their own will fall within the latitude of acceptance; those that resemble disagreeable positions will fall within the **latitude of rejection**.

Consider the case of Sarah, an animal rights activist. She argues that the university should stop using animals in laboratory testing. In her audience are Jake, a motorcycle enthusiast, and Anna, a pro-life activist. Jake has not thought much about animal rights in the past, but as Sarah presents her ideas he begins to compare the arguments against animal testing with laws requiring motorcyclists to wear helmets, a law he vigorously opposes. He views both positions as attempts to take away civil liberties. So Jake pushes Sarah's position into his latitude of rejection, contrasting it with his current attitudes.

Anna, on the other hand, compares the innocence of animals in lab testing to the innocence of the unborn child, and she assimilates Sarah's position into her own position; she embraces Sarah's proposition in her latitude of acceptance.

This example also illustrates the importance of ego-involvement in determining whether audience members will accept or reject propositions. As a reminder, ego-involvement refers to an audience member's commitment or strength of feeling on an issue. Although neither Jake nor Anna had a personal commitment on the issue of animal rights, both of them were ego-involved in issues *inherent* in the subject of animal testing. According to Sherif, Sherif, and Nebergall, *highly ego-involved audiences will have narrower latitudes of acceptance and broader latitudes of rejection*,[24] as illustrated in Figure 5.3.

THE AUDIENCE AND EGO-INVOLVEMENT

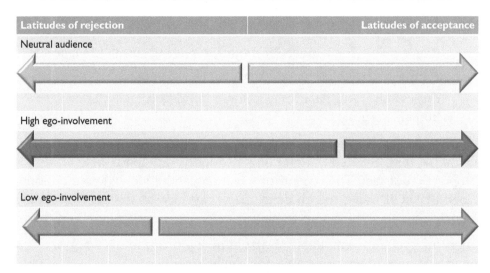

Figure 5.3 The audience's latitudes of acceptance and rejection vary according to their ego-involvement with the subject matter, as explained by social judgment theory.
Courtesy of Barbara Breaden

The question you must ask is whether, based on the audience's stance, the speech can be effective or the approach should be modified. If your proposition is likely to alienate the audience, you might modify the proposition to promote audience acceptance.

Modifying the Proposition

Let's get back to Sarah's speech on animal rights and the problem she faces in convincing Jake to oppose lab testing on animals. What if she could find a sub-issue on which Jake is more inclined to agree? For example, Sarah feels strongly that humans are self-centered in destroying animals for human gain. Is there a way she can link this to Jake's commitment to motorcyclists' rights? Motorcyclists, after all, are considered second-class drivers. We resent it when they hold up traffic in rush hour and when they consume an entire automobile parking space for one motorcycle. We take risks in passing them, nudging them to the side of the road. These risks surely endanger cyclists' lives for the sake of our convenience and our sense of vehicular superiority.

Now Sarah can argue that we view animals like cyclists, as second-class species. Notice that in arguing this way, Sarah has probably caused Jake to identify with her position without pushing him to agree that the university should stop using animals for lab testing. Consequently, Jake may become more sympathetic with Sarah's position. Sarah has applied the wisdom of social judgment theory by recognizing Jake's rejection of her position and by attempting to turn that rejection into acceptance—through a sub-issue in her proposition.

Here is Sarah's propositional shift:

Proposition 1: The University should stop using animals in laboratory testing.

Proposition 2: Animal testing assumes fundamental superiority of the human species.

In the first case, Sarah uses a proposition of policy that is action-oriented. In the second, Sarah is attempting to modify audience beliefs with a proposition of fact. The second proposition can be viewed as a building block that will move the audience part way toward the goal of ending animal testing.

There are probably countless sub-issues in any proposition. Look at a few more examples of how a proposition can be modified:

Proposition 1: Tax vouchers should be made available to parents whose children attend private schools.

Proposition 2: Private schools save state and local school systems money.

or

Proposition 1: A major earthquake will take place in the Midwestern United States this year.

Proposition 2: Geologic conditions created by fracking in the Midwestern United States resemble conditions that have ordinarily preceded significant earthquakes.

We can modify propositions of fact and value just as we modify propositions of policy. The *audience* should determine which proposition you choose to argue. You need not abandon your position in an effort to tell the audience what it wants to hear, but you should carefully consider, once you have come to know your audience, which position will be most practical and effective in reaching a shared outlook.

One speaker summarized a propositional shift he made to adapt to his audience's ability to take action:

> Since audience opinion was in my favor, I probably could have given a more radical proposition of action speech, such as all-out banning of old-growth [forest] harvesting. I decided that such a proposition would do little good because [my audience] had no power to carry it out. Instead I decided to propose something within the everyday means of audience members: use of young growth tree farms rather than forests to supply paper products.

As a rule, hostile audiences are more likely to accept a position that is not far from its own views. On the other hand, receptive audiences need strong enough messages to motivate them to listen. So sometimes you may want to strengthen your proposition, shifting from a proposition of fact or value to a proposition of policy, such as:

Proposition 1: Steroids endanger young athletes' health.

Proposition 2: College athletes should be tested twice a season for steroid use.

or

Proposition 1: Pilots over age 65 are capable of continuing to fly commercial jetliners.[25]

Proposition 2: The FAA should not link mandatory retirement to age.

If you already have selected a proposition of policy, you can appeal to the audience to take a personal stand or action. The key is to take an already favorable audience beyond simple agreement. By studying audience latitudes of acceptance and rejection you can strategically position your speech to avoid the pitfalls of irrelevance and alienation.

In Summary

Socrates maintained that an unexamined life is not not worth living. Just so, a speech is not worth giving to an unexamined audience. If persuasion is grounded in dialectic, to discover mutually beneficial positions and policies, the speaker speaks not *to* the audience but *for* the audience. The speaker, then, must *know* the audience.

You can collect audience information from observing or surveying demographic factors. If you can formally survey your audience, Likert scales, semantic differentials, fixed-alternative and open-ended questions will provide an array of audience perspectives. On the other hand, a source close to your prospective audience can be a rich source of information if a poll is not feasible.

The lessons of social judgment theory demonstrate how to navigate your audience's latitudes of acceptance and rejection. The time you devote to audience analysis is time well spent, for it enhances many times over the outcome of your persuasive speech.

Endnotes

[1] Peggy Noonan, *What I Saw at the Revolution: A Political Life in the Reagan Era* (New York: Random House, 1990), 64.

[2] Ibid., 64–9.

[3] https://www.surveymonkey.com.

[4] See Edwin P. Bettinghaus and Michael J. Cody, *Persuasive Communication*, 5th ed. (Wadsworth/Thomson Learning, 1994), 175.

[5] Carroll C. Arnold and John Waite Bowers, *Handbook of Rhetorical and Communication Theory* (Boston: Allyn & Bacon, 1984), 753.

[6] Daniel O'Keefe, *Persuasion: Theory and Research* (Newbury Park, CA: Sage, 1990), 179.

[7] Timothy R. Levine and Eugenia E. Badger, "Argumentativeness and Resistance to Persuasion," *Communication Reports* 6.2 (1993): 71–78.

[8] Herbert W. Simons, *Persuasion: Understanding, Practice, and Analysis*, 2nd ed. (New York: Random House, 1986), 154.

[9] O'Keefe, *Persuasion*, 32–33.

[10] Excellent summaries of these and other analysis techniques can be found in O'Keefe, 18–26, and Arnold and Bowers, 411–16.

[11] For ego- and issue-involvement, *see Audience Attitude and the Proposition* in Chapter 7.

[12] Aristotle, *The Art of Rhetoric*, trans. John Henry Freese (Cambridge: Harvard Univ. Press, 1975), 173.

[13] Marsha I. Vanderford, "Vilification and Social Movements: A Case Study of Pro-Life and Pro-Choice Rhetoric," *Communication Monographs* 75 (1989): 166.

[14] O'Keefe, *Persuasion*, 165–68.

[15] Saffron O'Neill and Sophie Nicholson-Cole, "Fear Won't Do It: Promoting Positive Engagement with Climate Change through Visual and Iconic Representations," *Science Communication* 30:3 (2009): 355–379.

[16] Kim Witte, "Putting the Fear Back into Fear Appeals: The Extended Parallel Process Model," *Communication Monographs* 59 (1992): 329–342.

[17] Daniel O'Keefe, "Guilt as a Mechanism in Persuasion," in J.P. Dillard, et al, eds., *The Persuasion Handbook: Developments in Theory and Practice* (Thousand Oaks, CA: Sage, 2002) 329 ff.

[18] George Packer, "The New Liberalism," *The New Yorker*, November 17, 2008, 86.

[19] Ibid.

[20] O'Keefe, *Persuasion*, 178. This is a complex question, and though there are many persuasive outcomes possible with a knowledgeable audience, this is clearly the most disadvantageous to the speaker.

[21] Robert J. Lifton, *Thought Reform and the Psychology of Totalism: A Study of Brainwashing in China* (University of North Carolina Press, 1989).

[22] Ibid.

[23] Carolyn Sherif, Muzafer Sherif, and Roger Nebergall, *Attitude and Attitude Change: The Social Judgment-Involvement Approach* (Philadelphia: W. B. Saunders, 1965). An excellent review of this work is included in O'Keefe, 29–35.

[24] O'Keefe, *Persuasion*, 33.

[25] The age limit was 60 in late 2007, when Congress passed legislation requiring a shift in mandatory retirement age for commercial pilots to 65. The Fair Treatment of Experienced Pilots Act implemented the age 65 limit in 2012.

Theory into Practice

1. To practice thinking about how audience demographics relate to speech subjects, construct a demographic tally sheet like the one on page 108–109. Include the demographic elements that would reveal important information if your speech was about
   a. increasing minimum job requirements at your place of employment
   b. volunteering for military service
   c. building a new rapid transit route
   d. more rigorous emission control requirements for cars
   e. labeling genetically modified foods

2. After constructing the audience poll (see below), make a list of elements you can adapt in your speech based on your findings, for instance:
   a. What potential counterarguments should I address? (See Chapter Seven.)

   _____

   _____

   _____

   b. What additional evidence is needed?

   _____

   _____

   _____

   c. What audience values, likes, and dislikes should I connect to?

   _____

   _____

   _____

Sketching out the Audience Survey

1. Proposition: _____

    _____

    strongly agree _____ _____ _____ _____ _____ *strongly disagree*

    $\qquad\qquad\quad$ 5 $\quad$ 4 $\quad$ 3 $\quad$ 2 $\quad$ 1

2. Demographic information—You can adapt these factors depending on your speech subject.

    age _____ employment status _____

    gender identity_____ annual income _____

    education _____ group affiliation _____

    religion _____ ethnicity _____

3. Experience questions—Your questions here should evoke audience feedback on background or exposure they have had (or lack) related to your subject.
    a. _____
    b. _____

4. Knowledge questions—Here you can ask respondents to describe their understanding (or lack of understanding) on an aspect of your subject.
    a. _____
    b. _____

5. Attitude questions—Insert statements below on which audience members can rate their level of agreement.
    a. _____

strongly agree _____ _____ _____ _____ _____ *strongly disagree*

5   4   3   2   1

b. _____

strongly agree _____ _____ _____ _____ _____ *strongly disagree*

5   4   3   2   1

Once you have a rough idea for the survey, you can develop it more fully, incorporating scale, fixed-alternative, and open-ended questions, as illustrated in this chapter. If online access is possible, you can transfer this survey plan into an online survey that will be emailed to prospective audience members and automatically tabulated by the survey instrument.

Part Three

Organization and Style: Speech Construction

Persuasive Speech Organization

To Make a Long Story Short ...

Because the human mind is grounded in order, organization provides the framework for understanding and accepting persuasive messages.

Key Concepts

- Core structure consists of an introduction, body, and conclusion, each with unique functions in the speech.
- Speech organization should be adjusted to suit the speech goal or proposition.
- The common topics help to organize your thoughts.
- An outline equips a speaker with a visible structure for speech content.
- The purpose of your introduction and conclusion is to adapt the speech to your audience's interest, understanding, and experience.
- Placement of counterarguments shapes audience response.

Key Terms

motivated sequence	climax/anticlimax order
counterargument	primacy
signposting	recency

Core Structure

We take comfort in organization. Remember your early school days when armed with a new 12-pack of number two pencils, a 64-pack of crayons, and a slick new binder, you felt *ready*. Now you may take comfort in having the oil changed on your car—or the bills paid by the end of the month. Organization drives us crazy when we are striving to be organized, but in the end it makes us feel invincible.

Organization is vital in a persuasive speech because the human mind interprets and reasons about incoming information by recognizing patterns and order in mental input.[1] Is it any wonder, then, that fear of public speaking is magnified when we are not prepared to speak? If we speak when our thoughts are disordered, we struggle to express the message, while the audience fails to grasp it altogether. On short notice, it helps to have a formula for minimal organization as a visible structure in your mind. This structure will help your audience understand, remember, and accept what you say. What's more, your speech organization enhances audience perception of your competence.

Any organized speech contains the core elements of introduction, body, and conclusion. Persuasive speeches are no exception. Here is a typical core outline:

    I. *Introduction*—gains the attention of the audience and introduces the subject

    II. *Body*—presents the bulk of the speech content

    III. *Conclusion*—summarizes and refocuses the speech

What goes into the body of the speech is the most troublesome aspect of speech organization. Minimally, a persuasive speech organization would contain these elements:

    I. Introduction

        A. Audience attention-getter

        B. Proposition statement (or a succinct opinion statement)

        C. Preview of reasons justifying this proposition

    II. Body

        A. Reason 1

        B. Reason 2

        C. Reason 3

    III. Conclusion—restatement of proposition or central idea

What goes into the body of the speech? You have lots of choices. One effective technique for incorporating substance in a short time frame is to plug in the common topics. Let's say you are proposing that the state maintain a coalmine near one of its premier cities, and your proposition is "The state should keep the Neptune mine open." Scanning the *topoi* we discussed in Chapter 3, you might recognize that you can use the topics of size, possibility, and comparison. See how these fall neatly into three substantial main points:

II. Body

   A. *Size*—The Neptune mine supplies power for more than 1.5 million homes in the state.

   B. *Possible and impossible*—The state currently has no accessible alternative sources of home heating energy. (That is, it is not possible to provide other energy sources.)

   C. *Comparison*—When a neighboring state shuttered its only nuclear power plant, 350 businesses and industries closed for want of affordable power.

This simple structure enables any speaker with limited experience to go before a group with something to say. Granted, you must have a working knowledge of the subject, but with that and with a firm proposition, you can plug the common topics into the most rudimentary speech format. If you know the subject and are familiar with the common topics, any speech can have depth and impact.

Core structure is both a first step in complex speech preparation and a fallback for impromptu presentations. In formal speeches, once you have roughed in your plan, you can pinpoint where you need to develop examples and evidence. In all speeches, like a good GPS, core structure boosts confidence that you are heading in a sound direction.

Organization and the Proposition

There is more than one way to organize a persuasive speech. Just as a farmer determines what crops to grow based on climate and soil, so does your purpose and proposition call for a suitable structure.

We have already mentioned in Chapter Two that the three kinds of propositions correspond with three persuasive purposes and contexts. Propositions of fact appear in *forensic* speech, the speech of the courtroom. Propositions of value are found in ceremonial speeches or speeches of praise or blame, that is, in *epideictic* speech, like an award speech or a eulogy. Propositions of policy, or *deliberative* speech, are common to legislative or decision-making groups. To prove your point, your organization needs to fit your proposition.

Propositions of Fact

You use a proposition of fact to establish the existence of something in the past, present, or future. The governor will be re-elected, red wine consumption contributes to a healthy heart, educational institutions are losing their most experienced teachers to the corporate world. You are not attempting to make a value judgment (as with a proposition of value); you are not attempting to move an audience to action (as with a proposition of policy). Your speech development should be straightforward, contributing to a factual tone, as in the following patterns.

Survey of Reasons Here your main points state the reasons that your proposition is plausible. In its simplest outline form, the survey of reasons proof would look like this:

    I. Introduction

    II. Body

        A. Reason 1

        B. Reason 2

        C. Reason 3

    III. Conclusion

Let's take a real example:

Proposition: Red wine protects against heart disease.

    I. Introduction (Scenario of life in France: beautiful architecture, late-night conversations in sidewalk cafés—and a healthy heart?)

    II. Body

        A. Reduces blood clotting

        B. Increases antioxidants

        C. Raises HDL, good cholesterol

    III. Conclusion

The survey of reasons structure is the most basic of structures—simple, straightforward, and adaptable to any proposition of fact.

Common Topics Survey Another approach to proving a proposition of fact is to develop your subject by using the common topics. As you can see, the body of the speech is much like the survey of reasons structure.

I. Introduction

II. Body

    A. Common topic 1

    B. Common topic 2

    C. Common topic 3

III. Conclusion

An actual outline will look like this:

Proposition: Governor Roberts will be re-elected.

    I. Introduction (Story of Roberts youth, her tenacity and ambition)

    II. Body

        A. *Testimony*—The speaker of the House and Senate majority leader feel she has the support of the electorate.

        B. *Possible/impossible*

            1. Polls indicate she is six percent ahead two weeks before the election. *(possible)*.

            2. Opponent has not been endorsed by any public organizations. *(impossible)*.

        C. *Comparison*— Current status mirrors her lead four years ago, when she won by a landslide

    III. Conclusion (Recap and end with Roberts anecdote.)

As you can see, this format is simply another survey of reasons why the proposition should be accepted. Either of these first two methods can be effective with a neutral or uninformed audience. Since the audience has no preconceptions about the subject, you can present factual information directly, as a list of reasons for agreeing with the proposition.

Cause-Effect Method If the audience has some background in the subject or is seeking an explanation for incidents that are difficult to grasp, the cause-effect structure can be useful:

I. Introduction		
II. Body		II. Body
A. Causes	OR	A. Effects
B. Effects		B. Causes
III. Conclusion		

You can see that this format uses one of the common topics (cause and effect) as an entire speech. With sufficient background information you can *inform* an uninformed audience and *interpret* information for a confused or uncertain audience. This format often appears in historical or political analyses, which try to explain history and current events by assigning causes. For example:

Proposition: A U.S. military buildup in Ukraine will result in armed conflict.

    I. Introduction (Recall similar situation in history.)

    II. Body

        A. Causes

            1. Numbers of troops and weapons

            2. Russian perception of buildup as a threat

        B. Effect = armed conflict

    III. Conclusion (We no longer can avoid or ignore the obvious.)

The cause-effect method can guide an uncertain audience lacking rigid opinions by providing a plausible interpretation of events.

Elimination Method When the speaker and audience are at odds or the audience hostile to the speaker, you may need to seek accord on views that both oppose. This is a little like my son's method for selecting from a menu appetizers for a group of people to share, where each person gets to eliminate a choice. Usually you wind up with something everyone can live with.

Suppose for your speech you want to propose that to escape its water crisis, Southern California should be allowed to divert water from the rivers of the Pacific Northwest. Residents of the Northwest would rally to oppose your proposal. You proceed, therefore, by eliminating possible courses of action, hoping to achieve your own as a last resort.

Proposition: Southern California's water shortage will require diverting water from the Pacific Northwest.

    I. Introduction

    II. Body

        A. Common topic 1—what is *not* the case

        B. Common topic 2—what is *not* the case

        C. Common topic 3—what is *not* the case

        D. Therefore, the only alternative is …

    III. Conclusion

Let's try this with actual arguments:

I. Introduction

II. Body

    A. *Definition*—Naturally semi-desert, California has limited regional water resources.

    B. *Size*—As the most agriculturally productive state, California cannot reduce water usage.

    C. *Possible/Impossible*—Current aqueduct systems are economically and competitively unsustainable.

    D. Therefore, the people of California are turning to their neighbors, asking for compassion and generosity in their time of need.

III. Conclusion (Good neighbors are California's last best hope …)

There you have four workable and logical ways that, with evidence woven in, can prove a proposition of fact. With any one you can have speech substance, a sensible structure, and a convincing case.

Propositions of Value

A proposition of value advances an *evaluation* of a person, place, thing, or idea. The proposition of value includes a value term, like *good* or *bad*, *beneficial* or *harmful*, *right* or *wrong*, and so on. Here are two useful structures for proving a proposition of value.

Survey of reasons method You can use this method to prove a proposition of value just as you would to prove a proposition of fact. In this case, the proof lists three reasons the value term is justified. For example, in proving that, "Pharmaceutical company incentives for doctors are dangerous to patients," your list of reasons could include:

II. Body (Pharmaceutical incentives are dangerous because …)

    A. Incentives pressure doctors to prescribe a drug that *approximates* the preferred treatment.

    B. Incentives raise the cost of all prescription drugs.

    C. Incentives influence doctors' perceptions of patient symptoms.

The survey of reasons method provides a simple organizational pattern for a proposition of value, but it may not be as convincing as the next strategy, the criteria-satisfaction method.

Criteria-satisfaction method This method follows the deductive reasoning pattern you will read about in Chapter Seven. You begin the criteria-satisfaction method by identifying your value term. Next you establish a general definition or set of criteria for that term. Finally, you show how the subject under discussion fits your definition (or criteria).

For example, for the proposition "Abraham Lincoln was an effective U.S. President," you would first want to pick out the value term, the word that evaluates the subject. Here the word *effective* evaluates positively Lincoln's presidency. So for the first segment of the proof, you will define what makes a presidency "effective." For the second segment, you will apply that definition (or set of criteria) to the subject, Abraham Lincoln. The outline of your proof might look like this:

Proposition: Abraham Lincoln was an effective U.S. President.

    I. Introduction (Some doubted he could win over powerful party leaders, some believed the country would never elect a "hayseed" from the frontier, and some wondered whether he could survive his first war-torn term ...)

    II. Body

(criteria)   A. An *effective presidency* means

        1. The President confronts problems rather than backing away from them.

        2. The President appoints independently minded aides.

        3. The President seeks long-term good for the country as a whole.

(satisfaction) B. President Abraham Lincoln

        1. Directly challenged the problem of slavery.

        2. Appointed strong aides who would question him, to promote high quality solutions that met the test of diverse viewpoints.

        3. Sought to remove the inequality and inhumanity of slavery as a stain on national integrity and character.

    III. Conclusion (We can say that Lincoln was an effective President.)

Again, the organizational technique is 1) *criteria* (definition) and 2) *satisfaction* (applying the criteria to the subject). For the next example, ask yourself what is the value term in the proposition. Then figure out an appropriate proof before looking at the one provided.

Proposition: Home-schooling is a sound educational alternative to public-schooling.

    I. Introduction (the story of Alex, a 13-year-old boy who slipped continually through the cracks of the local public school system)

    II. Body

(criteria)   A. What makes an education *sound*?

        1. A sound education adapts to a child's needs.

        2. A sound education provides individualized instruction.

        3. A sound education stimulates creativity and independent thought.

(satisfaction) B. Home-schooling provides sound education.

        1. Home-schooling adapts to each child's developmental level.

        2. Home-schooled children experience abundant individualized instruction.

        3. Home-schooled children have been shown to surpass their public-school counterparts in creativity and critical thinking skills.

    C. Conclusion (So we need not worry about Alex and thousands of children who like him are home-schooled every year …)

You may have noticed that the criteria-satisfaction proof is based on the common topic of *definition*. First, the speaker *defines* (establishes criteria for) the value term, and second, the speaker shows that the subject considered fits the definition (criteria).

In a criteria-satisfaction structure, where would evidence go? You can insert evidence both where you establish criteria and where you apply them. You can validate your criteria for *sound education* by citing studies and educational theory experts. For section II-B, you could cite studies and authorities on home-schooling. Your finished speech will be structurally logical and will demonstrate your command of the subject, thus enhancing your credibility.

Propositions of Policy

The Motivated Sequence Though presented last, the proposition of policy is neither the least common nor the most difficult of persuasive speeches. In fact, it is the type of speech most often associated with persuasive speech, and it is arguably easiest to prove, largely thanks to the work of Alan

Monroe, author with Douglas Ehninger of *Principles and Types of Speech Communication*.[2] Monroe called his structure for proving propositions of policy the **Motivated Sequence**.

Monroe considered audience psychology the basis for persuasion: what motivates an audience to change their mind? He maintained that the very structure of an argument can motivate attitude change. Monroe's structural pattern interfaces neatly, too, with Festinger's theory of cognitive dissonance (see Chapter One). Monroe proposes that the speaker trigger cognitive imbalance in audience members, and then provide the means to restore balance.

The result is a problem-solution pattern consisting of five steps:

1. *Attention*—The speaker arouses audience attention.

2. *Need*—The speaker establishes a need for a change—that a problem exists.

3. *Satisfaction*—The speaker satisfies the need by proposing a solution to the problem.

4. *Visualization*—The speaker points out the benefits of adopting the solution.

5. *Action*—The speaker asks the audience to do something to help achieve the solution.

Here is how the motivated sequence would psychologically *motivate* audience concern and attitude change. First, the attention step, ordinarily a part of the introduction, helps to rivet audience minds to the subject. Next, the speaker establishes that a problem exists, by offering various forms of evidence—examples, statistics, testimony from authorities, for instance. The need (or problem) step agitates cognitive imbalance within listeners. Why imbalance? Because the if the speaker can create a striking picture of an imminent problem, the audience will perceive a threat to themselves or to what they value.

With the satisfaction (or solution) step, the speaker offers an escape from the imbalance, a way out of the problem. The fourth step, the visualization, enhances the appeal of the solution by showing its benefits and that it will work, reassuring the audience that restored balance is still within reach. The fifth and final step stirs the audience to become a part of the solution by taking action against the problem.

Look at the motivated sequence in outline form:

Proposition: The city should declare all public gathering spaces tobacco-free.

I. Introduction

   *A. *Attention* (Remember the last time you were caught in a smoke cloud at the Farmers' Market ...)

   B. Introduce subject.

   C. State the proposition.

   D. Preview main points of the body.

II. Body

   *A. *Need* (*problem*)—Smoking in public areas poses a problem to all citizens.

   *B. *Satisfaction* (*solution*)—We can prohibit smoking in public gathering spaces.

   *C. *Visualization* (*benefits*)—Imagine being able to stroll through the market without health risk or physical discomfort.

III. Conclusion

   A. Review main points. (problem, solution, benefits)

   B. Restate proposition.

   *C. *Action* (*You* can help by signing this petition ...)

Now, if you prefer, you can switch up this strategy by using the common topics as pieces of the motivated sequence, such as in developing the problem.

II. Body

   A. *Need* (*problem*)—Smoking in public areas poses a problem to all citizens.

     1. *Size*—Nonsmoking citizens outnumber smokers 15 to 1.

     2. *Cause-effect*—There is little doubt that second-hand smoke is a public health problem, for smokers as well as for non-smokers. According to reports from the American Cancer Society ...

     3. *Possible/Impossible*—This would not be a problem if there were gathering spaces constructed for smokers apart from the main public areas, but the fact is that there are not, and are not likely to be, in the city's current financial crisis.

Propositions of policy can be exciting for both speakers and their audiences. The motivated sequence is both a classic and modern persuasive formula that ignites audience enthusiasm.

Dealing with Counterarguments

You may be impeccably prepared and eloquent, but that will not make you immune to audience opposition. Their opposing arguments we call **counterarguments**, since they run counter to (or oppose) the speaker's position. What is to be done with counterarguments?

If you have a proposition of fact, you can admit there are those who deny your claims. With a proposition of value, you can acknowledge testimony opposing the validity of your criteria. With a proposition of policy, you could recognize that some people deny a problem exists or that the solution you have proposed solves the problem.

Wherever you acknowledge counterarguments, you need follow them with refutations (arguments *against the opposition*) to reinforce your position, as shown below in the policy speech we just constructed:

II. Body

A. *Need (problem)*—Smoking in public areas poses a problem to all citizens.

1. Supportive argument

2. Counterargument

3. Refutation

B. *Satisfaction (solution)*—We can prohibit smoking in public gathering spaces.

1. Plan

2. Counterargument

3. Refutation

C. *Visualization (benefits)*—Imagine being able to stroll through the market without health risk or physical discomfort.

1. Plan will benefit us because …

2. Counterargument: Plan will be harmful because …

3. Refutation

Or as an alternative, you could save all the counterarguments until after you have presented your case:

II. Body

    A. *Need (problem)*—Smoking in public areas poses a problem to all citizens.

    B. *Satisfaction (solution)*—We can prohibit smoking in public gathering spaces.

    C. *Visualization (benefits)*—Imagine being able to stroll through the market without health risk or physical discomfort.

    D. *Counterarguments and refutation*

        1. Arguments

        2. Refutations

It is tempting to ignore difficult counterarguments against your position, but as we will explain more in Chapter Seven, to be persuasive you must include and confront them.

Looking over the Outline

Ideally you will use your outline as speaking notes. With this brief and clear-cut structure, you can remember what you want to say and communicate clearly to your audience. We have not stressed outline form just yet, but you can see that each example has adhered to a consistent and simple structure. If you begin to *think* repeatedly about this form, it can become ingrained in your speechmaking, increasing the probability that your speeches will be dependably organized.

You can see how the outline examples in this chapter state the proposition at the top. This does not mean that the first remarks in your introduction would be your proposition. But your proposition, as your guiding principle, should be evident to you throughout your preparation. You also may have noticed that we mostly have dealt with the body of the speech (since this is the most difficult part of the speech to develop), but our outline examples show three parts to a persuasive speech: introduction, body, and conclusion.

Finally, you see that the outlines are indented from I and II to A and B, and from A and B to 1, 2, and 3. The farther to the left each number or letter is, the more critical that point to speech content. When you indent these points, you indicate that they support more important, general points. The indentations also show at a glance where you are in the flow of the speech. Look at an outline without these indentations:

    I. Introduction

    A. Attention

    B. Introduce subject

C. State proposition

D. Preview main points

II. Body

A. First main point

1. What authorities say

2. How many people affected

B. Second main point

1. Example

2. Statistics

C. Third main point

III. Conclusion

A. Recap

B. Restate proposition

When you set main points apart from supporting (or subordinate) points by indentation, you can locate your place quickly, whereas in the faulty example above, all the points look the same. Yet another error in outlining is to indent supporting points inconsistently:

I. Introduction
A. Attention
B. Introduce subject
C. State proposition
D. Preview main points
II. Body
A. First main point
1. What authorities say
2. How many people affected
B. Second main point
1. Example
2. Statistics
C. Third main point
III. Conclusion
A. Recap
B. Restate proposition

There is no logic to this format, since there is no consistency in the number and letter notations. If the structure of the speech is not obvious to you

Figure 6.1 The Occupy Wall Street movement began in September, 2011, in downtown Manhattan. Protesters rallied against economic inequality as exemplified by the country's financial sector (the "1%") at the expense of the greater citizenry (the other "99%.") Such clashes vividly illustrate the reality of contrary viewpoints and the necessity of counterarguments to defuse opposition.
© lev radin/Shutterstock, Inc.

as you speak, you are bound to appear disorganized to your audience. Organization gives you confidence as you speak. This confidence translates into credibility with the audience. Moreover, the only audience that will be persuaded is the one that can understand and follow the speech's logic.

Introductions and Conclusions

Introductions

After you have a solid sense of the body of your speech, like selecting the filling for your sandwich, you can figure out a complementary wrapping, in this case your introduction and conclusion.

Attention

Your speech will not go far if its hearers do not attend to the message. Thus the first task of the introduction is not to state your name and credentials, not to state a title to your speech, and not to state your proposition. To begin you must first *capture the attention* of your audience. There are as many ways to do this as there are speakers and subjects, including

- stating a startling fact or statistic
- reciting a memorable quote
- referring to the audience's experience
- asking a thought-provoking rhetorical question
- telling a story; revealing an interesting example or anecdote related to the subject

The Primacy of Stories

If you find yourself torn between these strategies for introductions, contemporary presentation theory heavily favors the anecdote, or story, as a hook. Nancy Duarte is both founder and CEO of Duarte Design, a communication consulting firm featuring presentation design and branding. Her career took a giant step when she assisted former Vice-President Al Gore in developing visual content for his award-winning documentary on climate change, *An Inconvenient Truth*. So why does Duarte recommend stories? She explains,

> Stories build suspense by introducing a hero, a challenge, a journey, and finally, a resolution that delivers the hero into an improved reality . . . [and stories] cause chemical, physical, and emotional responses in listeners. When stories make people feel things like trust or kindness, the brain releases oxytocin, which motivates cooperation by enhancing empathy.[3]

In 2018, *The New York Times'* podcast, "The Daily," described how Anthony Romero, executive director of the American Civil Liberties Union, recognized the superior public relations of the National Rifle Association on the basis of their ability to make their story personal:

> Back in 2013, I think the NRA and the ACLU were of comparable size. But if you asked me who had had a greater impact on American society and politics and government, I'd have to say it was the NRA. I was trying to understand why is it they punch so much above their weight, if they're the same size as we are . . . Their website was very different from our website. It was much more narrative. There were stories; there were videos . . . They don't talk about [the second amendment] in legalistic terms. They talk about it in very personal lifestyle terms. That was when the light bulb went off in our heads, because when we talk about liberty . . . we're not only talking about the first, or fourth, or fifth amendment . . . We're talking about . . . making sure that you have the right to live the life you choose to have.[4]

Hence, the ACLU changed their PR tactics by telling the stories of people whose rights were under siege. As a case in point, in 2018, when the Department of Justice began to separate undocumented immigrant children, including toddlers, from their parents, the ACLU did not try to convince the public with a fifth amendment argument, but with the stories of children taken from their parents, the parents deported, and the children left behind, lost in the system. Audiences understand human stories. As an introductory technique, the story's bonus feature is its potential to weave through the speech and into the conclusion, sustaining interest from start to finish.

Connect Audience and Issue

Once you have secured audience attention, you want to hold it by providing reasons for them to care. To *draw your audience into the speech*, stimulate their interest in and concern for the subject. Since the persuasive speech deals with a public problem (see Chapter Two), you can stir up audience concern by referring to the connection between the problem and the audience. If the speaker's subject is airline safety, refer to your audience's future travel plans; if they do not travel much by air, people they care about may. If your subject is disposable diapers in landfills, you can refer to audience members who are parents or to those who intend to become parents or to sanitation hazards that threaten public health. Whatever your subject, you want the audience to recognize that they have a stake in it.

 Since You Asked...

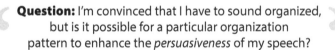 **Question:** I'm convinced that I have to sound organized, but is it possible for a particular organization pattern to enhance the *persuasiveness* of my speech?

Answer: Yes, some of the more interesting organization studies address these questions:

1. Where should I put my most important arguments?

2. How should I intersperse counterarguments and refutations with the rest of my speech?

3. Is it more powerful to speak first or last?

The first question deals with climax as opposed to anti-climax organizational schemes. The **climax order** builds momentum and impact toward a rousing finish with less important or weaker arguments first and most powerful arguments last. The **anticlimax order** starts with a punch, then simmers down, placing most

(Continued)

important arguments first and less significant ones last. Persuasion scholar Daniel O'Keefe observes that studies suggest no preference for either order, although a speaker should insert important arguments first if there is a chance of being cut off early.[5] Likewise, if the speaker wants to capitalize on the emotional impact of an issue, a climax order may more effectively intensify audience emotions.

As for organizing counterarguments and refutations, a speaker probably has three choices:

Option 1:

    II. Body

        A. Arguments

            1. Argument 1

            2. Argument 2

            3. Argument 3

        B. Counterarguments

            1. Counterargument/refutation 1

            2. Counterargument/refutation 2

            3. Counterargument/refutation 3

Option 2:

    II. Body

        A. Counterarguments

            1. Counterargument/refutation 1

            2. Counterargument/refutation 2

            3. Counterargument/refutation 3

        B. Arguments

            1. Argument 1

            2. Argument 2

            3. Argument 3

Option 3:

    II. Body

        A. Argument 1

            1. Counterargument

            2. Refutation

Proposition

The third function of the introduction is to *state the proposition*. Because the subject of a persuasive speech is controversial, there may be some merit to withholding your point of view until the audience is "softened." To offset audience resistance to the message, you delay the proposition. Some theorists support this strategy, reasoning that speakers should emphasize points of agreement before trying to win acceptance on contentious points.[8] You might emphasize concerns you have in common with the audience, concerns discovered through your audience analysis. Ruth Anne Clark supports the value of invitational rhetoric in suggesting several other adaptations, such as expressing understanding for the audience's feelings and reassuring the audience so as to avoid threatening their interests.[9] Yet once you *have* taken care to adapt your opening statements to the audience and to modify the proposition if necessary (see Chapter Five), you should state the proposition directly so that the audience will know your intent.

Signposts

The last stage of your introduction will serve to segue into the body of the speech. Here you *preview your speech content*. Research is fairly conclusive on this aspect of message organization. When you provide a structural scheme for listeners, those listeners understand more, recall more, and learn more from the message.[10] This is **signposting**, where you tell the audience, as a signpost on the road would tell, where they are going, where they are presently, and where they have been. In the introduction, a signpost tells the audience what is to come, as in this example:

> If we really want to tackle the problem of homelessness in the city, let's first track the *scope of the problem* and then suggest some *solutions* that can relieve their burden and ours.

> First, how many homeless do you think populate our city? ...

The speaker has told the audience that the speech will discuss the problem first and the solution second. Then launching into the body of the speech, the speaker reiterates the first signpost—the problem. In the example above, the body of the speech begins with a rhetorical question as a signpost. Lastly, addressing the solution, the speaker announces

> Now that we know our homelessness problem is critical and that it threatens our town's productivity and safety, let's consider our options in solving the problem.

Because you signpost the solution phase of the speech, the audience never loses sight of where the speech is headed. The signposts in the introduction set the audience up for the structure of the entire speech, and this clarity ensures audience comprehension. See how one speaker developed a smoothly conversational introduction that accomplished each of these objectives:

*This **attention**-getter first sparks curiosity and second subtly establishes identification with a cultural value.*	Individualism. What is it to you? If you are like most people in the United States, you consider yourself an individualist. So do I. It may surprise you that inside this apparently conservative mother beats the heart of a rebel.
*The speaker **introduces the subject**—home-schooling.*	Maybe this is why I did not flinch at bucking the norm when my children entered school. I wanted to seize the reins of their education instead of mounting them on the plodding old mare of our local school system. I chose home-schooling.
*This direct appeal to audience members makes the **proposition** absolutely clear.*	Whether you know it or not, whether you have children now or will one day, public schools will matter to your life and theirs. You may be in for a wild ride. This is why I believe so firmly that **parents should consciously choose the course of their children's education.**

*The speaker introduces three **signposts**.*

But let's back up a little. First, let's examine the problems facing public schools, second, whether the schools can overcome these problems, and third, whether home school parents have discovered a better way.

Conclusions

As Richard Petty and John Cacioppo observe, "A conclusion is usually helpful or necessary for the audience to understand and remember fully the message arguments and advocacy."[11] But as these scholars point out, if the audience is motivated, the issue engaging, and the speech clearly developed, a speech may be more persuasive when the speaker allows the audience to draw conclusions independently. In most persuasive speeches, however, absolute speech clarity does not exist, and as William McGuire puts it, "It is not sufficient to lead the horse to water; one must also push his head underneath to get him to drink."[12]

If the introduction tells the audience what you're going to tell them, and the body tells them, then the conclusion tells them what you've told them. The primary goals of the conclusion are to confirm your point and to rouse your listeners.

Review

The telling them what you've told them part of the persuasive speech is not difficult. You simply *recall for the audience the points you have covered*:

> We know the homeless are not going to disappear without help, and we know we *can* help.

With this brief statement, you recall the problem and solution phases of the speech.

Recall the Proposition

Above all, you want your audience to leave with a clear idea of what you said and where you stood. For this reason, it's a good idea to restate your proposition, preferably as a paraphrase of the way you presented it in the introduction. If the proposition is *The city should be proactive in managing homelessness*, the paraphrase might state *If through negligence our city has made homelessness more dangerous for residents and homeless alike, then it should move toward a managed homeless policy that will enhance public safety.* By paraphrasing the proposition, we optimize its force, and our audience, fortified with evidence and arguments, is primed to accept it.

Reinforce Audience Connection

Finally, the conclusion should *rekindle audience involvement in the subject.* If you began with a story, bring it full circle in the conclusion by updating us on the status of its main characters. If you have a proposition of fact or value, you can remind the audience of its stake in the issue. With a proposition of policy, however, you would make a final *appeal to the audience to take action.* You might ask the audience to sign a petition, to write an email or letter of advocacy, to talk to another person, to become involved in an organization. The speaker on home-schooling stated her appeal to action figuratively:

*The speaker **recaps** the problem and solution.*

Our plodding public schools may be struggling to leap the barriers in their paths, but they are tripping over them instead. Home-school parents are determined, they are dedicated, they are focused. They are not falling; they are taking every hurdle in stride as they stride toward the finish line. And their children are coming away with the prize.

*The **proposition** paraphrase is concise and figurative.*

*The **appeal to action** may be a little over-the-top metaphorically (see Chapter Eight), but it engages the audience with a sense of urgency.*

Parents need to take the reins of their kids' education. Don't let them slip through your hands, and don't abandon your charge. Teach your children to ride before turning them loose on the bucking bronco of life.

Unfortunately, an audience's resolve to take action begins to fade the moment the speech is over. You will be more likely to get the audience to take action if you provide a tangible means of doing so. One persuasive speaker sought to remedy poor sanitation standards in local day-care centers. She gave listeners cards for their name, address, and telephone number and for citing one complaint against a particular day-care center's practices. She then forwarded these comments to the county's Children's Services Division. Another creative speaker who had two epileptic children spoke about rampant misinformation in our society about epilepsy. What the audience could do, she said, would be to donate toward the purchase of an epilepsy fact book for the library. The audience was moved to do just that. Practical and effective.

In Summary

Psychologists and neurologists have made much of the human propensity for order. If we are to reach others' minds through communication, our messages will need to accommodate their innate sense of order. You can choose from a number of organizational schemes, depending on your subject and proposition.

You can approach propositions of fact by reviewing reasons that support the fact or reasons to reject opposition to the fact. Propositions of value require you to define and defend the value term. A proposition of policy will likely work best using the motivated sequence.

Whichever organizational method you choose, you must examine and refute counterarguments to the proposition to address the audience's resistance to persuasion.

You can capture your organization in an outline that serves as your speaking notes. The outline provides a simple, readable, and memorable record of what you want to say. The *last* additions to your outline, the introduction and conclusion, generate interest and prepare the audience for what follows. In the end, by recalling your points, rekindling interest, and stimulating action on the proposition, you can reinforce the value of this rhetorical moment.

Endnotes

[1] See, for instance, Mark P. Mattson. "Superior Pattern Processing is the Essence of the Evolved Human Brain." *Frontiers in Neuroscience*, vol. 8, no. 265, 22 Aug. 2014, https://www.ncbi.nlm.nih.gov/pmc/articles/PMC4141622/, and Ting Qian and Richard N. Aslin. "Learning Bundles of Stimuli Renders Order as a Cue, not a Confound." *Proceedings of the National Academy of Sciences of the United States of America*, vol. 111, no. 40, 27 Aug. 2014, http://www.pnas.org/content/111/40/14400.

[2] Raymie E. McKerrow, Bruce E. Gronbeck, Douglas Ehninger, and Alan H. Monroe, *Principles and Types of Public Speaking*, 16th ed. (Upper Saddle River, NJ: Pearson, 2006).

[3] Becky Bicks, "Improve Your Storytelling Presentation Skills and Get Your Ideas Adopted." *Duarte*, 10 Mar. 2018, https://www.duarte.com/presentation-skills-resources/storytelling-presentation-skills/.

[4] Podcast interview with Anthony Romero. "Why the ACLU Wants to Be More Like the NRA." *The Daily, The New York Times*, 30 July 2018, https://www.nytimes.com/podcasts/the-daily.

[5] Daniel O'Keefe, *Persuasion: Theory and Research*, 2nd ed. (Thousand Oaks, CA: Sage, 2002), 158.

[6] See, for example, Gordon L. Dahnke and Glen W. Clatterbuck, *Human Communication: Theory and Research* (Belmont, CA: Wadsworth, 1990), 162.

[7] Ibid., 183.

[8] Ibid., 247.

[9] Ruth Anne Clark, *Persuasive Messages* (New York: Harper and Row, 1984), 42–45.

[10] Robert N. Bostrom, *Persuasion* (Englewood Cliffs, NJ: Prentice-Hall, 1983), 174–175.

[11] Richard E. Petty and John T. Cacioppo, *Attitudes and Persuasion: Classic and Contemporary Approaches* (Boulder, CO: Westview Press, 1996), 76.

[12] Ibid.

Theory into Practice

1. For practice, sketch out an outline for the following propositions:
   a. The increasing trend of severe hurricanes in coastal regions will result in persistent land loss issues for coastal communities.
   b. Government subsidies for oil exploration benefit the American consumer.
   c. The Environmental Protection Agency should increase its financial commitment to controlling industrial waste that exacerbates climate change.

2. For the following proposition of fact, consider three organizational options for developing a speech. Which do you think would be the most workable?
   Proposition: The cosmetic industry affects animal health by its laboratory testing procedures.

3. Select an opinion piece from a news source. Think of three counterarguments you could present against this point of view. How might the writer refute your counterarguments?

4. For each of the subjects in Exercise 1, write an introduction, performing each of the four functions of the introduction. Try using various attention-getting techniques, as suggested in this chapter, or create your own techniques. Evaluate your efforts: what works and what doesn't?

5. Repeat Exercise 4, this time writing and evaluating conclusions.

Oral Practice

Jot down several policy proposals in recent news reports. In the spaces a through e under each proposal, note how you would express the five stages of the motivated sequence for that subject. Try delivering one of these aloud (about two minutes' worth of speaking)—in front of a listener, if possible.

Policy Proposals:

1. _____

    a. _____

    b. _____

    c. _____

    d. _____

    e. _____

2. _____

    a. _____

    b. _____

    c. _____

    d. _____

    e. _____

3. _____

    a. _____

    b. _____

    c. _____

    d. _____

    e. _____

Outline Worksheet for Speech of Fact

(See pages 138 to 141 for the suggested structures for this type of speech. Fill in the appropriate information in the spaces provided. This outline can be used as your speaking notes.)

I. Introduction
    A. Attention
    B. Introduce subject
    C. Proposition
    D. Signposts
        1.
        2.
        3.

II. Body
    A. Issue 1
        1. Evidence/example
        2. Evidence/example
    B. Issue 2
        1. Evidence/example
        2. Evidence/example
    C. Issue 3
        1. Evidence/example
        2. Evidence/example
    D. Counterarguments/refutation
        1. Counterargument
            a. Claim
            b. Refutation
        2. Counterargument
            a. Claim
            b. Refutation

III. Conclusion
    A. Recap main points
    B. Paraphrase proposition
    C. Rekindle audience concern

Outline Worksheet for Speech of Value

(See pages 141 to 143 for suggested organizational patterns for this type of speech. For a survey of reasons method, use the format for a speech of fact; for a criteria-satisfaction method, use this format. This outline can be used as your speaking notes.)

I. Introduction
    A. Attention
    B. Introduce subject
    C. Proposition
    D. Signposts
       1.
       2.
II. Body
    A. Criteria for value term
       1. Criterion 1
       2. Criterion 2
       3. Criterion 3
    B. Why the value term is appropriate to the subject
       1. Reason 1
       2. Reason 2
       3. Reason 3
    C. Counterarguments/refutation
       1. Counterargument
          a. Claim
          b. Refutation
       2. Counterargument
          a. Claim
          b. Refutation
III. Conclusion
    A. Recap main points
    B. Paraphrase proposition
    C. Rekindle audience concern

Outline Worksheet for Speech of Policy

(See pages 143 to 146 for the motivated sequence structure. This outline can be used as your speaking notes.)

I. Introduction
   A. Attention
   B. Introduce subject
   C. Proposition
   D. Signposts
      1.
      2.
      3.
II. Body
   A. Need (existence of problem)
      1. Evidence/example
      2. Evidence/example
      3. Evidence/example
   B. Satisfaction (how to solve the problem)
      1. Step 1
      2. Step 2
      3. Step 3
   C. Visualization (solution will work/is beneficial)
      1. Reason 1
      2. Reason 2
      3. Reason 3
   D. Counterarguments/refutation
      1. Counterargument
         a. Claim
         b. Refutation
      2. Counterargument
         a. Claim
         b. Refutation
III. Conclusion
   A. Recap main points
   B. Paraphrase proposition
   C. Appeal for audience action

7 Reasoning and Refutation

To Make a Long Story Short...

The study of reasoning describes systematic ways humans learn to think.

Key Concepts

- Persuasive speech preparation includes constructing reasonable arguments and defending against unreasonable opposition.
- Some common reasoning faults include fallacies of generalization conformity, cause, and comparison.
- Your speech should recognize and refute opposing arguments.
- Effective refutations challenge the claim, reveal the claim's error, and provide an alternative interpretation of facts.
- Persuasion is more durable when you "inoculate" your audience against counterarguments and refutations.

Key Terms

reasoning	*ad hominem*
premise	appeal to conformity
deduction	false cause
induction	faulty comparison
fallacy	refutation
hasty generalization	inoculation theory
stereotyping	

The Nature of Reasoning

There are many wonders in nature, but the human brain may be the most complex and unfathomable natural wonder of all. From infancy, humans learn to understand language: the word "cracker" produces a cracker, the word activating a predictable pattern of thought. This is one of our early reasoning processes.

When we speak of **reasoning** we are referring to patterns of thought. Experience teaches us what is reasonable. When the word "cracker" no longer produces the thing, a child may conclude that the word-thing connection is no longer valid. When we speak of reasoning, then, we are not referring to abstract formulas but to ways humans learn to think, or to ways they find expressed thoughts reasonable.

Still, not all thinking is reasoning. We can think without reasoning, just as we may be fit without working out. As Irving Copi points out, "Reasoning is a special kind of thinking in which . . . conclusions are drawn from premises."[1] The goal of reasoning is not simply to operate the mind, but to determine whether our conclusions follow from the premises.[2] By **premise** we mean an assumption, or a reason for accepting a conclusion.

By examining the reasoning patterns below, you can understand ways to defend your views in a persuasive speech and to argue effectively against opposing views. Thus, the study of reasoning can help you *form* reasonable arguments and *refute* unreasonable ones.

Forms of Reasoning

Review the following reasoning patterns, considering what deductive or inductive arguments you could use to defend your point of view.

Deduction

In Chapter One, we referred to *beliefs* as accepted data about the universe. Beliefs, those statements we hold to be true, can become premises in our arguments. Deduction begins with such premises or *general beliefs*. Deductive reasoning demonstrates that what is true according to general beliefs is also true in particular aspects of that belief. Look at a couple of examples:

Example 1

    General—Art classes are enjoyable.

    Particular—Life Drawing is an art class.

Example 2

>*General*—Denzel Washington films are worth seeing.

>*Particular*—Malcom X is a Denzel Washington film.

Both of these belief progressions suggest conclusions. In Example 1, you could easily conclude that Life Drawing is an enjoyable class. In Example 2, you conclude that *Malcolm X* is worth seeing. The reasoning process goes like this:

Example 1

>*General (premise)*—Art classes are enjoyable.

>*Particular (premise)*—Life Drawing is an art class.

>*Conclusion*—Life Drawing is an enjoyable class.

Example 2

>*General (premise)*—Denzel Washington films are worth seeing.

>*Particular (premise)*—Malcolm X is a Denzel Washington film.

>*Conclusion*—Malcolm X is worth seeing.

A deductive reasoning process says this: If we know that a general statement is true, whatever is contained within that statement is also true. What is true of the whole is true of its parts. Look at some other examples of deductive reasoning:

>*General (premise)*—The countries of the Middle East are oil-rich.

>*Particular (premise)*—Saudi Arabia is a Middle Eastern country.

>*Conclusion*—Saudi Arabia is an oil-rich country.

>*General (premise)*—Opioids are addictive drugs.

>*Particular (premise)*—Fentanyl is an opioid.

>*Conclusion*—Fentanyl is an addictive drug.

What is the use of deduction in a persuasive speech? If you know that an audience holds a general belief, you can demonstrate that your position aligns with that belief.

To demonstrate how you might develop a deductive argument to support a persuasive proposition, look at the 2013 case of Edward Snowden, a 29-year-old security worker for the National Security Agency and the CIA, who sought refuge in Hong Kong as cover for the impending fallout over the fact that he had leaked vast classified information documenting global U.S. surveillance against other countries and its own citizens.[3]

After these revelations emerged, Snowden was accused of espionage and labeled variously a spy, a traitor, a whistleblower, and runner-up to Pope Francis for *Time* magazine's Man of the Year.

If you were to speak on this subject, proposing that Snowden should be protected from prosecution for his actions, by the Whistleblower Protection Act,[4] you might follow this pattern:

> *General premise*—The Whistleblower Protection Act defends employees who disclose information to protect others from abuse of authority.

> *Particular premise*—Edward Snowden revealed the NSA's abuse of authority.

> *Conclusion*—Therefore, the Whistleblower Protection Act applies to Edward Snowden's actions.

What makes deduction useful in this case is that many people might be inclined to oppose leniency toward Snowden, but the speaker could gamble that between U.S. security and individual right to privacy, the privacy right was paramount in the minds of the audience—and this is what the deductive argument supports.

Deductive reasoning is a thought pattern we use to make sense of the unknown or to determine what we can reasonably claim.

Induction

While deduction reasons from a general belief to particular cases, **induction** reasons from particular instances to general conclusions.

There lies the problem with induction, or as Nassim Taleb poses in his best-selling study, *The Black Swan*, "how can we *logically* go from specific instances to reach general conclusions?"[5] If I generalize to a belief about cats, that cats have tails, on the basis of my experience of having seen only tailed cats, the certainty of my conclusion is limited by the scope of my experience. Here is Taleb's case in point:

> Consider a turkey that is fed every day. Every single feeding will firm up the bird's belief that it is a general rule of life to be fed every day by friendly members of the human race "looking out for its best interests," as a politician might say. On the afternoon of the Wednesday before Thanksgiving, something *unexpected* will happen to the turkey. It will incur a revision of belief.[6]

As Taleb points out, "There are traps built into any kind of knowledge gained from observation,"[7] as in the following series:

> *Observation*—The Cubs won their first series against the Mets.
>
> *Observation*—The Cubs won their second series against the Cardinals.
>
> *Observation*—The Cubs won their second series against the Pirates.
>
> *Conclusion*—The Cubs will win the World Series this year.

In this case you could attend fifteen games or more in a season and see the Cubs win every time. But a major league season consists of more than 160 games per team, and to win the World Series, the National League champion must then play the American League champion, reducing the odds of a correct conclusion. Of course, if you know anything about the Chicago Cubs baseball team, you probably know the Cubs went from 1908 to 2016 before winning a modern World Series, and those who bet on a 2017 repeat lost their bet.

In fact that last statement, too, demonstrates the problem of induction; from experience of the Cubs having been a losing team, I infer that they will continue losing. Taleb calls this reliance on the evidence of experience "naive empiricism." What is improbable is improbable on the basis of our current knowledge. What's more, any generalizations from observation are backward-looking or retrospective, since they depend on what has happened in the past. They have little predictive value: *"the same hand that feeds you can be the one that wrings your neck."*[8]

Despite the problem of induction involving probabilities (and unstable probabilities at that—remember the turkey), the human mind is inclined to find inductive reasoning reasonable. With an inductive thought pattern, we perceive a *probable* truth: The turkey will continue to live a pleasant life among beneficent humans; the Cubs will win the World Series. In contrast, a deductive pattern leads to a certain truth, as long as the general belief and particular case are true.

To sum up the value of deduction and inductive reasoning, then, Howard Kahane, a leader in the critical thinking movement in education, observes that the two basic kinds of arguments we recognize as valid are deduction and induction.[9] The difference between these two forms of argument is that "the conclusion of a deductively valid argument is just as certain as its premises, while the conclusion of an inductively valid argument is less certain than its premises."[10] Nonetheless, the fact that people find inductive reasoning reasonable suggests that we can use inductive arguments in our speeches, but we also can learn how to refute an opponent's inductive argument as uncertain.

Causal Reasoning

For many engineers-in-training, persuasive speech is a required course. If a persuasive speech course was not required for you, you might still have determined that a course in persuasive speech is what you need to upgrade your professional skills. You have made this judgment by *causal reasoning*, when you reason that one factor or event will bring about another factor or event.

Causal reasoning may work another way: If you listen to a presentation by a skilled engineer, you suppose that this speaking ability was acquired by (caused by) speech training. In the first case you reasoned from *cause to effect*, and in the second from *effect to cause*. Causal reasoning is often used in the field of health care. A doctor observes that a patient's obesity will eventually cause more serious problems, such as heart disease or diabetes (cause to effect). Or a doctor predicts that from the symptom of a tennis player's tender right elbow, the player has tendinitis, inferring that it was caused by playing tennis. An argument from cause might look like this:

Effect to cause (effect = swollen eyes; cause = hay fever):

Observation—Carmelo's eyes are red and swollen again this spring.

Conclusion—Carmelo must be suffering from hay fever again.

Cause to effect (cause = investment; effect = earnings):

Observation—I have invested $2500 in a money market account earning five percent interest.

Conclusion—I expect to earn $125 from this investment the first year.

Either type of causal reasoning is a form of induction because you are reasoning from one or more particulars to a conclusion. Like any inductive argument, causal reasoning works in the realm of probability rather than certainty,[11] which is why neither medicine nor investment can be considered an exact science, depending on the number of cases that form the basis for a conclusion.

Comparison

In 1971, the state of Oregon passed what was then an innovative law, a bottle bill, setting a deposit on soft drink and beer cans and bottles, which would then be recycled when they were returned to redeem the deposit. Since then ten states (and eight Canadian provinces) have followed Oregon's lead, often arguing that if it worked in Oregon, it could work in their own states. By 1991 Oregon legislators pressed Congress for a federal bottle bill, with Senator Bob Packwood arguing, "The recycling effort is

Figure 7.1 You can reason causally based on images you see as easily as from arguments you hear. Are you inclined, for instance, to infer health effects among this group of smokers gathered outside a cigar shop In New York City?
© cdrin/Shutterstock, Inc.

in full swing in my home state of Oregon, where we have a 93 percent recycling rate for beverage containers,"[12] By using the Oregon precedent in their reasoning, congressional legislators were reasoning by comparison or analogy.

You have probably heard people in the United States argue in favor of legalizing marijuana for recreational use by comparing the criminalization of marijuana to alcohol prohibition from 1920 to 1933, which ended in failure by most accounts. If alcohol prohibition did little to restrict alcohol consumption, and it led to higher crime rates as well as more violent (and virulent) organized crime, what was the value in restricting it? And by comparison, in what way does prohibiting marijuana discourage its use or benefit society? This argument can be schematized like this:

> *Observation*—The illegalization of alcohol in the 1920s was unenforceable and damaging.

> *Conclusion*—Marijuana illegalization must also be unenforceable and damaging.

Like causal reasoning, reasoning by comparison is inductive. You take one or several examples as a basis for comparison. The more similarities you can find between the things compared, the more probably valid your conclusion, and the more evidence that the things compared *are* similar, the firmer your conclusion.

Vulnerable Reasoning and Fallacies

As you look back over the examples of arguments given so far in this chapter, you can see that some of the conclusions are questionable. Superficially the arguments are plausible, but any argument can fall apart under scrutiny. Thus you will want to use only those arguments you can support with sound premises and evidence. Likewise, by becoming familiar with typical argument structures, you also can probe opposing arguments to locate holes and faults within.

Holes in reasoning show up like holes in a poorly knit sweater; to the untrained eye they seem to fit in as a part of the design but to the skilled practitioner, they reveal their sloppiness. We label such weaknesses in reasoning as fallacies. A **fallacy** is a vulnerable argument or reasoning pattern—one that is easy to attack. Of course, conscientious persuasive speakers will want to tighten the progression of ideas in their speeches to eliminate fallacies. With practiced focus on how premises and conclusions fit together, both speakers and listeners can train themselves to find weak reasoning in others' claims as well.

Faulty Reasoning

To develop a deductive or inductive reasoning pattern is not necessarily to construct a valid argument. Look again at our first deductive example:

> *General (premise)*—Art classes are enjoyable.
>
> *Particular (premise)*—Life Drawing is an art class.
>
> *Conclusion*—Life Drawing is an enjoyable class.

For a deductive conclusion to be true, the premises on which it is based must be true. If art classes are *not* entirely enjoyable or if Life Drawing is *not* an art class, the conclusion does not follow. Here is a flawed deduction:

> *General (premise)*— Jennifer Lawrence films are top box office draws.
>
> *Particular (premise)*—*The Devil Wears Prada* is a Jennifer Lawrence film.
>
> *Conclusion*—*The Devil Wears Prada* was a top box office draw.

Maybe the initial premise here is true, but the second premise is not; Jennifer Lawrence did not produce, direct, or act in *The Devil Wears Prada*. Once again, because one of the premises was not true, the conclusion is not logically valid; it does not follow from the premises.

Finally, a deduction also is invalid if it does not follow the form of whole and part of the whole, for example,

All baseballs are round.

Oranges are round.

Therefore, oranges are baseballs.

In this case, the second (particular) premise must be part of the general class, *baseball*, rather than sharing the descriptive characteristic of that class, *round*. In the same way, we would have a defective deduction if our *The Devil Wears Prada* example did not follow the whole and part of the whole formula, as follows,

Jennifer Lawrence films are top box office draws.

The Devil Wears Prada is a top box office draw.

Therefore, *The Devil Wears Prada* is a Jennifer Lawrence film.

Again the descriptive term in the general premise cannot be used as the *whole* of which the particular premise is a *part*.

As you see, it is possible to encounter *untrue premises* and to encounter *defective deductive forms*. To deconstruct and refute deductive arguments, you need to show that either

1. at least one premise, general or particular, is not true, *or*

2. the conclusion does not follow from the general and particular premises, *or*

3. the deductive argument does not adhere to proper deductive form arguing that what is true of the whole is true of a part of the whole.

Discovering a loophole in an inductive argument is far simpler than untangling a deductive argument. We deconstructed our earlier example of the Chicago Cubs on page 173 and we saw how untrustworthy were the turkey's expectations based on experience.

An inductive argument is easily faulted because it assumes the claims leading up to the conclusion are the rule and not the exception. To dismiss an inductive argument, then, one need only point out that exceptions happen, indeed exceptions *may* be the rule. Nevertheless, audiences and speakers alike do recognize the value of inductive reasoning in determining what is not yet known. In the interest of reasonable dialectic, then, we can say that a *valid inductive argument requires that the examples on which the conclusion is based are* representative *and not isolated or exceptional instances*.

Types of Fallacies

Hasty Generalization, Stereotyping, and *Ad Hominem* Arguments

"One swallow does not a summer make," but why? A swallow is a *sign* of summer, but not a guarantee. Likewise if it rains each of three times you are in New York City, and you conclude that it always rains in New York, you have jumped to a conclusion. A **hasty generalization** is a form of jumping to conclusions; we take too few specific instances to reach a general conclusion.

Here is another example:

> Wal-Mart is always busy. I was in there three different times last week, and they were swamped each time.

You could suspect here that the speaker shopped during Wal-Mart's three busiest times of the week, or even the month. The conclusion is vulnerable because the listener can find exceptions to the claim, asking "But were you in there Thursday morning at eight or Monday night?"

Stereotyping follows an inductive reasoning pattern, but in this case, the reasoning attributes to an entire class a real or potential characteristic of one or few people. For instance, "Men are slobs," "Asians are mathematical whizzes," "Models are anorexic," and "Americans are obese," all are stereotypes. You

Figure 7.2 If I insisted that cats have tails, based on my experience with only tailed cats, my inductive conclusion that all cats have tails would be a hasty generalization. Here is a Manx cat, a breed of cat whose "primary feature is its lack of a tail,"[13] disproving my claim.
©Robynrg/Shutterstock, Inc.

can see how this claim bases a conclusion on occasional unsubstantiated assertions. As an inductive argument and a broad generalization applied to all members of a class, a stereotype is easily disputed, but difficult, nonetheless, to dislodge from audience minds.

Ad hominem arguments work a little differently. The Latin *ad hominem* means "against the man" or "against the person." Thus an *ad hominem* argument is a personal attack, for instance, on another's personality, appearance, family, or even previous misfortunes, rather than on the substance of a person's views. A successful deflection of an age-discrimination *ad hominem* occurred in the 1984 presidential campaign between Ronald Reagan and Walter Mondale, Reagan then 73 and Mondale 56. The debate moderator had asked Reagan if he thought he would be able to function effectively as President at his age. Reagan's responding quip turned the table on the issue with his declaration, "I want you to know that I will not make age an issue of this campaign. I am not going to exploit, for political purposes, my opponent's youth and inexperience." Reagan's wit sidesteps the *ad hominem* of too old for the job, while dismissing the question of why an age would be too old—or too young.

Ann Richards, former governor of Texas, spoke against George H.W. Bush at the 1988 Democratic National Convention, saying "Poor George, he can't help it. He was born with a silver foot in his mouth." With one swipe she was able to attack both Bush's privileged birth and his proclivity for saying the wrong thing at the wrong time. Was Bush born into wealth? Yes. Had he committed verbal gaffes in public? Yes. But did Richards address his political performance or policies with this adroit barb? Not so much.

With each of these fallacies, you can grasp the implications: Reagan is too old and Bush too rich and gaffe-prone to be President. But in each case issues are not seriously addressed, and the statements remain vulnerable to evidence-based refutation or as ill-mannered taunts.

Appeals to Conformity, Popular Sentiment, and Tradition

It is difficult to access any media without being bombarded by advertisements appealing to conformity, to popular sentiment, or to tradition. We see crowds of young people glued to cell phones (appeal to conformity), happy gatherings of beautiful people at a lively tavern (appeal to popular sentiment) and heartwarming dramatizations of family holiday reunions (appeal to tradition), these advertisers tugging hard at emotions entwined with our sense of self.

An **appeal to conformity** implies that you should adopt an attitude, value, belief, or behavior because everyone else does. The attitude, value, belief,

ETHICS WATCH

Although *unethical* and *illegal* are distinct concepts, defamation law recognizes that people may not damage a person's reputation with unsubstantiated accusations. *Defamation* refers to false and malicious statements designed to injure another's reputation. "Unethical" name-calling (*ad hominem*) arguments can be proved illegal under certain conditions.

If a speaker's defamatory words are heard by a significant number of people and the "defamatory sting" sticks, we have *slander*. *Libel*, on the other hand, is also defamation, but via a tangible medium, such as print or video recording.

If, for example, Congressman Michael Hernandez hears that at a small dinner party Governor Jeremy Todd charged that Hernandez took bribes from lobbyists, Hernandez would probably not file charges of slander. If, however, Todd made his accusation in a television interview or a public forum, Hernandez would have the makings of a slander suit.

Consider then…

1. Under what circumstances would Todd's remarks be considered *libel*?

2. How are the terms *unethical* and *illegal* distinct?

3. If slander and libel are illegal, how would you determine whether they are also unethical? (Hint: see Chapter Twelve for some guidelines.)

or behavior *may* be reasonable, but to suggest that it is reasonable because lots of other people think it is reasonable is a *tautology*, a statement that affirms itself while giving no actual support for its validity.[14]

The *appeal to popular sentiment* and *appeal to tradition* follow the same pattern. According to this logic, you should accept the truth of a statement because it expresses an age-old viewpoint because that is the way things have always been. There may be good reasons for agreeing with public sentiment or with continuing a tradition. Americans tend not to favor eliminating turkey for Thanksgiving dinner, for instance. But the strongest argument for continuing a tradition is to examine the worth of the tradition.

These three appeals are faulty deductions. Formally, they might be written like this:

General belief (premise)—Everyone drinks whiskey.

Particular case (premise)—I am one of everyone.

Conclusion—I drink (or should drink) whiskey.

As we discussed earlier, to demonstrate the weakness of a deductive argument, point out that one of its premises is false. Here, of course, we can question the claim that everyone drinks whiskey.

Figure 7.3 Misleading listeners by fallacy can lead to unfortunate consequences. In this case, advertising promotes conformity to the potentially dangerous popular sentiment that there is no such thing as being too thin.

© Slawomir Fajer, 2014. Used under license from Shutterstock, Inc.

False Cause

You don't have to live on a farm to observe that roosters crow and the sun comes up. The problem is when we believe that the rooster's crow makes the sun come up. The Latin name for a false cause fallacy describes it well: *post hoc ergo propter hoc* or "after this, therefore because of this." The **false cause** fallacy asserts that because one thing preceded another, it *caused* the other. This is the logic of superstition. Determined to win the baseball championship, Max eats two cups of Wheaties, omits brushing his teeth, and wears a sweatband around his head because that's what he did when his team won the first and second playoff games. Max dismisses the opinion of his sister, who contends that the team won as a natural consequence of hard work, practice, and skill.

What makes a cause false? To create a sound argument establishing causation, you need more than a simple assertion, as we see in the following examples.

Greenhouse gases have produced climate change.

Easy availability of guns leads to school shootings.

These two issues gained traction in the late twentieth and early twenty-first centuries but have suffered blowback from climate-change skeptics and progun rights advocates. As with any fallacy, the claims may be true, but they remain vulnerable and are not broadly accepted until sufficient evidence emerges to support them.

In the United States, climate-change skeptics have considered the evidence of climate change anecdotal and inconsistent. At this writing, several decades into the issue, a majority of scientists and people support the evidence that climate change is a real and perilous threat, but resistance persists. In the same way, after each school shooting, much of the country's population has rejoined the battle over restricting access to guns. Although indicators mount that more controlled gun access could curb school shootings, again there are those who point out other plausible causes of school shootings, such as laxity in law enforcement or a perpetrator's mental illness.

Acceptance or rejection of causal arguments hinges on establishing the validity and proven impact of one or more causes. *Post hoc ergo propter hoc* relies on a prior event as a single cause, while other false cause arguments inadequately support the cause–effect relationship.

Faulty Comparison

Dante and Jesse are the sons of Ernie, a world-class track star. As they grow up, family and friends predict extraordinary athletic ability in both sons. Dante is better known as a great student and eventually a successful lawyer while Jesse follows in his father's footsteps, training in track and field events from an early age, culminating in his advance to the world championships. Dante, in spite of his academic success, is haunted by the ghost of his father's athletic reputation. In this case, friends, Ernie, and even Dante himself have accepted a faulty comparison. A **faulty comparison** in a persuasive speech is much the same; you assume that if two people, places, things, or events are alike in one or few respects, they are alike in many respects. In Ernie's family, the presumption of similarity is based on a blood relationship, but not on skill, desire, or interest.

One speaker proposed that people should not buy cut Christmas trees. Rather they should buy live trees. Seems reasonable. But the speaker's reasoning was that trees should not be harvested because they register pain when cut; cutting down a tree is akin to murder. Of course the problem with the speaker's logic was in drawing a comparison between trees and people. On the one hand, both are living organisms, but on the other hand, you cannot cut human beings off at the knees and stick them in a bucket of water for a couple of weeks to sustain their life. There are too many dissimilarities between people and trees for the reasoning to stand on the basis of the comparison alone; thus the conclusion fails. A comparison will be more valid the more points of similarity between the items compared. If the speaker had drawn significant similarities between trees and people, the claims would have been more credible, though still pretty far-fetched.

Building a Refutation

Of all the pitfalls to avoid, perhaps the most serious in persuasive speaking is the assumption that your arguments are strong enough to stand on their merits without acknowledging the opposing side, as if telling your audience to take it or leave it. In doing so you are sweeping away as nonexistent a host of unanswered questions and objections. Ideally, when you deliver a persuasive speech, you have anticipated opposing arguments and considered carefully how to refute them. A **refutation** is a response that attempts to discredit opposing arguments. With a dialectical approach to persuasion (see Chapter One), refutation is not meant to bludgeon the opposition. We still strive to join our position with the audience's, to seek common ground for future action. However, we refute claims to ensure that shoddy reasoning, research, and dishonesty are confronted and exposed.

Your counterarguments will emerge through your research and audience analysis. As you read and listen to arguments on your subject, you will undoubtedly come upon opposing viewpoints. Likewise, if you find out anything about your audience's attitudes toward your subject, that audience analysis may reveal the arguments audience members harbor against your position. As you examine opposing views, you may find that your own arguments have weaknesses. If opponents have the weight of evidence on their side, you will want to re-evaluate your position to see if you have made an error in judgment. But if you are still convinced that your position is more reasonable and supportable than the opposition's, you can refute counterarguments to strengthen your position.

In Chapter Six, we saw where to place counterarguments and refutations in the speech outline. Now let's consider how to develop their content. To begin refuting an argument (See Figure 7.4), you should

1. *State the claim* you want to challenge.

2. *Show what is wrong with the claim.*

3. *Provide your more accurate or reasonable interpretation* of circumstances, evidence, or facts of the case.

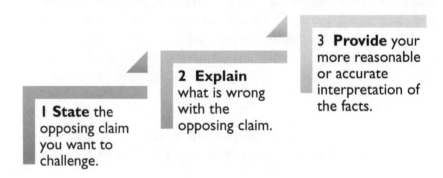

STEPS TO REFUTATION

3 **Provide** your more reasonable or accurate interpretation of the facts.

2 **Explain** what is wrong with the opposing claim.

1 **State** the opposing claim you want to challenge.

Figure 7.4 Three-Step Method of Refutation.
Courtesy of Barbara Breaden

Your refutation strategies are limited only by your imagination, but your refutations should be prompted by the needs of the situation. Below are a few straightforward strategies that can be applied in many cases.

Denial If someone makes false claims about information, events, and circumstances, you can deny the charge. For example:

1. *State the claim* to be challenged. "Jacob says I accepted a bid by Fortis Builders because I was paid off, that is, bribed."

2. *Show what is wrong with the claim.* "But if I was paid off, what did I receive, and what is the proof that I received anything from Fortis? Jacob provides no evidence to support this charge. There is none."

3. *Provide an alternative interpretation* of the circumstances, evidence, or the facts of the case. "In fact, Fortis won the contract because they had the best bid. Here are the competing bids. See if it is possible to draw any other conclusion than that there was no payoff, no bribery."

Questioning evidence Occasionally the opposition has an argument that sounds reasonable, but the evidence given fails one of the evidence tests mentioned in Chapter Two. Look at the case below, where the speaker exposes inaccurate use of evidence.

1. *State the claim* to be challenged. "Dr. Tobin cited *Politifact's* statement that mass shootings occur in other countries, even though they have stricter gun-control laws."

2. *Show what is wrong with the claim.* "Well, that's not exactly what *Politifact* said. What they stated was (and I quote), 'Mass shootings do happen in other countries. But they do not happen with the same frequency as in the United States.'"

3. *Provide an alternative interpretation* of the circumstances, evidence, or the facts of the case. "In fact, according to the article she cites, the frequency of mass shootings and numbers of victims in the U.S. is greater than eleven comparative developed countries *combined*. So *Politifact* does not support Dr. Tobin's view; it upends it."

 Since You Asked...

Question: Must I refute counterarguments to make my speech persuasive?

Answer: As we have pointed out, the audience is not always on your side. If persuasion is part dialectic and part rhetoric, you know you need either to discover a mutually acceptable view of the controversy or to demonstrate the soundness in your interpretation of the controversy. You may be tempted to ignore arguments against your position, rather like ignoring a red traffic light and just as risky. You might proceed through your speech heedless of opposition, only to find the audience seething or hurling insults afterward. Whatever arguments you don't bring up, the audience will mentally nurture. They may leave the speech unpersuaded and more firmly entrenched in their position.

So it makes sense to acknowledge and expose counterarguments against your position. William McGuire's **inoculation theory**[15] reinforces this idea. McGuire offers two choices: 1) present *supportive* arguments only for your proposition, or 2) present both *supportive* and *refutational* arguments.

The key elements of inoculation include *exploring threats* to existing beliefs, and to *providing defenses* against future attacks.[16] You strengthen your argument by forewarning the audience of impending attacks on their views. "Taken as a whole," say scholars Arnold and Bowers, "research evidence suggests the superiority of the refutational pretreatment over the supportive message strategy."[17] Arguments are most effective when they support a viewpoint *and* refute opposing ones.

McGuire's theory has been used to explain how to make people resistant to brainwashing. Audiences can be immunized, just as people can be immunized against polio or measles.

According to McGuire, you undercut opposing arguments by refuting them, and you ensure that your audience will not flip as soon they encounter a contradictory message. In short, when you inoculate your audience against counterarguments, your message becomes more durable.

Questioning credibility You may be able to question whether someone is qualified to make certain judgments or whether their sources are believable. Here the speaker questions whether speakers possess the credentials they claim.

1. *State the claim* to be challenged. "You want us to accept that Harvey Weinstein was a consummate film professional. We should believe him when he says he never assaulted or abused women."

2. *Show what is wrong with the claim.* "But even a casual glance at Weinstein's testimony shows he brought to his room dozens of women, one by one, after he'd hired them for roles in his films. They were objects of his power. He met them in secrecy. Their stories tell of the same ploys to seduce them, and when that did not work, to assault them. You defend him as believable, but no one who has worked closely with him is calling his behavior defensible."

3. *Provide an alternative interpretation.* "Yes, I recognize that one is innocent until proven guilty, but you have provided no substantial reasons why this man is worthy of belief."

Questioning reasoning Knowing what you know now about forms of reasoning, both viable and faulty, you can pinpoint logical flaws in your opponents' views. Here is a critique of inductive reasoning:

1. *State the claim* to be challenged. "For my colleague to say that all the 2018 lawmakers were timid and self-serving during the legislative session is inaccurate."

2. *Show what is wrong with the claim.* "She cites three legislators who did compile an undistinguished and even embarrassing record. But look at Will Merton, Thalia Shamir, and Rashad Bowman. These legislators and other bold members like them stood up to the governor's ludicrous tax plan, vowing to go down with it."

3. *Provide an alternative interpretation* of the circumstances, evidence, or the facts of the case. "Well, the tax plan passed, I'm sorry to say, but not because there were no voices opposing it. It was simply because there were not enough of them."

Exposing fallacies As with exposing faulty reasoning, once you are aware of what makes reasoning fallacious, you can recognize and refute it. Here the speaker challenges an opponent's appeal to conformity:

1. *State the claim* to be challenged. "Raul wants us to throw our support behind the Board's move to save money by removing the school's

two police officers. In spite of all our concerns, Raul says we should just go along; the Board knows best."

2. *Show what is wrong with the claim.* "But think about this. Yes, removal of our officers will save money up front, but what will it cost us later? Will our gang problems magically disappear? Can the Board guarantee our kids' safety if their last line of defense is removed?"

3. *Provide an alternative interpretation* of the circumstances, evidence, or the facts of the case. "We haven't even begun to study how officers have helped to protect our students—or how they have failed to do so. We haven't considered any alternatives to the Board's chosen course. Let's examine the facts and several possible courses of action before jumping on the bandwagon."

In each of the above examples, you can see how carefully the speaker walks us through the refutation. This is essential because a refutation that the audience cannot follow is as good as no refutation at all. The more you take the opportunity to practice this three-step refutation method, the more it will come naturally to you and you will remember the steps when you speak in both prepared and unprepared speech settings.

In Summary

Human reasoning follows our patterns of experience. These patterns teach us about certainties, probabilities, comparisons, and the relationship between cause and effect. They teach us, too, when a belief assumes too much, when a probability is far-fetched, when things are not comparable, and when causes and effects are not clearly connected. Thus, we are able to recognize faulty reasoning or illogic.

To be persuasive, you want to avoid faulty reasoning and logical fallacies because they reveal weakness or unreasonableness in your position. On the other hand, if you discover faulty or fallacious reasoning in opposing views, you can strengthen your position by exposing and refuting them.

The most effective way to refute a counterargument is to use a three-step method, where you state the claim to be challenged, state what is wrong with the claim, and present an alternative interpretation of the facts. By including sound reasoning and sound refutation of opposing views, you go a long way toward accomplishing the goal of persuasion—a well grounded perspective that helps to resolve a significant controversy.

Endnotes

[1] Irving M. Copi and Carl Cohen, *Introduction to Logic*, 13th ed. (Upper Saddle River, NJ: Pearson, 2008), 5.

[2] Ibid.

[3] Glenn Greenwald, Ewen MacAskill, and Laura Poitras, "Edward Snowden: the whistleblower behind the NSA surveillance revelations," *The Guardian*, June 9, 2013, 19 May 2014 <http://www.theguardian.com/world/2013/jun/09/edward-snowden-nsa-whistleblower-surveillance>.

[4] "Information on Whistleblower Protection Act and Whistleblower Protection Enhancement Act," *U.S. Securities and Exchange Commission*, December 23, 2011 19 May 2014 <http://www.sec.gov/eeoinfo/whistleblowers.htm>.

[5] Nassim Nicholas Taleb, *The Black Swan* (New York: Random House, 2007), 40. The thesis of Taleb's book is that inductive thinking establishes confirmation bias that causes us to see the variations as extreme (the black swan) rather than to be expected.

[6] Ibid.

[7] Ibid.

[8] Ibid.

[9] Nancy Cavender and Howard Kahane, *Logic and Contemporary Rhetoric: The Use of Reasoning in Everyday Life*, 12th ed. (Boston, MA: Wadsworth, Cengage Learning, 2014), 11.

[10] Ibid.

[11] Austin Freeley offers a valuable and extended discussion of argument from cause in *Argumentation and Debate: Critical Thinking for Reasoned Decision-Making*, 7th ed. (Belmont, CA: Wadsworth, 1999), 151–155.

[12] "National Bottle Bill Proposed," *Eugene Register-Guard*, June 19, 1991, 7A.

[13] "Manx," *The International Cat Association*, 16 May 2014 <http://www.tica.org/public/breeds/mx/intro.php>.

[14] W. Stanley Jevons, *Elementary Lessons in Logic: Deductive and Inductive* (London: Macmillan, 1957), 69.

[15] See Carroll C. Arnold and John Waite Bowers, *Handbook of Rhetorical and Communication Theory* (Boston: Allyn & Bacon, 1984), 450–455.

[16] Ibid., 451.

[17] Ibid.

Theory into Practice

1. For a single day, try keeping a journal of claims made by those you speak with or listen to, and list what reasons form the basis for those claims.

2. Later, look back over your journal (#1) and label the reasoning samples as induction, deduction, causation, or comparison, if the examples correspond to these forms.

3. Begin compiling a list of fallacies from letters to the editor, editorials, opinion pieces, and advertisements. Practice refuting these both mentally and orally.

4. Find an assertion with which you disagree and prepare an oral refutation, using the three-step refutation method.

5. This might make a good parlor game. With a partner, prepare a mini-debate on the current weather report for your area. One person should present reasons for the accuracy of the report, and the other should refute one or more of the reasons given, according to the three-step method given in this chapter. After this debate, reverse roles, arguing for the opposite point of view.

8 Verbal Style in Persuasive Speaking

To Make a Long Story Short...

Images in persuasive messages evoke vivid perceptions, with both positive and negative effects.

Key Concepts

- Images are a speaker's verbal visual aids.
- Images enable the audience to identify with the speaker's unique perception.
- Metaphor is a potent persuasive tool.
- The classical directives for language usage include clarity, vividness, and appropriateness.
- Ultimate terms can secure an audience's identification with the speaker.
- The persuasive speaker should avoid ultimate terms that alienate the audience.
- Effective word choice demonstrates sensitivity to issues of gender and labeling.

Key Terms

image/imagism
metaphor
puzzlement-recoil stage
tenor
vehicle
identification

consubstantial
ultimate term/god-term/
     devil-term
political correctness
inclusive language
gender-specific/gender-neutral

Language and Emotional Appeal

When you wrestle with persuasive messages, you often deal with abstract ideas—such as the federal deficit. Can you show your audience a picture of the deficit? You could show numbers or graphs to depict its size. Or you could show pictures of people and programs affected by the deficit—but can you depict the deficit as a visual entity?

If you were to describe the deficit itself, what would it look like? Like a huge vault—or more likely a huge sinkhole or drain, a pipe or a flood of money drained off the edge of the earth into . . . where? Or would it be a gargantuan creature (King Kong? A dragon?) towering over and devouring the life of the country: hospitals, schools, national parks, factories? The picture you create carries meaning and compels audience understanding with clarity and force. A word picture can reduce the words needed to express an idea while portraying that idea more vividly. You compel the audience to apprehend a perspective never before seen, or at least never seen in just this way.

The Persuasive Use of Imagination

Why Images?

In the early twentieth century, a group of poets and fiction writers developed a theory of writing to enliven the written word. Theirs was the Imagist school, led by T.E. Hulme, the "Father of Imagism,"[1] and Ezra Pound. According to literary critic Herbert Read, Hulme preferred the *image* to logic is an instrument of thought.[2] To Hulme, thought consists of the mind putting together different images. By **image** the imagists meant a succinct verbal construction to convey thoughts and emotions in an instant, as in T.S. Eliot's image of the fog in his poem *The Love Song of J. Alfred Prufrock*:

> The yellow fog that rubs its back upon the windowpanes,
> The yellow smoke that rubs its muzzle on the windowpanes
> Licked its tongue into the corners of the evening,
> Lingered upon the pools that stand in drains,
> Let fall upon its back the soot that falls from chimneys,
> Slipped by the terrace, made a sudden leap,
> And seeing that it was a soft October night,
> Curled once about the house, and fell asleep.[3]

In this selection, you "see" the image of the fog as both smoke and cat—two different pictures merged to create a single and compelling image. The imagists strove to use no extraneous words, no abstractions, and to use common but precise language—always the *exact* word, not the nearly exact or "decorative" word. **Imagism**, then, was characterized by economy and precision of words, which you will see is useful not only in poetry, but in speechmaking as well.

Metaphor and Persuasion

You probably have heard another person refer to someone as a monster, or an angel, or a pig. The speaker in this case is drawing on **metaphor**[4] to create an image of the person described. The image identifies people with what they are not.

This is where metaphor gets its power, by calling a thing what it is not. Consider the comparison used by Peggy Noonan, the speechwriter who prepared George H. W. Bush's acceptance speech for the 1988 Republican National Convention. The speech presented the future president's vision of America:

> At the bright center is the individual. . . . And there is another tradition. And that is the idea of community—a beautiful word with a big meaning. . . . For we are a nation of communities, of thousands and tens of thousands of ethnic, religious, social, business, labor union, neighborhood, regional, and other organizations, all of them varied, voluntary, and unique. . . . This is America . . . —a brilliant diversity spread like the stars, like *a thousand points of light in a broad and peaceful sky* [emphasis added].[5]

In her story, Noonan recalls how she created the "thousand points of light" image:

> It was my favorite phrase in the speech because its power is born of the fact that it sounds like what it is describing: an expanse of separate yet connected entities sprinkled across a broad and peaceful sky, which is America. . . . Why stars for communities? I don't know, it was right. Separate, bright, and shining, each part of a whole and yet discrete. Why a thousand? I don't know. A thousand clowns, a thousand days—a hundred wasn't enough and a million is too many.[6]

What Noonan considered is what we all consider when we create a metaphoric image. We let the thing we are describing speak to us in a picture. The audience, in hearing the image does not need to be urged or instructed to accept a point of view but is lit with a physio-emotional perception of an idea. Just as with our image of the federal deficit as a monster, something terrifying, and with Eliot's fog image we feel the fog as something sinister, so with Noonan's image we are uplifted.

Finding Places for Images

So images grab attention and rivet perceptions. How can this power be harnessed in speechmaking? Images and imagist principles can guide language choices throughout your persuasive speech. In your introduction an image can focus the mind of the audience. In Chapter Six we used the example of the 13-year-old boy, Alex, who slipped through the cracks of the local school system. But could you develop a more vivid image of Alex slipping? You could describe a young boy trying to climb a glacier—or a sand dune. Each time he takes a step he slides down until he realizes that the attempt to go forward is what is defeating him, and so he will attempt no more.

To begin your speech with an image like the one of Alex promotes audience sympathy for Alex and maybe good will for you for bringing Alex's plight to their attention. The image in the introduction engages audience attention and deflects their reservations toward home-schooling. It also cuts to the heart of the subject; without talking *about* Alex, you identify with his experience in an instant.

What about using images in the body of your speech? One possibility is to use an image to state succinctly each of the main points. Let's go back to the smoking in public spaces speech from Chapter Six. In this policy speech, rather than present a need statement saying that smoking in these gathering spaces poses a problem, why not present the idea as an image:

> Next time you board the 82 bus to campus, observe the jaundiced smog-burst you maneuver around to step aboard. The plume, stirred by your movement, chases you, flicks a sting into your eye, and rakes your silky throat membranes, churning up a dry choke.

You can use an image to animate the need or problem segment of the policy speech. Listeners then harbor your word picture in a corner of their minds throughout the speech.

Images help to explain data and other evidence. To describe the amount of an herbicide used along county roads last year, you could create an image to depict the statistic: "If Highway 20 were an enormous baguette sliced lengthwise and stretching from City Hall to the coast highway, this herbicide would coat the loaf generously and completely." To diminish the credibility of an opposition group, you could say, "The Concerned Citizens Alliance says their members represent the political make-up of all Texas. But according to a recent count, their numbers have about as much impact as a single olive on a sixteen-inch pizza." Your image can be flip or intense. Whichever tone you choose, the image illuminates evidence.

In the conclusion, you can drive home the subject's emotional weight with an image, as Martin Luther King's "I Have a Dream" speech accomplished so memorably, expressing his dream that

> "one day every valley shall be exalted: every hill and mountain shall be made low . . . . we will . . . hew out of the mountain of despair a stone of hope . . . to transform the jangling discord of our nation into a beautiful symphony of brotherhood."[7]

Here the metaphor of the dream is King's vision of the future; you have hope presented as a stone, a nugget or gem to be hewn from the mountains, and brotherhood as a symphony.

Your images can be simple, humorous, edifying, and moving. They can engage audience sympathy, clarify ideas, and inspire. You use images to tap and convey the heart of your message.

Since You Asked...

Question: How can metaphor accomplish more than direct explanation?

Answer: Metaphor is a powerful persuasive tool because of how it impacts the minds of listeners. Modern language philosopher I.A. Richards, in his *Philosophy of Rhetoric*, described how metaphor works.[8] The image-maker, let's say Shakespeare, describes the heroine in his tragedy *Romeo and Juliet*. He writes:

"But soft! What light from yonder window breaks? It is the east, and Juliet is the sun."[9]

Juliet is the sun? But the sun is a ball of flaming gas 93 million miles from Earth. Yet what else is the sun? Our source of light, warmth, the center of our lives, since we revolve around it. And here you find many reasons for calling Juliet what she is not. To Romeo, the connotations of sunlight, warmth, and radiance reside in Juliet. Shakespeare's metaphor brings together two disparate things—Juliet and the sun—and by conjoining them, you perceive an entirely new idea within a single image.

But why is metaphor persuasive? When you use a metaphor to combine two wholly different things into one new thing, you impel listeners to put together two ideas or images not ordinarily combined. Listeners must make sense of the juxtaposition; they begin to process the image, considering how these two things can be equated.

This process is called the *puzzlement-recoil stage* in decoding the metaphor.[10] The listener puzzles at the juxtaposition of two different

(Continued)

things, recoils to consider what it means, and eventually resolves the confusion by discovering meaning. Consequently, an audience learns something new. The "Aha!" moment when the juxtaposed meaning is realized becomes a source of satisfaction and allows listeners to see through the speaker's eyes. So what is persuasive about metaphor? By understanding the image the audience is *persuaded to perceive as the speaker does.* We are persuaded to see Juliet—warm, bright, and vivacious—as Romeo sees her.

In Shakespeare's image, the tenor is *Juliet*. The meaning of Juliet is created by the vehicle, *sun*. You discover the meaning of the tenor through the vehicle, as if you look at Juliet *through* the sun. By overlaying Juliet with the sun, you see each element, sun and Juliet, in a new way.

The more unusual or odd the juxtaposition of the two elements, **tenor** and **vehicle**, the harder it is for listeners to achieve the "Aha!" moment. This is not a bad thing—if you must work to understand something, your understanding is more valuable and the image more striking. This is why we consider some metaphors *clichés*, overused expressions that the listener no longer has to strive to understand. The meaning has become as direct as any commonplace word. Metaphors are more effective than simple description or direct explanation because they excite and identify the audience's perception with the speaker's.

BUILDING AN IMAGE

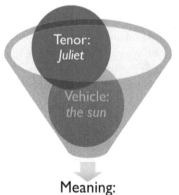

- The **tenor** is the *thing* that is given meaning.

- The **vehicle** is the *comparison* used to impart the meaning.

- The **meaning** is the *composite* of these two elements.

Tenor:
Juliet

Vehicle:
the sun

Meaning:

Juliet is the sun.

Figure 8.1 I.A. Richards explains that a metaphor takes its meaning from the confluence of two elements, the tenor and the vehicle.
Courtesy of Barbara Breaden

Creating Persuasive Images

You can enhance your image-making skills through exercise. Just as we created an image of the deficit at the beginning of this chapter, you can create an image to express your subject. Try asking yourself a series of simple questions about one or another aspect of your speech:

1. *What does the subject look like?*
   an animal?
   an object?
   a substance?
   an organism?

2. *What does the subject do? How does it behave?*
   gently/roughly?
   chaotically/systematically?
   artfully/mechanically?
   slowly/quickly?

3. *How does it sound?*
   loud/soft?
   abrasive/soothing?
   excited/calm?
   seductive/repugnant?

Figure 8.2 A picture may be worth a thousand words, but try to create a verbal image that captures the drama of this photograph.
© Gayvoronskaya_Yana/Shutterstock, Inc.

4. *How does it feel? taste? smell?*

Suppose you are preparing a speech on the issue of logging ancient forests. See how you can develop an image on either side of the subject—pro-timber and pro-environment—to set a mood and evoke the desired audience reaction.

How would you describe a logged forest?

	Pro-Timber	Pro-Environment
1. Appearance	Bountiful, like a cornucopia	Ravaged, like a wasteland
2. Behavior	Vigorous, replenishing and recurring faithfully, like "Old Faithful"	Beaten, chastened, like a defeated prizefighter.
3. Sound	Energy, productivity, the sound of wealth, money, buzzing, humming, laughing	Silence, emptiness, the eerie sound of desertion, spooky, a faint, low, enduring note
4. Other senses	Fresh smell of cut timber, pine, new wood, clean, dewy, alive	Suffocating heat, a blast of hot air, choking hot dust, dryness, dead

You can generate images by asking these sorts of questions about the subject of your speech—any speech. Insert images to enliven evidence or to make your main points vivid. When you have become accustomed to creating images, you will more naturally incorporate them. By adding images, your speech becomes more memorable, both for you (you can remember pictures instead concepts) and for your audience.

Terminology and Audience Identification

If you look back to T.S. Eliot's image of the fog "that rubs its back along the window panes," you may notice that he joins his perceptions with ours, or rather he compels us to join with his. This image-making and sharing is the basis of identification. According to Kenneth Burke's concept of **identification** (see Chapter Four), to be persuasive you must identify or unite your views with the audience's beliefs and values. As a speaker, you identify with the audience when you become **consubstantial** with the audience—when you experience common sensations, concepts, images, ideas, and attitudes.[11] That is, *experiencing common images makes us consubstantial* (of like substance) with the audience, as you see in Figure 8.3. You become *like* your audience (and vice-versa), and thus you become *identified* with them.

As Burke points out, images can be dangerously influential, as in the case of a child saturated with violent images becoming violent. If persuasive speakers expose audiences to images that promote harm to others, they

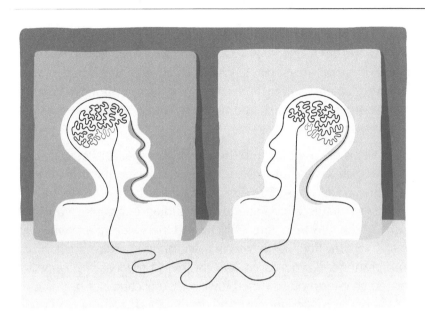

Figure 8.3 The image above illustrates the concept of consubstantiality. When a speaker presents a compelling image, the audience sees it their mind's eye. Thus the speaker and audience are now sharing the same vision; they are consubstantial in thought. As the figure suggests, the thought of one becomes the thought of another. They experience identification with one another's perception.

© robodread/Shutterstock.com

are treading on thin ice ethically. Such an issue emerged in 2010, when Congressional Representative Gabrielle Giffords was one of several representatives whose picture appeared in a political ad, her head centered in the crosshairs of a shooting target. Following the election, Giffords was shot in the head outside a grocery store in Tucson, Arizona. We cannot assume (a post hoc fallacy) that the crosshairs illustration caused the shooting, but the episode led to a national conversation on the dangers of political expression prompting public harm. Thus we consider a persuasive speaker bound to support public good over harm,[12] a standard that should be reflected in a speaker's images.

Ultimate Terms and Persuasion

It is not only images that create identification. So do words, especially **ultimate terms.**[13] Ultimate terms express both ideals (if positive) or wrongs (if negative). University of Chicago professor Richard Weaver divided ultimate terms into **god-terms** and **devil-terms.**[14] To illustrate, Depression-era children were often said to view *financial security* as a god-term and *fascism* as a devil-term. During the Vietnam War period, *peace* became a god-term, as it would for any period of war. More current ultimate terms include *sustainability*, *technology*, *human rights*, *diversity*, *tolerance*, and *privacy*. As for devil-terms, how about *racism*, *homophobia*, *partisan*, *obesity*, *inequality*, *injustice*, or *corporate greed*? In all eras in United States history, *freedom* and *equality* seem to remain god-terms, though Weaver would classify these as **charismatic terms**, those words that possess appeal across particulars of time and place.

Ultimate terms are important to the persuasive speaker because, like images, they unite speaker and audience. If you can locate the audience's ultimate terms, you can link those terms to your goals. In the first decade of the 21st century, if you wanted to persuade your audience to support an immigration measure, you could link your objective to the value of *economic growth* and contrast it with the devil-term *economic stagnation*. On the other hand, to oppose an immigration bill, you could link the bill to *terrorist threats*, an assault on the charismatic-term of *security*. However, your choice of oppositional terms would likely confront counterarguments that it is inaccurate and prejudicial to link immigration to terrorism or security risks.

Ultimate terms, then, change as times and audiences change. Consider these differences, including the fourth version, where the god-term of one becomes the devil-term of the other.

Era	God-Term	Devil-Term
1775	independence	monarchy
1863 (North)	union	slavery
2000	energy independence	foreign oil
2016	conservative	progressive
	progressive	conservative

As an example of ultimate terms at work in the heart of American politics, shortly after Barack Obama's 2008 election, *The New Yorker* detailed the campaign themes and ultimate terms for the opposing camps. The magazine's analyses contrasted the ultimate terms of *honor* on John McCain's (the Republican candidate) side and *change* on Obama's Democratic side.

On the McCain side, David Grann observed "the only way to understand McCain . . . is to grasp that he is driven less by ideas than by an almost chivalrous notion of honor."[15] The Obama campaign had only to link McCain to the popular view of George W. Bush's "dishonorable" (Republican) presidency[16] to discredit McCain's claim to the label of honor. Thus, McCain's ultimate term never grabbed the upper hand in the campaign.

On the other side, Obama campaign analyst Ryan Lizza demonstrated that the Obama strategy was to establish their candidate as "a change agent."[17] Citing Obama's chief pollster, Joel Benenson, Lizza explained, "The fundamental idea behind this race from the start has been that this is a 'change' election."[18] As Lizza goes on to relate,

> Obama almost never delivered a speech from a lectern unless it was festooned with the word *change*. On Election Day, thirty-four percent of the voters said that they were looking for change, and nearly ninety percent of those voters chose Obama.[19]

How could you use ultimate terms to achieve your speech objectives? Suppose you are an over-50 employee and have just been laid off your job at a technology company. The company is seeking "new blood" and a more youthful, edgy image. You argue that in the wake of the aging baby-boomer population age discrimination has become rampant with little enforcement of anti-discrimination laws. How can you argue this position before a youthful audience? First, you can appeal to their respect for *equality* under the law and an *end to discrimination* at either end of the age spectrum, establishing identification with them. You are saying, in essence, "I think as you do; I value your experience; my ideas contribute to our mutual good."

Figure 8.4 The unambiguous theme of President Barack Obama's first election campaign was *change*, this term decorating the rostrum and seating area at nearly all of his campaign appearances.

© spirit of america/Shutterstock, Inc.

Kenneth Burke maintains that we can always transcend differences to find some ultimate term on which we agree. For example, we may disagree on whether higher education is necessary to a productive life but agree that self-fulfillment is important to all. If you were to argue in this case for increased state support for higher education, you might meet opposition, but if you argue that you want to remove obstacles to fulfilling the American dream, you are saying the same thing in more abstract but possibly more acceptable terms. Successful politicians master this skill early.

In Donald Trump's 2016 campaign for president, no political stance resonated with supporters more than his promise to nip illegal immigration. In his speeches, Trump depicted the prospect of immigrants—and drugs—pouring into the country, soaking up jobs and social services and leaving behind U.S. citizens. Trump, the real estate developer, would build a wall. The wall would inhibit illegal immigration. The wall became his overarching image for healing the country's economic wounds.

Pressed for details on the wall, Trump obliged. How high would it be? How thick? What would it be made of? Would it be an ugly gash in the natural landscape of the border?

Over time, the wall image became more elaborate. It would be 35 feet tall. It would have strong doors, beautiful doors, that people would be able to pass through at times. The entire wall would be beautiful, President Trump said. He had developed "great buildings;" the wall was not as challenging as some of the buildings he had constructed. We would save jobs for U.S. citizens. We would provide services for U.S. citizens. We would build the wall beautifully, and it would be completed on time and under budget.

As Trump's wall image illustrates, transcendent goals are inherently conceptual. By appealing to transcendence, the momentum of a speech can become bogged down in abstraction unless you infuse the speech with images to add vivacity to those transcendent and unifying beliefs.

Political Correctness, Inclusiveness, and Ultimate Terms

Just as ultimate terms change with the times, you cannot *choose* an audience's ultimate terms. They depend on audience attitudes. The late twentieth century witnessed a controversial language movement known as political correctness. Political correctness examined how labels for minority groups or marginalized members of society made assumptions about people that were not altogether accurate. These labels had become "devil-terms" in that they triggered offense in the people referenced. Why was political correctness controversial? From a progressive standpoint, politically correct language neutralized language bias and stereotyping, but from a libertarian perspective, it substituted prescribed and sometimes awkward usage for freedom of expression.

In the twenty-first century, defenders of **political correctness** have continued to emphasize its intent: to avoid offensive language toward specific groups, especially with regard to race, ethnicity, culture, gender, age, disability, or sexual orientation.[20] Insofar as language shapes thought, using "incorrect" terms insults and excludes identity groups, while using "correct" terms reduces bias and marginalization.[21]

Inclusiveness

Later iterations of the political correctness movement have continued to frame the issue as one of **inclusive** and polite language usage. The Linguistic Society of America explains:

> Inclusive language acknowledges diversity, conveys respect to all people, is sensitive to differences, and promotes equal opportunities . . . [in order to] avoid past pitfalls or habits that may unintentionally lead to marginalization, offense, misrepresentation, or the perpetuation of stereotypes.[22]

Proponents of inclusive language adaptations recommend that as a matter of respect and good manners, speakers avoid exclusive or "incorrect" terminology for marginalized identity groups, turning instead to inclusive terms. This can be tricky. Like ultimate terms, preferred usage changes with the times, so that the inclusive terms suggested in Figure 8.5 may well slip from favor. Yet, as we mentioned in Chapter 1, speaking well starts with the good will of the speaker. Surely a good will suggests sensitivity to audience composition. While we may inadvertently offend our listeners, we at least can try to stay abreast of what constitutes inclusiveness and what gives offense.

Although the issue of political correctness in recent decades has drawn both support and opposition, it has not been a strictly contemporary issue. Other historical eras have "softened" or euphemized language. However, while inclusive language seeks to avoid giving offense, euphemism is used to conceal unpleasant or even brutal realities. As George Orwell demonstrated in his 1946 essay *Politics and the English Language*, **euphemisms** have provided cover for acts of brutality, the dropping of an atom bomb, for example. Orwell explained,

POLITICALLY "INCORRECT" VERSUS "INCLUSIVE" LANGUAGE

Identity group	"Incorrect" / Exclusive	"Correct" / Inclusive
Race	Colored, Negro, Indian	Black, Brown, African American, person of color, historically underrepresented group, Native American (or tribal /place-specific identity, e.g. Navajo)
Ethnicity	illegal alien, slang associated with ethnic or geographic origin	undocumented person, or specific national origin (Korean, Latino, African)
Gender	mankind, male nurse, actress, chairman, stewardess, founding fathers he or she, his or her (specific or binary gender identity) *The dean must give his approval.*	humanity, nurse, actor, chair, flight attendant, founders one, they, their (non-specific or non-binary gender identity) *Deans must give their approval* or *The dean must approve.*
Age	old, elderly, senile, senior citizen	older person, mature, an elder, experienced
Disability	deaf, disabled, handicapped	hearing impaired person, person with [insert specific] disability or special need
Sexual orientation	homosexual	lesbian, gay man, transgender person

Figure 8.5

> In our time, political speech and writing are largely the defense of the indefensible. . . . Thus political language has to consist largely of euphemism . . . . Defenseless villages are bombarded from the air . . . this is called *pacification*. . . .[23]

According to Orwell, we use words in this way to suppress the images they produce, to assign labels to things while stripping them of their "mental pictures." So it is that military terminology refers to the act of soldiers accidentally killing their own troops as "friendly fire." In this case a euphemism becomes an act of deception. Such deception may be grave, or it may be innocuous. The French, for example, refrain from referring to an "elderly woman," preferring *une dame d'un certain age* ("a woman of a certain age"). We soften our word choice to deceive or to conceal harsh realities—but also to be pleasing or ingratiating to others.

Inclusive Speech and Freedom of Speech

In the United States the custom in some settings, to soften blunt language with bland substitutions, has shifted from a cultural best practice to language codes that forbid offensive usage. One notable workplace example occurred in 2014, when Donald Sterling, owner of the Los Angeles Clippers' basketball team, made a series of crude racist remarks about black people to a friend, and his comments were made public.

The egregiousness of Sterling's behavior lay in the fact that nearly 75% of the National Basketball Association (NBA) players are black; they drive the engine of his wealth.

Black superstar LeBron James was among the most outspoken against Sterling, saying "There's no room for Donald Sterling in the NBA," appealing to NBA Commissioner Adam Silver to ban Sterling from the league. "It doesn't matter, white, black or Hispanic—all across the races it's unacceptable. As the commissioner of our league, they have to make a stand," James continued.[24] Consequently, Silver did fine Sterling $2.5 million and banned him from the NBA for life. After several dramatic twists, Sterling ceded ownership of his team and vowed to sue the NBA. He eventually—and voluntarily—withdrew the action.[25]

We can understand the grievous insult to NBA players in Sterling's case—and the hypocrisy of Sterling's behavior. On the other hand, does a person in his position have the right to speak freely to a friend, no matter how outrageous his comments? We have suggested that inclusiveness and avoiding offensive speech is both fundamentally polite and communicatively wise, but can and should it be enforced? After all, people do not agree on what constitutes offensive speech; what is offensive to one is acceptable to another. Second, avoiding particular ways of expression will not resolve conflict, disrespect, or hatred at the root of an offense. As Barbara Dority, Executive Director of the Washington Coalition Against Censorship, points out, "No one was ever won over to a more inclusive view of life via bullying and coercion. . . . Suppression merely allows unsupportable views to become stronger."[26] Social psychologist Ellen Langer looks at prescribed language another way, arguing that

> categorizing is a fundamental and natural human activity. It is the way we come to know the world. Any attempt to eliminate bias by attempting to eliminate the perception of differences is doomed to failure.[27]

In the evolution from Orwell to political correctness to inclusive speech, usage scales have tipped toward inclusive speech in the twenty-first century, yet the tension over appropriate language has persisted.

Universities in the United States have taken seriously the importance of promoting and protecting diversity among students by modeling inclusive communication. In turn, student and faculty groups have ramped up efforts to shut down objectionable speech preemptively by developing speech codes and by protesting speakers who espouse "offensive" points of view. As University of Chicago president Robert Zimmer described it, student groups proposed to model inclusion by excluding viewpoints they found objectionable.[28] Universities, hailed historically as bastions of free inquiry and debate, had begun proscribing freedom of expression.

In reaction, free speech advocates stepped up their defense against campus "thought police" and against the expansion of "bias response teams" that encourage students to report intentional or unintentional offensive speech to university administrators for corrective action. The FIRE organization (Foundation for Individual Rights in Education), for instance, declares as its mission

> to defend and sustain the individual rights of students and faculty members at America's colleges and universities. These rights include freedom of speech, freedom of association, due process, legal equality, religious liberty, and sanctity of conscience—the essential qualities of liberty.[29]

The FIRE staff is comprised of a hefty legal, policy, and journalism team that takes on free speech cases. In their Spotlight Database, they rate colleges and universities for their adherence to or violations of due process and freedom of expression. A "red light" shows that an institution has a policy that unambiguously restricts freedom of speech. A "yellow light" indicates a limited violation of free speech. A "green light" shows no violations. Over ten years of FIRE's reports on the state of free speech on college campuses, the percentage of colleges with purported free speech infringements has dropped consistently, yet they indicate that, as of 2018, almost a third of US institutions do infringe students' rights to free speech.[30] Clearly, at this writing the tug of war between inclusive speech and unrestricted speech in higher education remains fluid.

Finding a Middle Ground

The University of Chicago has placed itself at the nexus between inclusive speech guidelines and free speech precepts. Their "Statement on Principles of Free Expression" stipulates that the university "fully respects and supports the freedom of all students, faculty, and staff, 'to discuss any problem that presents itself,' free of interference." In addition,

> the University may properly restrict expression . . . that violates the law, is threatening, harassing, or defamatory, or invades substantial privacy or confidentiality interests. Moreover, the University may reasonably regulate the time, place, and manner of

expression to ensure that it does not disrupt the ordinary activities of the University. . . . Although faculty, students, and staff are free to criticize, contest, and condemn the views expressed on campus, they may not obstruct, disrupt, or otherwise interfere with the freedom of others to express views they reject or even loathe.[31]

We can consider these principles a starting point toward a balanced perspective on usage in our persuasive speeches. In all, we will do well to seek identification with all audience members in the following ways:

1. *Recognize each listener as an appropriate member of the audience you are addressing.* Strive not to alienate any individual or group by excluding their gender, age, ethnicity, disability, or sexual orientation from the group or subject you are addressing.

2. *Refuse to promote stereotypes.* Recognize the common humanity, individuality, and dignity of each person.

3. *Omit slang or slurs that denigrate an individual or group.* In referring to individuals or groups, use their preferred self-descriptors.

Gender and Ultimate Terms

For more than a century, feminism has ignited public awareness of terms that diminish women's importance or dignity. Gender-specific terms have become devil-terms. Unwitting persuasive speakers who use such terms risk distancing themselves from their listeners.

Unchecked, such terminology creeps into everyday usage. If you use the phrase *modern man,* you are being exclusive. If you refer to *male nurses* or *lady doctors,* you are indicating that you expect nurses to be women and doctors to be men. The problem with **gender-specific** as compared to **gender-neutral** language is that it excludes human possibilities; it "assumes more differentiation [in gender] than is, in fact, the case."[32]

Besides gender-specific language, you will commit stereotypes if you assume a duality in gender between men and women. As the American Psychological Association points out, "Gender refers to the socially constructed roles, behaviors, activities, and attributes that a given society considers appropriate for boys and men or girls and women."[33] But apart from social expectations, women can display and identify with traditionally "masculine" traits and social norms, just as men can with "feminine" traits and norms. Further, people can identify along a range or spectrum of gender assumptions. This makes it difficult to trust generalizations about a binary (either-or)

Figure 8.6 Just as it is difficult to identify these children as boys or girls, as a speaker you may not know the gender identity of your audience members. For this reason, you will want to strive for gender neutral and inclusive language in your speech.
© Monkey Business Images/Shutterstock.com

conception of what concerns and interests men versus women. When you assume such a duality, that men talk football and women shoes, you run the risk of annoying the woman football enthusiast (such as Condoleeza Rice, former Secretary of State, who holds a seat on the College Football Playoff selection committee) or the man who designs footwear (such as legendary University of Oregon track coach Bill Bowerman who designed the first Nike running shoes). If you approve certain personality characteristics for one gender and not another, you will find yourself in a similar bind. A successful male CEO may thus be characterized as "tough" and "demanding," whereas a successful female CEO may be labeled "emotional" or "controlling." Such double standards can constrict a woman's advancement and deny individual style across genders. They also may reduce productivity by insisting on uniform behavior and personality codes.

In your persuasive speeches, stereotypic assumptions might indicate that your perceptions are dated, limited, or inaccurate. They can alienate the audience, damage your credibility, and prompt your audience to dismiss broader issues that you are addressing. Though you cannot be all things to all people, you can demonstrate respect for individual dignity by using gender-neutral, inclusive language.

Other Perspectives on Usage

Classical rhetoricians summed up their requirements for language usage with the words *clarity*, *vividness*, and *appropriateness.* In clarity, they sought precise word choice. In vividness, they favored lively expression to capture listeners' imagination and emotion. In appropriateness, they recommended a style no more or less elevated than the level of the audience; the speaker should be conscious of the audience's education level and preference for formality or informality.

The concepts advanced in this chapter can help you achieve the characteristics the classicists preferred. Images and imagism supply precision and vividness. Ultimate terms and sensitivity to inclusive language reflect a speaker's sense of appropriateness, gender-neutral language being more universally appropriate than gender-specific language in the context of a speech. If you can *identify* with the audience through word choice, using terms suitable and sympathetic to their

ETHICS WATCH

If precise word choice is critical to getting your message across without ambiguity, speaking to children requires that we go beyond simple clarity, to methodically thinking through how children might be misled by careless comments. This skill was perfected by the quiet, award-winning children's television star and advocate, Fred Rogers, host of his educational children's show *Mr. Rogers' Neighborhood.*

Several years into Rogers' show, his producer and one of the series' writers conspired to develop a pamphlet that captured Rogers' strategies for talking to children. The entire methodology entails nine steps, but the gist of it follows:

1. State a message clearly, for example, "It is dangerous to play in the street."

2. Make it positive. "It is good to play in safe places."

3. Make sure the child can accomplish the advice. "Your parents will tell you where you can be safe."

4. Eliminate assumed certainty, and make the advice applicable to all, including to children who don't know their parents. "Your favorite grown-ups can tell you where it is safe to play."[34]

So consider . . .

1. In light of Fred Rogers' example, how can a lack of clarity or precision be unethical or lead to unintended consequences?

2. Is Rogers' concern for precision excessive? Why or why not?

3. Consider an audience you have addressed or plan to address. What might you clarify to prevent discomfort or confusion on the part of the audience?

perspective, you will go a long way toward meeting the classical standard of appropriateness.

In Summary

Images act as verbal visual aids, bringing speeches to life. Images, particularly metaphors, unite your perception with your audience's. Sharing images (and hence perceptions), speaker and audience become more alike, and becoming more alike they identify with one another. This identification is the foundation of persuasion.

You also can identify with your audience by using ultimate terms. These abstract ideals are unifying goals for a group of people. We have pointed out that a dialectical approach to persuasion requires awareness of opposing viewpoints, but you can adapt to your audience by discovering and tapping into their ultimate terms.

Finding your audience's ultimate terms is a tricky business. You need to look to your audience rather than to yourself. Likewise, you will want to avoid unwittingly favoring a group's devil-terms. Whatever god-terms and devil-terms you draw on should enhance your persuasive goals. In the final analysis, persuasive language should express identification through vivid images, inclusiveness, and respect.

Endnotes

[1] G. Hughes, *Images and the Imagists* (Palo Alto, CA: Stanford Univ. Press, 1931), 9.

[2] T. E. Hulme, *Notes of Language and Style*, ed. Herbert Read (Seattle: Univ. of Washington Press, 1929), 8.

[3] T. S. Eliot, *The Complete Poems and Plays: 1909–1950* (New York: Harcourt, Brace, and World, 1952), 4.

[4] Aristotle, *Poetics*, trans. W. Hamilton Fyfe (Cambridge: Harvard Univ. Press, 1927), 83.

[5] Peggy Noonan, *What I Saw at the Revolution* (New York: Random House, 1990), 311.

[6] Ibid.

[7] Martin Luther King, Jr., "I Have a Dream Speech," *American Rhetoric: Top 100 Speeches*, 2001, 24 August 2014 <http://www.americanrhetoric.com/speeches/mlkihaveadream.htm>.

[8] I. A. Richards, *The Philosophy of Rhetoric* (New York: Oxford Univ. Press, 1936), 97–109.

[9] William Shakespeare, *Tragedies*, ed. Peter Alexander (London: Collins, 1969), 236.

[10] Michael Osborn and Douglas Ehninger, "The Metaphor in Public Address," *Speech Monographs* 29 (1962): 223–27.

[11] Kenneth Burke, *A Rhetoric of Motives* (Berkeley: Univ. of California Press, 1969), 21.

[12] This premise is examined more fully in Chapter 12 where we discuss the task of evaluating a speaker's ethics.

[13] Burke, 19–20.

[14] Richard Weaver, *The Ethics of Rhetoric* (Chicago: Henry Regnery, 1968), 211–32.

[15] David Grann, "The Fall," *The New Yorker*, November 17, 2008, 61.

[16] This perception was based largely on President Bush's move to war in Iraq in 2003, a decision founded, as discovered later, on faulty CIA evidence pointing to the existence of weapons of mass destruction in that country.

[17] Ryan Lizza, "Battle Plans," *The New Yorker*, November 17, 2008, 47.

[18] Ibid.

[19] Ibid. The 2012 Barack Obama versus Mitt Romney presidential campaign themes were not as clearly defined as those of 2008. One of President Obama's slogans was "Forward," perhaps suggesting that Romney would lead in the opposite direction, while in this post-recession period Romney favored emphatic cries for "Jobs."

[20] Cynthia Roper. "Political Correctness (PC)." *Encyclopædia Britannica*, 29 Nov. 2017, https://www.britannica.com/topic/political-correctness. Accessed 4 May 2018.

[21] Ibid.

[22] "Guidelines for Inclusive Language." *Linguistic Society of America*, Nov. 2017, https://www.linguisticsociety.org/resource/guidelines-inclusive-language. Accessed 8 May 2018.

[23] George Orwell, "Politics and the English Language," *Shooting an Elephant and Other Essays* (London: Secker and Warburg, 1950), 10 May 2018 <http://orwell.ru/library/essays/politics/english/e_polit>.

[24] "LeBron says NBA must reject Sterling." *ESPN*, 27 Apr. 2014, http://www.espn.com/nba/truehoop/miamiheat/story/_/id/10844906/lebron-james-no-room-donald-sterling-nba. Accessed 16 May 2018.

[25] Nathan Fenno. "Donald Sterling Settles Lawsuit with NBA Over Sale of Clippers." *Los Angeles Times*, 18 Nov. 2016, http://www.latimes.com/sports/sportsnow/la-sp-sn-sterling-lawsuit-settled-20161118-story.html. Accessed 16 May 2018.

[26] Barbara Dority, "The PC Speech Police," *The Humanist*, 1992, 32.

[27] William B. Gudykunst, *Bridging Differences: Effective Intergroup Communication*, 3rd ed. (Thousand Oaks, CA: Sage, 1998), 31.

[28] Tunku Varadarajan. "The Free-Speech University." *The Wall Street Journal*, 17–18 Feb. 2018, A15.

[29] "Mission." *FIRE*, 23 May 2018, https://www.thefire.org/about-us/mission.

[30] "Speech Code Reports." *FIRE*, 23 May 2018, https://www.thefire.org/spotlight-on-speech-codes-2018/.

[31] "Statement on Principles of Free Expression." *The University of Chicago*, June 2012, https://freeexpression.uchicago.edu/page/statement-principles-free-expression. Accessed 16 May 2018.

[32] Barrie Thorne and Nancy Henley, eds., *Language and Sex: Difference and Dominance* (Rowley, MA: Newbury House, 1975), 15.

[33] "What is the Difference Between Sex and Gender?" *American Psychological Association*, 16 May 2018, http://www.apa.org/topics/lgbt/transgender.aspx.

[34] Maxwell King. "Mister Rogers Had a Simple Set of Rules for Talking to Children." *The Atlantic*, 8 June 2018, https://www.theatlantic.com/family/archive/2018/06/mr-rogers-neighborhood-talking-to-kids/562352/. Accessed 26 June 2018.

Theory into Practice

1. Once you have acquired some knowledge about your audience, try to generate a list of what you would expect six *ultimate terms* to be for members of your audience—three god-terms and three devil-terms.

2. Using the list developed in Exercise 1, try to align a persuasive goal to one or more ultimate terms.

3. Pinpoint the ultimate terms found within an opinion piece for a news source. What group or groups does the opinion appeal to? Would you expect it to offend any groups?

4. Keep a list of gender-exclusive or other stereotypic language you encounter within a given week. What does this language assume about the listener(s), and whom might the language exclude?

Oral Practice

1. To brainstorm potential images for your speech, create an image chart like the one on page 198. Imagine the appearance, behavior, sound, and other sense experience you associate the subject of your speech.

	Subject:
1. Appearance	
2. Behavior	
3. Sound	
4. Other Senses	

2. Now using the images you have generated, write out an attention-getter for your speech:

Part Four

Memory and Delivery: Speech Presentation

Chapter 9

Memory: Enhancing Recall and Reducing Anxiety

To Make a Long Story Short...

Your method of speech preparation and practice can determine how reliably you remember what to say when the time comes to say it.

Key Concepts

- Memory is fallible.
- You can develop firm memory paths by rehearsing and repeating your speech content.
- You can improve retention and recollection by organizing ideas (as through the common topics) and by using mnemonic devices.
- You can reduce speech anxiety by developing memory skills, by systematic desensitization, and by cognitive restructuring.
- Minimal speaking outlines are more powerful memory aids than are manuscript or full-sentence outlines.

Key Terms

retention   mnemonic device
recollection   preparation outline
short-term memory   speaking outline
long-term memory   systematic desensitization
working memory   cognitive restructuring

On the Accuracy of Memory

Elizabeth Loftus, psychology professor and memory expert, has gone a long way in her writings to debunk most of our cherished beliefs about memory: that all sense experience imprints the brain with information that can be recalled at will, that memories are accurate reflections of reality, and that we never absolutely forget. The fact is that we perpetually modify our storehouse of memories and throw away most of the stimuli we encounter.[1] What's more, says Loftus,

> Truth and reality, when seen through the filter of our memories, are not objective facts, but subjective, interpretive realities. We interpret the past, correcting ourselves, adding bits and pieces, deleting uncomplimentary or disturbing recollections, sweeping, dusting, tidying things up. Thus our representation of the past takes on a living, shifting reality.[2]

Memory is so unreliable that eyewitness identification of criminal suspects by photograph or lineup is "so error prone that false-positive identifications are the leading cause of false convictions in the United States."[3] Yes, false memories are a fact of life, and though they increase with age,[4] no one is exempt. Intervening forces and emotions corrode memory and cause people to believe what has not happened *did* happen.

How Memory Works

As one of the five canons of rhetoric, memory is inextricably intertwined with speech preparation. A speaker's great apprehension is to look ridiculous (a problem of credibility), to be heckled (a problem of audience analysis), or to forget the speech content (a problem of memory). Memory touches public and persuasive speaking in several ways. Memory is necessary for

1. *registering* experience and information to determine if it is worth remembering, as when you recognize in a news clip information that pertains to your subject or that is worthy of research.

2. *retaining* over time information pertaining to your subject—quotations, statistics, and lines of argument.

3. *retrieving* retained information either spontaneously or at will when you speak.

4. *maintaining* the retrieved memory in thought while it is being used, as you keep track of a point you are making while calling up information to support that point.

To understand how you can optimize your memory in persuasive speaking, it helps to know how memory works.

Aristotle makes a few fundamentals of memory clear. First, memory is comprised of **retention** (information storage) and **recollection** (information retrieval).[5] The nineteenth-century psychologist William James reinforces this perspective, but points out memory's limitations. We can have a good memory (retention) without being quick at recollection. Retention, says James, is *liability* to recall: "The retention of an experience is, in short, another name for the *possibility* of thinking it again, or the *tendency* to think it again."[6] There is no guarantee that we will recall what is "in our heads."

What makes memory work, James explains, is that our experiences form paths in the nervous system. Retention means only that the paths are there. But like a path in the woods, the longer it goes unused the more indistinguishable it becomes from surrounding brush. Our memory paths are like well-worn paths or trails: the more we use them, the clearer they become, the firmer our memory. Thus information is best remembered if it is recent, attended to, and repeated.

Modern memory researchers have validated James's theories. The writings of Professors Elizabeth and Geoffrey Loftus (1976)[7] explain that the memory's **short-term storage** capacity is limited. You might remember one telephone number, for example, not two. Although the information in short-term memory is lost within about fifteen seconds, you can retain the information indefinitely if you will continually repeat or rehearse it. The **long-term storage** capacity is unlimited; it stores information indefinitely, with the caveat that it can be difficult to retrieve.

More recently Alan Baddeley introduced the theory of **working memory**[8], a more descriptive term for short-term memory. While Baddeley reiterates that one's working memory has limited capacity (usually from four to seven items at a time), his research has led to new conclusions: that memory retains best when focused on individual rather than multiple stimuli (perceiving discrete items rather than "sweeping" several items at once), and that the information must be organized for efficient retrieval.

Clearly we do not know for sure how memory works, but through various theories, we can gather that

- our working memory holds limited information.
- the working memory holds information for a limited time.

- to retain information, you must focus on individual rather than multiple stimuli.

- to retain information, you need to rehearse and/or organize it.

Memory in Speechmaking

Is it sensible, then, to remember speech content by constant rehearsal? Rehearsal *may* transfer information to the long-term store, but this does not happen automatically. However, you can "tell" your brain to retain information; this is what you are doing when you organize that information or develop mnemonic devices to help you recall it.[9] You are instructing your brain to remember when you

1. *Attend* to your memory by thinking and talking about your subject, continually sorting and discarding information as you research and build your speech. This type of rehearsal keeps information active in the short-term or working memory.

2. *Review* information, thus keeping it *recent* and laying down memory paths to ensure retention.

3. *Facilitate* recollection

   - by finding a speech structure that makes sense.

   - by adding cues to your notes—key words to spark your recall.

   - by concentrating, or thinking about what you are saying, as you speak, sustaining your focus on your speech intent and content.

These strategies show that memory is connected to and can be strengthened within your speech's invention, organization, and delivery stages.

Memory and Invention

Even though ancient rhetorical scholars pronounced memory the fourth canon of rhetoric, after invention, organization, and style, memory is not the final preparation stage before delivering your speech. An ancient text attributed to Marcus Tullius Cicero calls memory "the guardian of all the parts of rhetoric.[10] Memory is engaged the moment you determine that you are going to speak, since this is when you begin to lay down "memory paths" that will ensure recollection at the moment of delivery.

Figure 9.1 Statue of Marcus Tullius Cicero, a prolific first-century BCE Roman rhetorician and orator. Cicero wrote some of the earliest works on memory and its importance to speech-making.
© Renata Sedmakova/Shutterstock, Inc.

Mnemonic Devices

To optimize your memory during speech preparation, you can use mnemonic devices (memory aids) as you begin to gather information for your speech. Your mental disposition at this stage should be "I want to remember this example (or this fact or this research)." By coaching yourself to remember, you will invoke memory strategies: such as visualizing vivid stories that illustrate what you want to recall.

If your subject is homelessness, for example, and you are learning about the struggles of the homeless in your community, you might picture them going through their daily routine—showering at the local YMCA, applying for food stamps, trying to stay warm—the hard facts become a personal story you will recall when you deliver your speech. You won't need to rely on words on paper. Instead you will rely on the story in your mind.

As you figure out the main points of your speech, you can condense them to key words and develop an acronym from the first letter of each main point. If your main points for your speech on homelessness were 1) locating resources for personal care and hygiene, 2) being able to eat, and 3) finding work, your acronym could derive from the key words *hygiene, eat*, and *work*: hew. Taking this a step further, you can create a mental narrative about the homeless, who, like sculptors hewing statues out of rock, *hew* a life for themselves out of essential raw materials. On the other hand, if you have a longer list of main points or a more complex acronym, you can repeat the representative letters rhythmically, just as when you learned how to spell *Mississippi* by repeating *miss-iss-ipp-i*. Whatever your mnemonic device, this effort will create a mental structure that makes information retrieval easier and recall surer.

Thinking and Talking about the Subject

The most fundamental memory strategy in the invention stage of speech preparation is to articulate a sound proposition. (See Chapter Two.) If you have no clear idea of what you want to say, how can you recall your message? You can fortify your memory by typing, handwriting, or speaking aloud the proposition. If someone asks you what your speech will be about, state it firmly and succinctly. You can mention your speech subject in conversations over lunch with friends. The more you return to your speech subject—formally (in dedicated speech preparation) and informally (in conversations with others)—the more secure your memory.

Gathering evidence provides another opportunity for reinforcing memory. If you commit each piece of evidence to memory as you select it, you'll find you have established memory paths more efficiently than if you had memorized later a block of manuscript. You can rehearse each piece of evidence, each startling statistic, which then becomes a conversation starter. The more you rehearse and use your evidence, the more reliable your recall at the time of delivery.

Grouping Arguments by Common Topics

Sixteenth-century scientist Francis Bacon pointed out that one obstacle to memory is the "infinity" of stimuli continually before us. But if we group pieces of information into chunks, we reduce the number of items we have to remember. Bacon claims that the common topics "materially assist memory and raise it far above its natural strength."[11] Loftus and Loftus illustrate Bacon's claim about chunking information. If you ask someone to remember the series of letters: FB-ITW-AC-IAIB-M, your friend probably will not be able to recall more than five or six letters at best. But if you ask your friend to recall the same letters, now chunked—

FBI-TWA-CIA- IBM—she or he will probably recall the list this time with no mistakes.[12]

Theorist and researcher George A. Miller found that "it is the length and not the diversity of materials that limits memory."[13] Like Bacon, he found that when we try to remember lengthy pieces of information we falter; not so when we chunk or group memory pieces. With the common topics, you can group arguments according to categories: *cause and effect, size,* and so on. By organizing you simplify what you need to remember and make long-term recall more likely.

Memory and Organization: Preparation Outlines versus Speaking Outlines

Often in life, the bigger the crutch, the greater one's fear of letting it go—the first day in pre-school without a security blanket; the four-hour interview without a cigarette; the realization that your speaking notes are at home on the kitchen counter. The more detailed your notes, the greater your panic. This is why we favor brief speaking outlines.

To compare the value of a **preparation outline** to a **speaking outline,** look at the following examples of introductions:

Preparation Outline

    I. Fast food is a way of life in the United States.

ETHICS WATCH

Kevin had been involved in his neighborhood organization in the roughest part of Glenwood, and the speech he intended to deliver to the city council the next day was important to him. It could impact whether he would continue to be surrounded by gangs and drug deals or by relative peace.

Kevin had researched the problem at police headquarters and at the district attorney's office, so he possessed the statistical ammunition he needed to make his case. The problem was that now he had forgotten to bring his notes with all those figures. After a moment of panic, Kevin reasoned, "I can fake it well enough to get by." He rolled through his speech inventing the numbers he could not recall, and the council accepted his proposal.

Consider, then, . . .

1. What is your best course of action when you cannot remember important details of your speech?

2. Does it make a difference if you simply cannot recall details as opposed to when you are found to have invented them?

3. In what way could Kevin's action damage the outcome of his speech?

A. This past week I made a point of going to a fast food outlet for lunch every day to see how busy they are.

   1. At McDonalds, there were six lines of seven to nine people each for the entire hour I was there.

   2. At Taco Time the line of twenty to twenty-three held for more than an hour.

   3. Subway had a brisk business with full tables and a line of six to eight people lurking in the aisles for a table for more than an hour.

B. Yes, we love our fast food, and that is why we should love the fact that these fast food chains have come to high school cafeterias—or should we?

C. C. Fast food companies should not be a part of high school food services.

   1. They lack nutritional balance.

   2. They discourage local food service providers.

   3. Their high costs hamper student savings.

D. Let's look at

   1. The fast food policies of the school district

   2. What fast food offers nutritionally

   3. How we can discourage fast food businesses in our high schools

As you can see, the preparation outline is essentially a manuscript; every word of the speech is scripted. There is the advantage that the speaker leaves nothing to chance. Since every word is filled in, you need no memory. This outline, like a teleprompter, is a sure thing.

In contrast, look at the speaking outline below. Instead of complete sentences, it uses brief phrases or single words only. The brief phrases are cues to jog memory. Cues are one of the best ways to stimulate recall.[14] Once you link information to the cue, the cue will trigger your recollection of the information you need. Of course, practice will help you secure the cue as a reliable prompter so that the cue will assist information retrieval.

Speaking Outline

    I. Way of life

        A. Experiment

            1. McD—6 of 7–9

            2. Taco Time—20–23

            3. Subway—tables full + 6–8

        B. Coming to high schools

        C. Should not allow

            1. Nutrition

            2. Loss of local business

            3. Costs

        D. Will cover

            1. School policies

            2. Nutrition

            3. How to discourage

With the speaking outline, you see key words to jog your memory about what to say. You are forced to *think* during the speech. It sounds scary, but consider the alternative for a moment. With a full-sentence preparation outline, the *outline* is the memory of what to say; you never have to remember anything. Yet if you read the speech without thinking about the message, you may lose confidence in your ability to speak, should you get lost in notes and have to ad lib. Speech anxiety is more likely to *increase*, not decrease, when you use a manuscript or full-sentence outline. Anxiety is more pronounced when memory is lax.

With a speaking outline you can practice saying the speech aloud from your key-word framework. The test run of several practices will show you that your speech can be delivered in a number of different ways. You develop flexibility in the way you speak. Practice with a speaking outline builds confidence and reduces anxiety.

Using Notes

Those who grew up reciting the Pledge of Allegiance every day in grade school need no prompting in recalling how it goes. The thought of having notes to say the pledge would be absurd. Likewise, if you have worked in a job, in a

© Sean De Burca/Shutterstock, Inc.

© Stuart Jenner/Shutterstock, Inc.

Figure 9.2 A brief-speaking outline liberates you from the manuscript and enables you to forge a relationship with your audience. You can see from this photo comparison that the simple act of ditching the manuscript alters completely our desire to hear the message, but it also establishes the speaker as competent and sincere.

front-office position, for example, you have had practice in delivering a similar message many times. You do not refer to notes to explain to callers that to apply for a position they will need to present identification and a résumé. In speechmaking the same is true. The more you practice, the less you rely on notes. What seems insurmountable in the first run-through grows more natural and fluent after a number of false starts.

You can begin your preparation with the full-sentence preparation outline, read through it a few times to increase your familiarity with what you want to say. As you become comfortable with the material, abbreviate the outline until it is reduced to keywords. The speaking outline is the final version of your speaking notes. Its format is a minor security blanket; it engages established memory rather than numbing it.

Additional Memory Aids

In Chapter Eight we noted that imagery makes a speech memorable for an audience, but images also help speakers. With striking imagery your recollection becomes more vivid. In the same way, visual aids help you and your audience remember the speech.

Since You Asked...

> **Question:** I find the evening before a speech stressful. Is it wise to repeat my speech continuously over several hours? If I stop practicing, will I forget it?

Answer: This question suggests that stress does not aid memory, a correct conclusion. The hippocampus, the memory region at the center of the brain "consolidates" or pulls together pieces of memory (visual and auditory elements, for instance) into a meaningful whole.[15] But the hippocampus performs this function best when one is relaxed. This preference for relaxation is why cognitive psychologists have found that during sleep the hippocampus more readily integrates the memory pieces stored in various brain regions.

Consider an real incident a student experienced that illustrates what the hippocampus can accomplish even while you sleep: You spend eight hours studying for a math test then head to bed, your mind crammed with seemingly unrelated mathematical fragments. All night you dream you are chased by little animated numbers; in the morning you wake to find the pieces fit together into a coherent whole.

Memory studies would say your math made sense because the pieces of memory were "assembled" by your hippocampus as you slept.

If you want to optimize your memory before an important speech, then, do practice it a number of times until you feel you have achieved familiarity with the content. At this point, allow yourself to relax and even to sleep. By breaking the pressure on the hippocampus, you can empower your memory to recall information more readily. When you return to the speech the next day, you probably will find your recall stronger and your speech more fluent.

Images are one way for you to remember your speech, but it also is important to remember "meaning over form."[16] That is, *instead of trying to memorize your speech word-for-word, think the thought.* You will need concentration and a willingness to let the words come as they will, but in the end your content is more secure recalled as ideas rather than as specific turns of phrase.

Finally, if you get stuck in the middle of a speech and cannot remember what comes next, you can "refabricate"[17] the message from bits and pieces that occur to you. If you lose track of what you want to say about trade relations between the United States and China, you can try to recite tidbits that you recall: the U.S. trade deficit, the strength of China's currency, and so on, until you have reconstructed the overall meaning of your message. Naturally this will not make for the most artful presentation, but it can keep you from folding altogether.

Memory and Speech Anxiety

As we have seen, memory failure is a primary source of speech anxiety. If you improve your memory skills, you can reduce anxiety. Still, if stress is getting the better of you before a speech, you can reduce communication apprehension further by an internal process known as **systematic desensitization**.[18] This is a method of conscious deep muscle relaxation in response to anxiety-producing situations. The first step of this strategy is to establish a hierarchy of anxiety-producing situations.[19] After this, when you think of each of those situations, going from least stressful to most stressful, you coach yourself, or have another coach you, through a series of muscle-relaxation messages. As you move through the hierarchy and tension begins to intrude, you retreat to a lower-anxiety level, trying to gain firm control by deliberate relaxation over your anxiety reactions. Eventually, you learn to associate the anxiety-producing situation with muscle relaxation rather than with muscular tension and anxiety.[20]

SAMPLE SYSTEMATIC DESENSITIZATION HIERARCHY

Speech situation	Anxiety level
Researching the subject	Lowest anxiety
Preparing a rough outline	Low anxiety
Finding a subject	Moderately low anxiety
Rehearsing the speech	Moderately anxious
Thinking about giving the speech	Moderately high anxiety
Talking in front of the audience	High anxiety
Looking at the audience	Highest anxiety

Is systematic desensitization enough, though, to assure speaking confidence? According to communication theorist James McCroskey, you need to substitute relaxation for anxiety (desensitization) but also to think about yourself differently. This is **cognitive restructuring**,[21] explains theorist William Fremouw. It consists of identifying negative and anxiety-producing self-statements ("I'm going to choke/throw up/faint/look like an idiot") and replace them with coping statements ("I think I can get through this/Only one more point to go/So far so good/Think the thought/Breathe").

For both of these strategies, you need to recall newly formed associations: anxiety-producing situations with muscular relaxation and rational coping statements in response to negative self-imaging. Thus pre-speech thinking, practice, and new positive memory associations combined can give you the confidence you need to press on toward delivering your speech.

In Summary

Memories are imperfect. We make mistakes. Awareness that your memory is faulty can induce fear and predispose you to speech delivery gaffes. But if you understand how memory works, you can boost recall and reduce anxiety.

The most reputable theories of memory emphasize the importance of repetition or rehearsal. Yet you can enhance memory with mnemonic devices at the invention, organization, and delivery stages of speech preparation by using brief speaking outlines, for instance, rather than manuscripts or full preparation outlines.

For additional help in reducing apprehension, you can apply the psychological self-training strategies of systematic desensitization and cognitive restructuring. Once your toolkit of memory aids is stocked, you need only put them to use.

Endnotes

[1] William James, *The Principles of Psychology* (Chicago: Encyclopedia Britannica, 1952), 447.

[2] Elizabeth Loftus and Katherine Ketcham, *Witness for the Defense: The Accused, the Eyewitness, and the Expert Who Puts Memory on Trial* (New York: St. Martin's, 1992), 23.

[3] C. J. Brainerd, V. F. Reyna, and S. J. Ceci, "Developmental Reversals in False Memory: A Review of Data and Theory," *Psychological Bulletin* 134, no. 3 (2008): 380.

[4] Ibid.

[5] Aristotle, *On Memory and Reminiscence*, trans. J. I. Beare, *The Works of Aristotle, vol. 1* (Chicago: Encyclopedia Britannica, 1952), 695.

[6] James, 427–428.

[7] Geoffrey R. Loftus and Elizabeth F. Loftus, *Human Memory: The Processing of Information* (Hillsdale, NJ: Lawrence Erlbaum, 1976). The Loftus's work is based on the Atkinson-Shiffrin multi-store memory system. See R. M. Shiffrin and R. C. Atkinson, "Storage and Retrieval Processes in Long-Term Memory," *Psychological Review* 76, no. 2 (1969): 179–193.

[8] Alan Baddeley, *Working Memory, Thought, and Action* (Oxford: Oxford Univ. Press, 2007).

9 Loftus and Loftus, 64.

10 [Cicero], *Ad C. Herennium*, trans. Harry Caplan (Cambridge: Harvard Univ. Press, 1968), 205.

11 Francis Bacon, *Novum Organum* (Chicago: Encyclopedia Britannica, 1952), 156.

12 Loftus and Loftus, 64. NB: At the time the Loftus team developed this device, a major airline in the United States was TWA (Trans World Airlines). TWA was acquired by American Airlines in 2001.

13 Carroll C. Arnold and John Waite Bowers, *Handbook of Rhetorical and Communication Theory* (Boston: Allyn & Bacon, 1984), 354.

14 Loftus and Loftus, 47.

15 See, for example, José L. Cantero et al., "Sleep-Dependent Oscillations in the Human Hippocampus and Neocortex," *Journal of Neuroscience* 23, no. 34 (2003): 10897–10903.

16 Loftus and Loftus, 108.

17 Ibid., 113.

18 Arnold and Bowers, 317.

19 Gustave Freidrich and Blaine Goss, "Systematic Desensitization," in *Avoiding Communication: Shyness, Reticence, and Communication Apprehension*, 2nd ed., eds. John A. Daly and James C. McCroskey (Creskill, NJ: Hampton Press, 1997), 177.

20 James C. McCroskey, "The Implementation of a Large-Scale Program of Systematic Desensitization for Communication Apprehension," *The Speech Teacher* 21, no. 4 (1972): 263. McCroskey advocates five to seven 50-minute sessions.

21 William J. Fremouw, "Cognitive Behavior Therapies for Modification of Communication Apprehension," in Daly and McCroskey, 212.

Theory into Practice

1. Practice reciting the main points of your speech from memory. Don't attempt to make coherent sentences, instead simply state them in order as points. Once you can do this without error, add two supporting points to each main idea. Repeat the points and sub-points until you can recall them all.

2. Think of three mnemonic devices for recalling your main points, such as making the first words of each main point into an acronym, or developing a rhythmic pattern, or beginning each main point with a word that makes the list alphabetical, and so on. Practice reciting the main points using each of the mnemonic devices.

3. If you are experiencing speech anxiety, try writing out a hierarchy of anxiety-producing components in speechmaking, from least anxiety-producing to most. Practice relaxing all of your muscles one by one from toes to head as you reflect on each of these. Whenever you find you are unable to relax in thinking about one of these levels, retreat to the preceding lower anxiety activity. Continue in this way until you are able to relax through each component.

Chapter
10 Delivery Decisions

To Make a Long Story Short...

Nonverbal elements in your speech heighten audience comprehension and recall.

Key Concepts

- Your speech delivery should suit the speech's physical context.
- Speakers transmit their personae through dress, voice, and movement.
- Adjusting your speaking approach to adapt to environmental factors such as setting, time, and space will optimize the speaker-audience connection.
- Visual aids used well fortify your credibility and promote audience understanding.
- Attractive, electronically projected slides, prepared with established presentation software, set the current standard for visual aids.

Key Terms

persona	proxemics
illustrator	affect display
chronemics	monotone
regulator	optimum pitch

The Dominance of Delivery

As you think about your speech, you will doubtless visualize the speaking venue. Is the space dark or bright, large and well furnished or small and makeshift? Imagine, too, your appearance. Are you upbeat and friendly, reserved, formally or informally dressed? Do you look at your audience as you speak, does your voice sound full and confident, or reserved and intense?

Your speech is not only ideas, audience analysis, organization, and words. Your speech is a live, physical event. Your preparation brings you to the point of delivery. As Roman orator Cicero pointed out, "the effect of all of these oratorical devices depends on how they are delivered. Delivery . . . is the dominant factor in oratory; without delivery the best speaker cannot be of any account at all."[1] When Demosthenes, reputedly the greatest orator of ancient Greece, was asked to name the three most important parts of rhetoric, he answered, "Delivery, delivery, delivery!"[2]

Your speech delivery will use dress, movement, space, light, timing, and sound to create a multi-channeled message.

Malcolm X, one of the world's most extraordinary modern orators, epitomized in his speech delivery a fluid adaptability to audience. One rhetorical scholar detailed his techniques pointing out that Malcolm used more precise articulation, a faster speaking rate, and a higher-pitched voice for his mixed or white audiences, such as those he might find on college campuses. Facing urban black audiences, Malcolm used what was considered his "grand style," characterized by a deeper yet more varied and emphatic pitch, a slower rate, a pulsing rhythm.

> The problem with the black community, he would say, was that blacks would not confront injustice: "You don't do any swinging; you're too busy singing;" . . . You and I have never seen democracy, all we've seen is hypocrisy. . . . We don't see the American dream; we've experienced only the American nightmare."[3]

The Persuasive Persona

Magnetic speakers like Malcolm X certainly communicate to an audience a persuasive *persona*, but then, so can you. Your **persona** is your image, the way others perceive the blend of appearance, personality, and character. A speaker's persona establishes a palpable relationship with the audience, based on his or her authentic self. Thus whatever persona you project, recall Shakespeare's dictum: "This above all, to thine own self be true." To achieve your distinctive rhetorical style, you must be yourself. Naturalness has value because it conveys sincerity and honesty.

Your most natural self may comprise hundreds of characteristics and attitudes. You might recognize aspects of your persona in the following scales:

DISCOVERING YOUR PERSUASIVE PERSONA

Subdued	Energetic
Mellow	Intense
Sober	Buoyant
Calm	Excited
Steady	Agitated
Detached	Engaged
Nonchalant	Riled
Ironic	Straightforward
Light	Serious
Content	Angry

Figure 10.1 Try to envision an accurate (that is, authentic) image of the persona you would like to project in your speech, based on the contrasting descriptors in this table.

Figure 10.2 There is a distinct persona expressed in each of these two political figures, (l) Sarah Palin, former vice-presidential candidate and Alaska governor and (r) Michelle Obama, former First Lady of the United States. Consider here how dress, gesture, posture, and facial expression communicate differences in personality and attitude.

Whatever your persona, it is this human element that gets inside the audience to make them "understand and feel what you want them to understand and feel,"[4] as speech scholar, Charles Woolbert and his collaborator, Severina Nelson, point out. They explain that just as when we watch a football game we wince, lean, and whoop in response to the action on the field, so audiences identify with the speaker's emotional presence along with the speaker's words. Woolbert and Nelson claim,

> Even as we face our audience, before we say anything, we are carrying meaning of some sort. It may be the wrong meaning, it may not be what we think it is, but it is meaning. We may be frowning or smiling or appearing bored or merely appearing to be something we are not. . . . . Because that first moment is of so much importance, [the speaker's] attitude will suggest an attitude to the audience. Unconsciously, the audience will tend to adopt the muscular tensions of the [speaker].[5]

These writers call for the speaker's "total bodily response" to the speaking situation. In the same way you should strive to adapt your physical delivery and total situational control to the message you are conveying.

Figure 10.3 Senator Cory Booker (D-NJ) demonstrates by dress, facial expression, posture, and gesture his focus and control in a 2011 speech.
© Eugene Parciasepe/Shutterstock, Inc.

Demonstrating Attitude through Dress

If you want to appear solemn, you can wear somber colors and formal attire—a business suit, for instance. If you want to establish a more relaxed tone, you would switch to more casual attire. In short, for an important speech, your apparel should conform to your goal. We watch Presidents and other elected officials in business attire for official work and in dress casual or hardhats for visits with the working public. Our attire must fit both the occasion and the audience.

Demonstrating Attitude through Voice

Ray Birdwhistell points out that although the English language is composed of only about forty-two sounds, "The number of sounds distinguishable from each other that the so-called vocal apparatus can make may run into the thousands."[6] We are capable of adjusting our voices to reflect what we say. Yet we have only four mechanisms for adjusting voice: pitch, rate, volume, and vocal quality. In any speech, we want to use these four factors to reinforce the attitudes we want to convey.

Pitch refers to how high and low, as on a musical scale, the voice registers. The speaker's pitch level may be habitually high or habitually low or somewhere in the middle. Excessively high pitches tend to be associated with excitement, tension, happiness, and energy, whereas low pitches tend to correspond with solemnity, sorrow, seriousness, and authority. Thus you can adapt your habitual pitch level to reflect an emotional tone. You should be aware, however, that an *unnaturally* high or low pitch will strain your voice, lead to hoarseness, and even cause permanent damage to your vocal folds, the primary mechanism of voice production. You should restrict your pitch adjustments to your natural or **optimum pitch**.

Aside from pitch level, your pitch *range*, or how widely you vary the pitch of your voice, also conveys emotion. For instance, ordinarily you would not speak in a **monotone**, or unvaried pitch, to demonstrate enthusiasm. To show sorrow, your pitch would not rise rapidly. Yet generally, to be expressive, you must stretch your pitch range, by incorporating more and varied pitch levels (see Figure 10.4).

By recording your voice, you can work toward a wide and varied pitch range. Often speakers feel that they are exaggerating pitch variation or sounding melodramatic, but when they hear themselves on a recording, they find their voices sound just about right and even pretty good. You cannot judge by listening to yourself out loud how effective your pitch variation is; you must listen with objectivity and detachment, as a recording allows you to do.

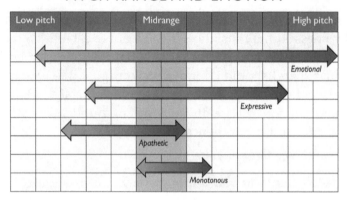

PITCH RANGE AND EMOTION

Low pitch   Midrange   High pitch

Emotional

Expressive

Apathetic

Monotonous

Figure 10.4 As this chart indicates, your vocal pitch suggests an underlying emotional state. You may not want to convey intense emotion, but to heighten your speech with expressiveness, your pitch must vary. Think of each horizontal space as a musical note. An expressive pitch range equates to a full octave, or eight notes, whereas a monotonous voice uses only about three notes.

Courtesy of Barbara Breaden

Rate While many communication theorists have concurred that a faster speaking rate is more persuasive and depicts higher intelligence, knowledge, and objectivity,[7] a speaker's attempt to produce a rapid rate may be disastrous. A number of negative speech characteristics also attend rapid rate. Most notably, the speaker's articulation may be slurred or otherwise unintelligible. With a faster rate, the speaker often does not have the time or agility to produce distinct speech sounds. If the reasoning in the speech is highly nuanced or if the speech presents many statistics, a rapid rate may make these incomprehensible. Last of all, a rapid speaking rate may undermine the mood the speaker is attempting to create.

Instead of striving for a fast speaking rate overall, you can use one or both of the following suggestions:

1. *Vary speaking rate.* Keep in mind that intelligible speech averages 120 to 180 words per minute. More than 200 words per minute, then, is considered relatively rapid. When information can be delivered quickly and with punch (without sacrificing important information), take advantage of the opportunity to speak more quickly. When the information becomes more complex, when it must be understood or emphasized, slow down.

2. *Pause.* If you use pauses or insert silence (think in terms of more than five seconds), while varying your speaking rate, you can avoid disfluencies and give your audience time to respond to the message, either orally or nonverbally. Pauses or silent moments

help the audience digest the message and may even demonstrate your competence or authority.[8]

The pause is arguably the most undervalued and underused of all speech techniques. If you ever heard now deceased radio commentator Paul Harvey, you heard a master of the pause. Why did he pause? For dramatic impact. In the same way, the pause is evident as a stylistic device of Native American delivery. This silence gives the listener time to reflect on and absorb the impact of the spoken word. Writer Kent Nerburn cites Chief Luther Standing Bear of the Teton Sioux in pointing out that for Native Americans, silence shows poise, respect, calm, and "thoughtfulness before speech."[9]

Chances are you have a point in your speech (or maybe several points) where you could pause for emphasis. If so, try to record your speech with the pause. Try to stretch the pause until it becomes daringly long. This may feel uncomfortable because when you pause, all eyes focus on you. Yet when you hear a long pause on your recording, you will see that it creates dramatic impact.

Volume The fundamental requirement of a voice is that it be audible. Still, audibility encompasses a range of volumes, particularly if you have access to a microphone, whereby you can speak softly and still be heard. Beyond the fact of audibility, however, the key to speech volume is appropriateness. Once again, you must consider the attitude you want to convey. For instance, a loud volume may depict strong feeling, but on the other hand, it may signal a dogmatic style. Even though you want to show enthusiasm or sincerity, audiences rate dogmatic speakers less attractive than non-dogmatic speakers.[10] Once again, the oratorical traits of Native American speakers are instructive. Rhetorical scholar Daniel Henry describes naturalist John Muir's acceptance by Alaskan natives, in part based on Muir's low-key delivery, in which his loudness level "rarely breached dinner table volume."[11] Of course, while some audiences prefer low key, if you feel you are perceived as weak, you might want to demonstrate strength either by increasing loudness or gaining attention by suddenly reducing volume to a hush or stage whisper. As with other components of voice, you should aim for variety and adapt loudness to cultural expectations as well as to your speech goal.

Quality Vocal quality is difficult to describe, yet you know that the voice qualities of Gilbert Gottfried (the voice of Iago, the parrot, in Disney's *Aladdin*) and James Earl Jones (Darth Vader in the original *Star Wars* series) are not alike. We usually like a speaker whose voice is full, rich and open, a quality that can be achieved by opening the mouth fully, articulating sounds energetically, and keeping the throat and shoulders relaxed by simulating a yawning feeling in the throat.

These descriptors help to define what makes a poor or grating voice quality: one that is hollow or dull (Sylvester Stallone as *Rocky*), one that is hoarse or raspy (Marlon Brando in *The Godfather*), or one that is frail, weak, or breathy (Marilyn Monroe), as opposed to rich and firm (Julia Roberts or Jennifer Lawrence).

There are times when a speaker wants to convey a persona or to create a "character" voice by mimicking these traits. Some people have amassed great wealth taking advantage of "substandard" or character voices. This goes to show that we cannot prescribe a single voice quality as superior. Nonetheless, if your audience hears pleasant vocal characteristics, you may be perceived as more intelligent, competent, and dynamic.

ETHICS WATCH

Adolf Hitler was said to have hypnotic power over audiences, that audiences more or less fell under his spell. Speech historian Houston Peterson says that Hitler "had a weird talent for holding an audience," and Emil Ludwig wrote in 1939 that "Hitler fascinates the Germans because his speeches have something of Wagnerian music—repetition of a few impressive leitmotivs, sobbing and shouting, and above all, a foggy conglomeration of gods and heroes, blood and race."[12]

So consider . . .

1. Does hypnotic control over an audience serve the goal of persuasion?

2. In the 21st century, post-Hitler, is a speaker's purpose still "holding an audience?" Do we refer to this goal in other ways in our current era?

3. Based on Ludwig's description of Hitler's speeches, would audiences today be as susceptible to their reputed power?

Demonstrating Attitude through Body Action

We cannot prescribe bodily actions that are guaranteed to express what you intend. As Birdwhistell explains, the effect depends upon the audience's point of view: "After searching for 15 years, we have found no gesture or body motion that can be regarded as a universal symbol."[13] Still, you can use gestures in a number of ways to fortify your persuasive message:

> As *illustrators*—Gestures can depict or explain a concept or describe something, as in giving directions.
> As *regulators*—Gestures can control audience responses, as in holding up a hand to request silence.

As *affect displays*—Gestures can show emotions, as a fist may show strong feeling, a pointed finger may show accusation or certainty, or dropped arms and upturned hands may show openness or helplessness.

Your task is to determine your goal and to use gestures as a natural part of your total bodily response.[14]

The face, like the voice, is enormously adaptive. Birdwhistell points out that "The human face alone is capable of some 25,000 different expressions."[15] Again you need not look for a prescription; rather, you want to use your eyes, mouth, and all facial muscles to reflect accurately and sincerely your attitude. Of course, you want to look at the audience throughout most of the speech, since eye contact will boost credibility; low eye contact can denote your lack of enthusiasm or even dishonesty.[16] On the other hand, *too much* direct or intense eye contact can seem overbearing, dominating, intimidating, or threatening. And there will be times when you disengage eye contact, by looking aside or off into the distance, as if visualizing a solution.

Figure 10.5 German Chancellor Angela Merkel's varied gestures suggest a multiplicity of attitudes and reflect her relationship with her audience.
©360b/Shutterstock, Inc.

Perhaps the best guide to facial expression comes from Cicero, who said,

> It is impossible for the hearer to feel grief, hatred, prejudice, to be reduced to tears and pity, unless all the emotions which the orator wishes to arouse in the [audience] are seen to be deeply impressed on the orator himself.[17]

Cicero attributed his own success "not so much [to] his talent as to his capacity for experiencing the feelings he expressed."[18] The true measures of apt facial expressions are naturalness and faithfulness to your message and goal.

A Word about Delivery Style

Examine the four traditional delivery styles listed below to consider which has the best chance of presenting a compelling delivery:

Memorized As noted in Chapter Nine, the potential for memory loss heightens speech anxiety. Why, then, do speakers memorize speeches? With a memorized speech, you are completely free of notes, able to gesture freely and engage eye contact. You are not tied to a podium, so that you can move where you would like, taking control of the speech climate. The downside of a memorized speech is that speakers can suddenly forget what they wanted to say and freeze up entirely. They have sacrificed the skill of thinking as they speak, so that they have difficulty regaining composure.

Manuscript Although it is easy to understand the advantages of a complete script, a manuscript delivery must be the worst choice for a delivery style. An inherent disadvantage to this method is that a written out speech is likely to conform to written style, as opposed to *oral* style, the written version often more formal and less conversational. If you aim for an interactive delivery, a manuscript makes interaction more difficult. Another drawback is that a manuscript may make it challenging for you to escape a visual lock on your notes. You wind up grasping or turning pages, tying up your freedom of movement. Do cue cards or teleprompters make manuscript deliveries more acceptable? Watch a national news commentator. Are the eyes connected to an "audience?" No, they are roving back and forth across a script.

Impromptu With this most spontaneous delivery style, you will have few if any notes, and you will be more flexible nonverbally. But because you will not have time to clearly articulate a goal or proposition, your remarks can lack polish and can fall short in conviction that comes from living with the speech over time. The abrupt preparation period for impromptu speeches can undermine your confidence as well, damaging credibility.

Question: Although the 21st century has brought us the TED Talk, can we say that public speakers (or orators) today compare favorably with the ancient orators?

Answer: True, today we see the democratization of public speaking in proliferating TED Talks, Toastmasters groups, and communication consultants. Whenever we stream a town hall meeting or a stump speech, public speaking becomes more visible and accessible. Of course stylistic differences abound among all venues, from informal, direct interaction with audiences to slick computer-generated visual presentations. But in ancient Greece and Rome, like today, the state of public speaking was judged by live political oratory. We probably find fewer great orators today, amidst a sea of uninspiring and even embarrassing public speakers, but the past century has brought forth such speakers as Winston Churchill, Martin Luther King, Jr., Margaret Thatcher, John F. Kennedy, Ronald Reagan, and Barack Obama.

Based on the studies of classical scholars, we discover that a distinguishing characteristic of the ancients was their passionate conviction, their ability to bring a subject to life emotionally. As W. Robert Connor wrote of the great Greek orator Demosthenes, "What distinguishes him from his lesser contemporaries . . . is his singleness of mind . . . until the emotions he seeks 'come alive in the listener's soul.'"[19]

M.L. Clarke writes of a Roman orator named Servius Galba, who was noted for his force and emotional power. In one speech, "Seeing that his case was hopeless, he brought his two sons and infant ward, and saved the situation by his own tears and those of the children."[20] Another Roman, Gaius, impressed Cicero so that he remarked "Gaius' eyes, voice, and gestures . . . were such that even his enemies could not refrain from tears."[21]

Finally, wit appears to have been a characteristic Roman oratorical weapon. Crassus was particularly well known for his sharp wit, and in one case "produced many amusing examples of what would happen if one followed the letter as opposed to the sense of the law, "and thus induced a general atmosphere of mirth and gaiety."[22]

It is not that the ancient orators foreswore invention and reason. Their peculiar force seems to derive from their ability to wed logos and pathos. Their vocal flexibility enlivened audience attention to prompt an emotional response that would confirm intellectual conviction.

Extemporaneous An extemporaneous delivery—prepared, yet delivered differently each time it is presented—is most speakers' ideal speaking style. It has a conversational feel. Delivered from minimal notes, such as the speaking outline shown in Chapter Nine, one side of one page may suffice, and this can be set on a table or podium for occasional reference. In this way you are free from manipulating notes. With an extemporaneous speech, you are called upon to think the thoughts you want to express, making your sincerity and competence more evident.

Regardless of the advantages and shortcomings of each method, you should select whichever delivery style meets the needs of your content, setting, and audience.

Climate Control

Nonverbal communication goes beyond how we present ourselves. Just as you can control an indoor climate by setting a thermostat, so you can adjust the situational climate to enhance your persuasive efforts. The place or physical context of your speech, the time (*chronemics*) in which it occurs, and the space (*proxemics*) in which it is presented will factor in its impact.

Physical Context

You may find yourself speaking in a large or a small room, in a stuffy or frigid space. Your speech may take place out of doors, in a public or private venue. You can make use of the space to convey a mood. If you want a sense of intimacy in spite of a large, cold space, you might step away from the podium to mingle with audience members, looking at and addressing them directly. On the other hand, if you want to demonstrate formal competence in a relaxed atmosphere, you can stand while others sit and show a high level of preparation and fluency rather than a few casual remarks.

You can arrange seating, if seats are moveable and you arrive in advance of your audience. You can also arrange for the use (or disregard) of a microphone to establish your relationship with the audience. It is not so much the setting but the way you *treat* the setting that determines its effect on the audience.

Time

Time in your speech can refer to one of several factors:

- *the speaker's timing within the speech*—for bringing up issues, for moving from one point to another, for using humor

- *the time at which the speech takes place*—because an address at midnight will have a different mood from one at noon

- *the time of the speech in relationship to other events, that is, historical time*—the year, the season, what has come before and what we anticipate coming after

As a speaker, *you* have most control over timing; you can move along quickly when listeners are restless or dwell on an issue when they are rapt. It is not as easy to control the time of day, but if it *is* possible, you can choose a time that offers the best opportunity for your targeted response. If you want a lively reaction, evening may work better than early morning.

The key to coping with historical time is adaptation. You need to demonstrate awareness of the historical element. If you speak during a religious season, such as Christmas, you may use elements of charity to good effect. At the time of the September 11, 2001 terrorist attacks in the United States, speakers successfully appealed to sentiments of patriotism and American unity. Your sensitivity to time can gain attention by tapping into audience experience.

Space

Apart from your physical setting, you need to consider the spatial relationship between you and your audience. For a speaker who wants to establish authority over a group, as with a military commander, or to assert competence, a favorable position can be one that is somewhat removed from them in a place that suggests a focal point, such as the head of a table or a podium. If you want to seem friendly or emphasize your equality with the audience, you would rather remove the elements that create distance—the podium, a head seat, and so on.[23]

You also would want to be aware of your distance from the audience. If you choose to approach audience members, be wary of breaching acceptable distance barriers, coming only so far within the four to twelve-foot "bubble" that anthropologist Edward Hall found to be appropriate social distance in the United States.[24] In all, climate control for the persuasive speaker means

1. considering the speech's audience and cultural context.

2. recognizing the characteristics of the speaking environment.

3. adapting the environment to establish an atmosphere that will advance your goal.

The Visual Aid Decision

Let's say you're ticketed for what the officer calls an illegal left turn, though you considered the turn reasonable and prudent, given the snarled traffic. You decide to plead this in court, and on the appointed date, pack along a neat diagram of the intersection in question. The judge sees the diagram, gets your point, and boom, you're not guilty.

Visual aids do have their advantages:

- They engage audience *attention and interest.*
- They can improve your *professional image.*
- They can simplify your message, aiding *comprehension.*
- They can make your speech *memorable.*
- They can help you *remember your content*, as speaking notes.

Presentation Software
Managing Data

The purpose of data (or statistics), as we mentioned in Chapter 2, is to support assertions and to promote audience understanding and acceptance of your proposition. As Scott Berinato points out in his excellent *Good Charts*, the purpose of data is to help the audience visualize a simple message. To be able to communicate accurately what the data illustrates is key.

Thus, Berinato suggests that in creating a chart for a visual aid, you first set aside the data and simply sketch out a rough version of the idea you are trying to demonstrate,[25] using only two or three variables, as in the drawing you see here. In this case, you are comparing the relationship between (1) salaries and (2) insurance costs over (3) an eight-year period.

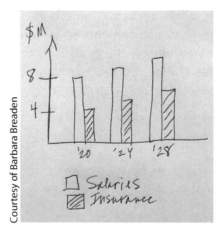

Courtesy of Barbara Breaden

The drawing exercise ensures that you have a firm grasp of the data and can keep that overall *meaning* foremost in your message. As a result, you will be able to communicate it confidently. Another benefit to hand drawing your chart is that you are more likely keep the chart simple and focused so that *audiences* can digest it as well.

At this stage, it helps to practice explaining your chart out loud to friends or colleagues. Show them your sketch and then listen to their responses and questions.[26] Revise your conception to "purify" and finalize it. Once you decide what your final version should look like, you can convert your hand drawing into a nice-looking visual by plugging the data into a Microsoft Excel, Google Charts, or PowerPoint version.

Only after you have managed your data and formed it into a chart, are you ready to import the chart into your chosen presentation software.

Presentation Choices

If you think most readily of a flip chart or poster board as an easy and effective visual aid, better think again. The visual aid standard at this writing is the one developed with presentation software.

Admittedly, many of us feel we have experienced death by PowerPoint, seated in a semi-padded chair to hear a thirty-minute speech comprised of 60 slides or more, each loaded with dozens of words sorted alongside a column of bullet points, with stark or tri-colored backgrounds, maybe a kitschy image tacked on the first and last slides. The speaker reads from a manuscript exactly the same words you see on the screen—and calls this presentation an act of public speaking.

Nevertheless, Microsoft's PowerPoint remains at this writing the go-to presentation software. There are alternatives, to be sure, two notable competitors being Haiku Deck and Prezi.

PowerPoint[27] (along with its clones, Apple Keynote and Google Slides) is still the standard-bearer.[28] It provides a variety of slide themes and layout designs, smart art for producing 3-D diagrams, graphs and charts to illustrate processes or relationships between items, all in an array of complementary colors. Thus your presentation can look pretty, if you have a good aesthetic sense. Yet PowerPoint presentations often are found predictable, stilted, and boring. Because they most often produce a linear progression of words, they lack a compelling story and fail to inspire creative thought.

Haiku Deck[29] is similar to PowerPoint, in that it produces a series of slides. Haiku Deck instructions promote thoughtful presentation skills, such as focus on only one big idea for each slide show and developing (optimally) three main points that derive from the big idea. Each main point can be expanded into multiple slides, but the content retains its focus. Each Haiku Deck slide is image-based, rather than word-based, which is Haiku Deck's primary difference from a PowerPoint style. It emphasizes visualization over verbal explanation.

Benefits of high-speed train

- Relief from traffic congestion

- Clean air

- Reduce fossil fuel consumption

Figure 10.6 The typical PowerPoint-style presentation consists of a heading and a list of bullet points. In this slide, you see the bullets supplemented by an image of an empty highway to enhance the notion that a high-speed train will reduce highway traffic and its natural consequences.

Image © portumen/Shutterstock, Inc.

Road relief
Cleaner air
Oil independence

Figure 10.7 The layout of Haiku Deck presentations favor image over words. In presenting this slide, you could reveal each word line separately, further minimizing the distraction that comes with excessive verbiage.

Image © hans engbers/Shutterstock, Inc.

Prezi[30] has generated excitement in the world of presentations for its innovative, non-linear presentation format. With Prezi, you begin by selecting a theme for a big-picture (the canvas) slide that depicts all of what you want to present at a glance. The program allows you to zoom into the details of the big picture and out again, running through a dizzying panoply of images, videos, PDFs and word entries. Since the presentation is non-linear, characterized by this zooming movement, many consider Prezi more dynamic than PowerPoint, though Prezi has its downsides. Its presentations can appear confusing, as a disconnected jumble of bits. Another advantage is also a shortcoming: it is web-based software, stored in the cloud, but users access it by subscription, which can get expensive.

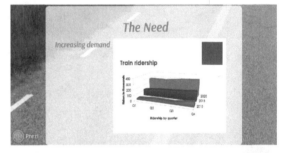
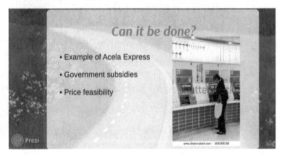
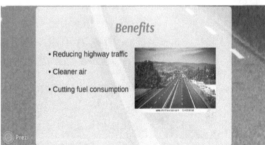

Figure 10.8 As you can see in this series, with Prezi presentations, each slide is a part of the big-picture "canvas," and the presenter follows a path that zooms from this overview into the separate aspects of the issue. The movement within this presentation presents a storyline to generate interest and motivate audience engagement.

Both Haiku Deck and Prezi have built on PowerPoint's weaknesses (often drab and wordy), aiming to amp up audience engagement by the dynamism of the presentation.

Presentation Guidelines

You might think of the various forms of presentation software as special effects in a movie. You can watch a movie, enjoy its special effects, and leave without a message of any kind. That's fine, since we don't always go to a movie for a message. However, we do listen to a speech to receive a message. Visual aids give us special effects tools, but they will not do the work of invention, organization, and style for us.

The lesson in dueling software platforms shows it's not the software that determines presentational effectiveness; it's the presenter. Presentation expert Nancy Duarte, CEO of her own presentation design firm, Duarte (at this writing, the largest in Silicon Valley), points out that people wrongly treat a presentation as a report, a document that provides information, as opposed to a presentation that provides experience, or connection with a storyline context.

Duarte might observe that the movement of Prezi, for instance, reflects a key component of a presentation: the presence of a developing story. According to Duarte, "Information is static; stories are dynamic."[31] The goal of your presentation is to connect the audience to the idea embedded in your speech, and the best way to connect is to involve the audience in a story that reminds us of what exists now and suggests what *could* be.

Visual aids will either complement or undermine your speech, depending on how you use the tools.

1. *Design and structure your presentation to reflect a logical or dramatic order.* If your slides move through a list of facts to prove a point, build these as a story leading from one way of looking at the issue toward revealing another. A motivated sequence organization is dramatic in itself; your visual aid can illustrate the drama that goes from problem to solution.

2. *Your presentation should be visually striking and consistent in its design*: its style, background, font, and use of color. If you select a design template at the outset, this consistency is more likely.

3. *Limit the words on a slide to what can be grasped in a few seconds.* Haiku Deck's design is built on restricted wording, as a matter of fact. To sustain the audience's attention, it is important to *restrict your wording* to key words or brief phrases. Another strategy is to time the entry of words to screen, so that they are revealed at the moment they are introduced orally, not before. This prevents the audience from being overwhelmed by verbiage.

4. *More is not better.* First, limit the number of slides you use, probably not more than one every 45 to 60 seconds. Second, limit each slide's content; empty space will make your presentation more readable.

5. *Use appropriate and high-quality images* relevant to the subject of the slide, and they should maintain high resolution when enlarged and projected on a screen.

6. *Be familiar with the software's navigation system*, so that you can move easily around the pieces of the presentation, whether a single main slide, as in Prezi, or a series of slides, as in PowerPoint.

7. Check to *make sure your presentation is compatible* with the computer or tablet and projection system you will be using—and have a backup plan in case technology fails you.

The fact that presentation technologies are ever-changing should signal the importance of being able to use computer presentations for visual aids. If you produce a homey substitute, be aware of what you are up against. Because the programs we have mentioned consist of cutting edge design elements that allow you to import audio, video, and online components, they add an air of competence and currency to your presentation.

You can hire out graphics, but it is still critical to be confident of their content and practiced in using them. Otherwise your visual aids may give the impression of a child with an oversized baseball bat, more quaint than credible.

When to Use Visual Aids

Once you have reached this point in speech preparation—proposition, content and evidence developed, organization set, a few compelling images and turns of phrase—you begin to hone your presentation with the thought, "How can I make it better?" Visual aids *may* be a good idea, or not. As you glance over the parts of the speech—introduction, issues in the body, and the conclusion, you can imagine how different visuals could enhance each part. In the introduction you can have a simple but striking graphic of the subject or a startling statistic to gain attention.

In the body of the speech, any of the evidence brought to bear on your subject can be projected in visual form—pictures of famous people, diagrams of complex processes, or a bullet-point outline of main ideas. Yet the most practical use for visual aids is to illustrate statistical information, as shown in the "Need" slide of Figure 10.7. Numbers are hard to digest, and lots of numbers are even harder. A graphic program can make fast work of statistics. Visualizing numbers gives them life while it helps your audience grasp and recall them, as long as your charts are simple and you provide a context, an explanation of what the chart *means*.

As in your introduction, visuals in your conclusion can rekindle your audience's interest, bringing them back to the core of your message, completing the storyline, and inspiring them to take action.

What Can Go Wrong: A Word of Caution

Most beginning textbooks on public speaking will list a number of standard precautions on the use of visual aids, but one law is primary: Murphy's Law—whatever can go wrong will go wrong. Therefore keep the following in mind:

1. *Practice speaking with—and without—the visual aid,* preferably with another person as audience. Request honest feedback about whether your visual aid is pleasing, distracting, clear, or unclear. Through practice you will gain confidence in using the technology of your choice. But if the technology should fail, you need to know your message well enough to forge ahead *without* the visual aid. A picture may be worth a thousand words, but if you lack the picture, you still have words.

2. *Make sure the visual aid is visible to the entire audience.* If you practice with another person you can also request their opinion on whether the visual aid is visible. Rather than excuse yourself with "I know you can't see this, but . . . ", if the visual aid cannot be seen, do not show it. It may not be visible if it is too small, if it is set at an angle blocking the view of some audience members, or if you are standing in front of a screen. Incidentally, a visual aid usually is not visible when you stand in front of it looking backward to admire your work, thus the adage, "Look at the audience, not the visual aid."

3. *Don't overdo it.* A few well-selected slides add impact to the speech, but if a slide show becomes a "sideshow," you lose the message to the medium. Use only those visual aids that add to or clarify the message; if they add nothing, delete.

4. *Present visual aids in such a way as not to detract from the message.* Resist the urge to pass items around the room as you speak. We're not listening anymore; we're looking for our turn to see what you passed. Don't show your visual aid *before* you are ready to talk about it. Present your information with its accompanying slide, then move on.

   The flip-side to this rule applies. If you have displayed the visual aid, explain it. A graph *may* be self-explanatory, but since the audience is looking at it anyway, you can expound on its implications. If a graph shows 63 per cent of the state's population, you might restate the figure in terms relevant to your audience: for example, "This is essentially the size of Portland." Finally, if you think your audience will find it difficult to understand your visual aid, why are you keeping it in your speech?

In Summary

To deliver your speech well, you must begin with a goal—what do you hope to achieve? In particular, what persona and attitude do you hope to transmit to your audience? Once you have envisioned this, you can link all the nonverbal elements of your speech to this goal.

Your dress, voice (including pitch, rate, volume, and quality), and action (including gesture and facial expression) reflect and reinforce your attitude. You also can adapt the climate of your speech—the setting, the time, and the use of space—to reinforce your goal.

Finally, you can use visual aids, most likely digital presentation programs, to tell your story, enhance your credibility, demonstrate your competence, and add another layer of appeal to your message.

Endnotes

1 Cicero, *De Oratore, Book III,* trans. H. Rackham (Cambridge: Harvard Univ. Press, 1968), 169.

2 Edward P. J. Corbett, *Classical Rhetoric for the Modern Student,* 4th ed. (New York: Oxford Univ. Press, 1999), 22.

3 John Illo, "The Rhetoric of Malcolm X," rpt. in Corbett 576.

4 Charles H. Woolbert and Severina E. Nelson, *The Art of Interpretative Speech,* 4th ed. (New York: Appleton-Century-Crofts, 1956), 213.

5 Woolbert and Nelson, 214.

6 Ray L. Birdwhistell, *Kinesics and Context: Essays of Body Motion Communication* (Philadelphia: Univ. of Pennsylvania Press, 1970), 7.

7 Loretta A. Malandro et al., *Nonverbal Communication,* 2nd ed. (New York: McGraw-Hill, 1989), 244. This has been disputed by Daniel J. O'Keefe in his *Persuasion: Theory and Research,* 2nd ed. (Thousand Oaks, CA: Sage, 2002), 185.

8 Malandro et al.

9 Kent Nerburn, *The Wisdom of the Native Americans.* New World Library, 1999, p. 9.

10 Carroll C. Arnold and John Waite Bowers, *Handbook of Rhetorical and Communication Theory* (Boston: Allyn & Bacon, 1984), 303.

11 Daniel Lee Henry, *Across the Shaman's River: John Muir, the Tlingit Stronghold, and the Opening of the North.* U of Alaska P, 2017, p. 120.

12 Houston Peterson, ed., *A Treasury of the World's Greatest Speeches* (New York: Simon and Schuster, 1965), 756.

13 Birdwhistell, 81.

14 Malandro, 100ff.

15 Birdwhistell, 8.

16 Steven A. Beebe, "Eye Contact: A Nonverbal Determinant of Speaker Credibility," *The Speech Teacher* 23, no. 1 (1974), 21–25.

17 M. L. Clarke, *Rhetoric at Rome: A Historical Survey* (London: Cohen and West, 1968), 59.

18 Ibid.

19 W. Robert Connor, ed., *Greek Orations* (Ann Arbor: Univ. of Michigan Press, 1966), 7.

20 Clarke, 42.

21 Ibid., 43.

22 Ibid., 47. It is difficult, however, to match the standard of wit found in British Parliament. Winston Churchill and Lady Astor, his nemesis, were responsible for a number of such quotable moments. Once in a House of Commons' debate on agriculture, Churchill broke off Lady Astor's remarks charging, "I'll make a bet she doesn't even know how many toes a pig has." The adroit Lady Astor replied, "Why don't you take off your little shoosies, and we'll count them together." Another, more-broadly reported incident, occurred when Lady Astor scoffed to Churchill, "If I were married to you, I'd put poison in your coffee." Without missing a beat, Churchill replied, "If I were married to you, I'd drink it."

23 Malandro, 161 ff.

24 Edward T. Hall, *The Silent Language* (Garden City, NY: Anchor Press/ Doubleday, 1973).

25 Scott Berinato, *Good Charts: The HBR Guide to Making Smarter, More Persuasive Data Visualizations.* Harvard Business Review P, 2016, pp. 75–76.

26 Ibid., 78.

27 Microsoft Corporation, 2014, PowerPoint, 11 June 2014 <http://office. microsoft.com/en-us/powerpoint/>.

28 "Top 10 Best Presentation Software of 2018—PowerPoint or Alternative App?" *Consumers Advocate*, 12 June 2018, https://www.consumersadvocate.org/ presentation-software/best-presentation-software. Accessed 9 July 2018.

29 Giant Thinkwell, Inc., Haiku Deck, 2014, 11 June 2014 <https://www. haikudeck.com/>.

30 Prezi, Inc., 2014, Prezi, 11 June 2014 <http://prezi.com/>.

31 Nancy Duarte, *Resonate: Present Visual Stories that Transform Audiences.* John Wiley and Sons, 2017, p. 17.

Theory into Practice

1. Define for yourself what attitude you would like to convey to your audience. How do you want them to feel toward your subject? What mood or atmosphere would you like to establish in your speech?

2. Consider the setting for your speech. How does this contribute to or thwart the objective you want to achieve? Can you adjust the space by rearranging seating, your position, and your use—or not—of a microphone?

3. Consider the effect of time on your speech.
   a. How much time to you plan to allot to each part of the speech?
   b. How will the time of day affect audience reception, and how can you adapt to this factor?
   c. What relationship does your speech have to the seasonal current political events and activities the audience will experience prior to or after your speech? What adjustments can you make in your delivery to refer to or adapt to external events?

4. If you do not already possess it, begin a personal campaign to improve your literacy in computer presentation software. You can begin to explore online the programs footnoted at the end of this chapter, and if you have the opportunity, participate in a workshop or class that will allow you to prepare sample presentations. If you already are adept in using these programs, produce at least one slide or small slide series for an upcoming speech.

Speech Delivery Checklist

<table>
<tr>
<td colspan="2">Speech Goal:</td>
</tr>
<tr>
<td>How can your dress contribute to your goal?</td>
<td>Possible attire:</td>
</tr>
<tr>
<td>How can your voice contribute to your goal?</td>
<td>Voice factors to consider (to be tried out by recording, listening, and evaluating the effect)</td>
</tr>
<tr>
<td>How can your gesture and movement enhance your goal?</td>
<td>Possible gestures/movements for an important part of this speech:</td>
</tr>
<tr>
<td>How can your facial expression enhance your goal?</td>
<td>What sort of facial expression might be appropriate at a key moment in your speech? (Naturally, this involves working with a mirror.)</td>
</tr>
<tr>
<td>Would visual aids help to achieve your goal? (Brainstorm potential visuals on the right.)</td>
<td>I. Introduction

II. Body

III. Conclusion</td>
</tr>
</table>

Part Five
_____

Beyond the Speech: Adaptation and Analysis

Chapter

11 Adapting the Persuasive Speech

To Make a Long Story Short...

While a persuasive speech setting and style may change, the fundamentals of persuasion remain the same.

Key Concepts

- Advocacy calls for *policy* persuasion that champions social or political action.
- Dialectical discovery of consumer needs lays the groundwork for sales persuasion.
- Public deliberation and deliberative polling present useful alternatives to debate for resolving contentious policy differences.
- Debate rebuttals correspond directly to persuasive speech refutations.
- Social commentary is a discrete rhetorical genre that stimulates inquiry, discussion, and novel perspectives on social issues.
- The highlight of legal persuasion is the summation, which usually pleads propositions of fact or value.
- The advocate in a legal summation is obliged to respect, adapt to, and emotionally engage the jury.

Key Terms

advocacy

commentary

affirmative

negative

public deliberation

soundbite

inherency

solvency

fairness doctrine

Speeches of Advocacy

When we advocate we speak in favor of an action. Thus **advocacy** is active support for a cause, be it political, social, or personal. We advocate all the time, often privately, less often publicly. Persuasive speaking is not just for study; it is for life. Practical skill in the art of persuasion makes us instruments of change in our personal lives and in our communities. As we become practiced advocates, we can use the early chapters of *Speaking to Persuade* to prepare for the task.

Ordinarily, advocacy promotes policy change. Whether we sell, promote or debate socio-political action, we deal in policy, applying the principles of policy persuasion.

Social or Political Advocacy

Although most people prefer not to give speeches, if you were the parent of a child who needed an outlawed medicine, you might be motivated to speak not once but repeatedly to campaign for its legalization. Dr. Tim Vogus is a Professor at Vanderbilt University's Owen School of Management, in Nashville, Tennessee. Known for his research in reducing medical error in health care systems, Vogus had learned that cannabidiol, a form of medical marijuana, might relieve his son, Aidan, from his nightly seizures from intractable epilepsy. Along with a committed cadre of medical marijuana

Figure 11.1 Throughout your life you may need to invoke your advocacy skills unexpectedly, as in the case of a public hearing, where individuals have an opportunity to articulate their positions.

© stock_photo_world/Shutterstock.com

supporters, Vogus and his wife, Jen, organized a panel of presenters at Vanderbilt to discuss a bill that would legalize cannabidiol in the state of Tennessee.

As Tennessee happens to be one of the most socially conservative states in the U.S., even with a sympathetic audience of like-minded progressives, the bill would not pass the legislature if Vogus and others failed to lay groundwork for the bill's broad acceptance by honoring values shared by Tennesseeans at large.

Notice how in this speech Vogus establishes identification with the immediate and statewide audience (this hearing would be broadcast and later covered by two local stations), and develops a proof corresponding point-by-point to the Motivated Sequence, not because this was an assigned speech in a classroom, but because it is effective strategy: a problem-solution pattern, followed by counterargument, refutation, visualization of benefits, and a call to action. Vogus' speech demonstrates that social and political advocacy tools are for real people to be used to impact the challenging circumstances of daily life.

Get Kids the Meds They Need[1]

I have an 11-year-old son, Aidan, and he's the reason I'm here. Aidan loves Tennessee. He loves all Tennessee has to offer him. He loves the Aquarium of Chatanooga and Gatlinburg. He loves the air shows in Smyrna, Lebanon, and Tullahoma. He loves seeing the Black Keys at Bridgestone Arena. He loves Mule Day and the Harley dealership in Columbia, riding in helicopters in the Smokies, the Railroad Museum in Lynville, Tennessee. He loves Marathon Motor Works in Nashville and the water tower there.

With this introduction, Vogus reaches out to all parts and all people of Tennessee, expressing appreciation and pride in its diverse and distinctive features. Tennessee's attractions have won the affection of Vogus' child, Aidan.

But Aidan suffers from a rare genetic condition that has caused seizures since he was five weeks old. His seizures are devastating. They're violent, myoclonic clusters that have worsened over time, and many times he's stopped breathing during these seizures.

Aidan's seizures have been unresponsive to eighteen different medications. To even try some of these medications, we've had to sign

This kicks off an extensive catalog of the problems needing to be addressed:

1. *Aidan suffers from devastating seizures.*

2. *The seizures are unresponsive to medications*

3. *The seizures have not responded to surgical "correction."*

4. *Nor can the seizures be controlled by diet.*

5. *The medications are endangering Aidan beyond the seizures themselves.*

And here Vogus has an opportunity to introduce Aidan, who walks into the back of the hall with his mother. He's a handsome child, composed, with an open, cherubic face, presenting a startling contrast between the child and the struggle Vogus details.

A solution to these problems is available.

waivers that said if he goes blind from this medication, that's on us. Some of the medications we've tried have the word *rage* associated with them, which is not a good thing to have associated with a medicine. He's also not been helped by a surgery to implant a vagal nerve stimulator that would send pulses to his vagal nerve, shown to help some kids with seizures. Not with him. He's tried a special seizure diet. That didn't help either.

Many nights his seizures are so severe that we have to administer an emergency medication—he's coming in right now; that's the man—we have to administer an emergency medicine called diastat just to get the seizures to stop. Diastat is a concentrated Valium that is both addictive and is required in increasing doses to be effective. Some nights the seizures are so bad we've been told we should give him a double dose: massive amounts, forty milligrams of Valium, concentrated. We're the ones having to make that call in the middle of the night.

The seizures have cost Aidan dearly. He desperately wants to tell us much, but the seizures have taken his speech and left him at the highest risk of sudden death from epilepsy.

But there's hope in the form of this bill proposing to make cannabidiol, a high-CBD, low THC substance, available to Aidan. The cannabis-based substance will be turned into an oil, put into a capsule and added to his food, just like any medication. Supportive research on adults and animals consistently shows the anti-seizure properties of CBD, [as] is famously documented by Dr. Sanjay Gupta in a widely seen [news] special.

Charlotte Figi, a little girl in Colorado, suffered up to 1200 seizures a month, but now after taking this high CBD medicine suffers only one or two. Another boy very similar to Aidan, named Zaki Jackson, went from having upwards of 200 seizures a night to a year seizure-free on this medicine.

A recent survey from Stanford University showed 70% of kids treated with high-CBD cannabis experienced a 50% reduction in seizures. These are kids for whom an additional medication would usually yield nothing. And these kids who've been helped by high-CBD strains of medical cannabis have increased alertness, development, and better mood. For children with intractable epilepsy, these results are remarkable.

But obviously there are concerns that remain. Representatives are trying to get other people to sponsor this bill, and they're probably hearing, "Well, we're with you, but it's an election year." No one's going to touch this in an election year. Well, I would argue that it's poor electoral strategy to let a child like Aidan suffer one night more, to have the chance of dying, when his parents are sitting up worried sick every night about him.

More importantly, the electoral argument relies on the myth that this bill is really for Cheech and Chong, but it's not for Cheech and Chong. It's for Piper Koozer and Millie Mattison, so they can quell their seizures and their families can come back home. This bill is for stopping the seizures of Ryne Gilbert, Corbin Wright, and Wally Peterson. And it's most certainly for Aidan Vogus

This bill isn't about abstractions and our fears of what *could* happen, but about helping those in the greatest need during their most desperate hour. And looking at this crowd, in all its diversity, this issue is not an electoral loser.

The solution has been shown to work.

*The most significant counterargument to a proposed bill is that it cannot gain legislative support. Vogus turns this argument into a reason **for** legislative support: This is the bill the people of Tennessee **want**, one that will serve children and families.*

A second counterargument, that the proposal was a cover to provide marijuana for druggies, is defused by replacing this image with the image of suffering children and displaced families left unprotected by the state. Here Dr. Vogus gestures toward his son sitting in the back of the room; the audience erupts in prolonged applause.

*Finally Vogus banishes the phantom argument of **possible** outcomes and refocuses on specific conditions and real people who need tangible help.*

Vogus visualizes this solution—legislative and voter support—as a win-win combination.

Vogus closes as he began, in solidarity and identification with people and values across the state.

Vogus leaves the audience with an appeal to action: speak up and vote.

Four months later, the bill passed 130 in favor to 4 opposed, stunning bipartisan support for a bill that had been in the works only four months. At this writing, Aidan's seizures have become a rare occurrence, thanks to his access to cannabadiol, in large part due to his parents' advocacy.

We're eager to back those who back us. The majority of Tennesseans, after hearing specific stories about real people will support this bill. We need to prove this to the legislators. That's on us.

Lastly, this bill embodies Tennessee values. Tennessee values say we prize family and attract the best from around the nation because of the opportunities, community, and quality of life—that's why my family came here—not to force families to leave when they need us most. Tennessee values say we give people tools to help themselves. Tennessee values say we take the steps to solve tough problems together, not shy away because we fear the worst.

So let's make clear that this bill is pure Tennessee values, this bill will help people and save lives across the state, and this bill is what the people want.

Sales Persuasion

In most cases, a sales presentation is fragmented; you walk the consumer step by step through the process of pinpointing needs and adapting product choice to those needs. The salesperson is not so much a public speaker as an advocate in a small group or interpersonal communication transaction. In any sales setting, the principles of persuasive speaking remain consistent with what we have described in Chapters One through Ten.

Sales as Dialectic

As with all persuasive speech, sales speech is grounded in dialectic. To engage in dialectical discovery, the seller establishes a dialogue with the buyer. This give and take over what the seller can offer, what buyers think they want, what is good and not so good in a product, captures the extent to which you must adapt to the buyer as speaker to audience. The key to sales success is not format, then, but the total package of the salesperson's "situational fluency," as Keith Eades and Timothy Sullivan explain in *The Collaborative Sale*,[2]

> The sales conversation can no longer focus on the seller's products and services; it must be about the buyer's business results. Buyer 2.0 specifically wants to talk about and do business with sellers who understand buyers' business, situations, challenges and opportunities . . . . Buyer 2.0 wants sellers to collaborate with them . . . .[3]

Coming to understand the buyer's role, to identify with the buyer's concerns, and to respond based on the buyer's unique needs are the seller's foremost obligations. As Susan Adams points out in *Forbes*, if you are trying to sell an iPad, there is little you need to know about the buyer; the product sells itself. But in most cases, "questions are better than answers"[4] to discover an individual buyer's particular situation.

If invention is the foundation for an effective persuasive speech (see Chapter Three), so it is in sales speaking. Your relationship as seller to buyer depends on dialogue and requires the push and pull of dialectical discovery to uncover salient issues. A problem-solution format makes sense, then, as long as the seller recognizes that the problem is not to sell a product but to come to know a buyer's needs, and potential resources for a solution.

Considering Form

A sales presentation, then, is a policy speech. You are saying that someone *needs* the product you are selling. As policy persuasion, a sales presentation can follow, if loosely, the problem-solution format:

1. *Identify the need (that is, the problem) to be addressed.* The problem is an unfulfilled need or want that the consumer is experiencing, whether for a car, an attorney, or a business investor. You can offer an appropriate solution only insofar as you understand the buyer's need.

    Psychologist Abraham Maslow reasoned that people are motivated to act when prompted by their needs, from basic survival needs to the ultimate need to achieve (or at least to strive toward) their potential. According to Maslow's Hierarchy of Needs (1954), our happiness depends on meeting and surpassing survival and safety needs. We are motivated to push beyond these to experience love and belonging, the respect of others, and personal fulfillment—what Maslow called *self-actualization*.

Although Maslow stressed that we must meet basic needs before attending to "higher" needs, recent follow-up on Maslow's findings shows that people seek to meet all of these needs all the time.[5] For a motivational sales approach, then, by reviewing Maslow's needs hierarchy (see Figure 11.2), you can assess a buyer's most salient needs. Those needs become the focus, the problem segment, of your rhetorical appeal.

2. *Suggest a solution, or a range of solutions, to the problem.* As with the Motivated Sequence (Chapter Six), the sales speech proposes to satisfy the buyer's need, which may not be your product. In the interest of sustaining your credibility for the long term, the most appropriate solution may be one that you do not sell. This openness to alternatives achieves a dual purpose: 1) as market research, to build your awareness of what products you should offer, and 2) to confirm you as a trustworthy resource.

3. If your product fulfills the need, you may go on to *visualize the benefits of the product* and *suggest the consumer proceed with the purchase,* as you would in the final two steps of the Motivated Sequence.

MASLOW'S HIERARCHY OF NEEDS

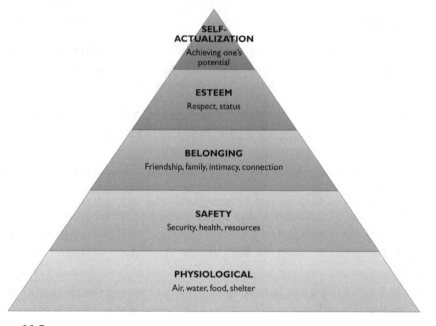

Figure 11.2
Courtesy of Barbara Breaden

The Elevator Pitch

Sometimes salespeople do give real speeches, as in the "pitch," a pre-packaged presentation to a potential customer or group of clients. As described by StartupNation, a website for entrepreneurs, a twenty-first century phenomenon of sales is the "elevator pitch." The elevator pitch may be as brief as thirty seconds or still less, as in the following,

> I provide a spick and span house cleaning service to upscale clients in Beverly Hills. I bring all the supplies needed, and clean with baby-friendly organic cleaning products. And of course, I'm bonded, discreet and reliable. I currently have an opening, would you know of anyone who could benefit from my services?[6]

Or the elevator speech can be a fully prepared and rehearsed speech that an entrepreneur who wants to woo investors must have ready when that momentous opportunity arises: you are standing in an elevator going from the lobby to the tenth floor within a single minute. Thus your pitch must be fluent, clear, concise, and credible. For example:

Figure 11.3 The elevator pitch should last about the amount of time it takes to go from the lobby to the executive floor of an office building–about a minute, give or take thirty seconds.
© Doreen Salcher/Shutterstock, Inc.

Our company is called ConstructionBoots.com, an e-commerce website that sells brand name construction boots. There are currently no companies serving this niche exclusively.

ConstructionBoots.com will drive traffic to the site by linking to other websites catering to the construction industry as well as through word-of-mouth. In industry surveys, over 90% of construction workers have these three traits: 1) they have a favorite brand of boots, 2) they know their size, and 3) they hate shopping at stores. In our own polling, over 70% indicated that they would prefer to buy their boots online and have them delivered. Accordingly, we expect a great market response and rapid sales ramp-up.

We need $1.5 million in funding to get to the point where the company is self-sustaining. This should happen in the middle of our second year. Right now, we're seeking $500,000 of initial funding in exchange for a 30% ownership stake in the company. I am the CEO with lots of operational experience and deep contacts with boot manufacturers. Our Marketing Director was instrumental in the growth and recent sale of a very successful e-commerce clothing company. If we hit our numbers, we expect to be able to sell ConstructionBoots.com to a 'brick and mortar' retailer within 3 years.[7]

Note the brief, straightforward introduction, followed by need or problem segment: availability of boots online.

The speaker demonstrates how market research has led to a unique solution. The rest of this segment establishes solvency: what the speaker has to offer will resolve the need.

The speaker visualizes potential success and appeals for action— sweetening the deal by hinting at potential rewards for investment and by establishing their entrepreneurial credibility.

You can sense in this pitch the entrepreneur's energy and positive approach, and that a dialectic has taken place in advance (through market research) to identify necessary adaptations in response to market needs. You also can see how the construction boots pitch follows the strategy for a policy speech, including capturing the stages of the motivated sequence. This format, grounded in a seller-buyer dialectic, characterizes effective sales in a 21st-century marketplace.

Informal Debate

There are many instances when a speaker may wind up informally debating an issue. The chair of a taskforce or other problem-solving group may invite those who hold strong views on a subject to debate it. A school board may set aside its agenda to debate opposing viewpoints in a pressing controversy over redistricting. And we know that political candidates for many offices agree to public debates. But why debate?

The Public Deliberation Option

Indeed, there *are* alternatives to debate as a means of civic engagement. The most productive of these may be public deliberation. Stanford communication scholar, James Fishkin, explains an experiment in democratic governance he calls deliberative polling.[8] His strategy involves convening a group of citizens who reflect demographic diversity and a range of attitudes. Next, he provides a setting for those gathered to engage in evidence-based discussions for and against proposals.

The goal of such deliberation is to motivate participants to become more informed, as opposed to changing opinions. To reach workable conclusions or solutions, participants must be on guard against distorting information and must repel domination by any particular viewpoint.[9]

Fishkin has implemented this strategy in the United States and other countries. He has found that "when a random sample of ordinary citizens deliberate in moderated small groups, they actually listen to each other and make decisions based on the substance of policy choices." Ultimately, the group endorses measures that reflect their findings. In a number of instances, state legislatures or local governments have used the group results to draft laws or to reform public policy. In Mongolia, the government adopted a law that would *require* public deliberation to screen constitutional amendments.[10]

Is There Value in Debate?

Linguist and communication scholar Deborah Tannen makes a case against *agonism*, the kind of combative discourse you find in contentious intellectual discussion. Agonism is problematic, says Tannen, because it frames opinion differences as battles. Its competitive nature causes participants to distort information to achieve "victory."[11]

Tannen favors an approach found in Asian cultures, where people resist polarized dualities—that is, where one side of an issue is deemed right, the other wrong, and opposing sides on an issue are considered irreconcilable. Typically, in China, polarities—the yin and yang—are complementary. They "interact to form a higher synthesis,"[12] with each side respected.[13] To Tannen, intellectual honesty and constructive opposition require that opposing parties strive not to annihilate one another, but to integrate a multiplicity of positions.

Tannen goes on to discuss the value of ritualistic fighting in some cultures: cockfighting in Bali, sheep-rustling in Crete, and, yes, boxing or wrestling in the United States. She describes human fights (generally between two men) on the Gaelic Tory Island in Ireland. The men threaten and curse one another. They create a big fuss as a fight heats up to the point where one man begins to take off his coat—and his friends struggle to restrain him. Eventually, he is held back by his supporters. Typically, the mother of one of the men is called in, and she begs her son to break off and come home.

As the fight disperses, the supporters on each side slap one another's backs and dissect the finer points of the skirmish—even though the men never came to blows. What is the purpose of this ritual? Tannen calls it a communal form of entertainment that deflects tension and creates harmony. The appearance of a great brawl is a kind of catharsis where both sides recognize but move past their differences toward peaceful coexistence.

What does this have to do with debate? In some ways, a debate resembles ritualistic combat. In debate, as in any athletic competition, conflict and struggle are integral; flat out differences are expected. You can mercilessly rip into your opponents' views. You can call them wrong, foolish, ignorant of certain information, then shake hands at the end and walk away in peace, both contenders satisfied at having made the best case for their position.

In a good debate, each side must listen to the other to refute opposing arguments. Consequently, the most resilient arguments rise to the top and become the talking points of further discussion. The audience benefits from hearing two distinct positions and new evidence to ponder. Debate efficiently informs, opposes positions, and proposes solutions that we carry forward for further action—not so different from ritualistic fighting, and not altogether useless.

A "Culture of Debate"

While debates sometimes appear to be nothing more than contentious posturing, these interchanges can be good for the public and for society. Democracy can benefit from a "culture of debate" to educate the public and clarify each side's position. *New York Times* columnist David Brooks pointed out, in discussing weaknesses in President George W. Bush's administration that good public policy requires debate. To Brooks, the absence of debate over two Bush terms constituted a fatal flaw:

> The real problem was there was no debate. . . . There were a lot of intellectual mediocrities who . . . did not have the intellectual chops to have a debate. And so what you had was a culture without debate . . . . no culture of testing decision-making.[14]

As we pointed out in Chapter One, the conflict we encounter in a dialectic or opposing positions promotes discovery of alternatives. Brooks recognizes the pragmatism of a debate culture in a healthy democracy.

Alternative proposals are put to the test, the better arguments withstanding scrutiny. Extended debate in policy-making bodies works best when proposals are revised through deliberation and adapted to overcome weaknesses. Over time, well crafted policy minimizes harms and maximizes benefits.

But does this tug of opposing positions really occur in public affairs? For many years, through the end of the twentieth century and onset of the twenty-first, the US government has struggled to resolve the issue of illegal immigration, especially along its southern border with Mexico. Political instability, poverty, and violent crime in Latin, Central, and South America drove people northward in hopes for political asylum and a better standard of living in the United States. Because thousands of undocumented immigrants have come to live in, work in, and blend into US culture, the country faces challenges in firmly upholding immigration laws in face of the vital role these undocumented members of US society have played.[15]

For example, beginning in 2001, the Development, Relief, and Education for Alien Minors (DREAM) Act sought to provide protection against deportation and to craft a pathway to citizenship for children brought to the United States illegally, but who had been acculturated and educated in the United States.[16] The DREAM Act became an exception to immigration policy. In 2017, the new administration of President Donald Trump vowed to enforce immigration law and threatened to halt the "Dreamer" movement. Yet a groundswell of bipartisan and popular support for Dreamers (including from the President himself) demonstrated that any enforcement of immigration policy should assure DREAM Act protection. Through assertion and counter-assertion of what US immigration policy should accomplish, a commonality emerged in public discourse. So it is that public conversation in the United States continues to uncover standards and guiding principles toward developing acceptable immigration policy.

Establishing Format

Most public debates do not replicate formal competitive debate, although they surely can become as intense. When debate functions as social or political advocacy, speakers once again are dealing with policy persuasion.[17] Debaters should have some say about how the debate will proceed: establishing time limits, how many times each debater speaks, and so on. With three speaking opportunities, each speaker would have two opportunities to develop a case and one to respond to the opposition. Each speaker's time should be uninterrupted, except perhaps for points of clarification. In labeling this informal debate, the format may not be rigid, but the more predictability you can build into the format the more you can concentrate on your message or case without the anxiety of anticipating unconstrained squabbling.

Isolate the Proposition

You may have seen informal debate take off without either side knowing or paying much attention to what they are debating. Both debaters must negotiate a proposition so that they concur on what is being debated. You can refer back to the guidelines in Chapter Two for stating the proposition. Social or political advocacy propositions will probably be worded as "should" statements: "The city should recycle glass," or "The state should increase incentives for new businesses," or "The school district should freeze new administrative hires."

Define the Terms of the Proposition

Why define the terms being debated? To advance the debate, each side should make clear what it means by key terms in the proposition. For example, in the incentives for businesses proposition above, what is meant by incentives: property tax breaks? income tax breaks? building fee waivers? And to what new businesses are you referring: large corporations? small businesses? green energy companies? technology start-ups? Since propositions can be interpreted variously; the debate will make more sense to debaters and listeners if each side nails down terminology early.

Determine Affirmative and Negative Positions

The person who speaks in favor of the proposition is the affirmative speaker; the opposing side is the negative. In laying out the debate, each side must take time to identify its position. Both sides should know whether they are speaking for or against the proposition as it has been stated. Obvious, right? Not necessarily. If the proposition states that *The school board should not support anti-choice sex-education programs*, does the negative debater support or oppose choice in sex education? (The negative would want the school board to oppose choice.)

It is customary for an affirmative speaker to present a case first. Negative speakers defend the status quo and need to recognize what policy proposals they are arguing against. In a political debate, the affirmative speaker is the candidate who challenges the incumbent and opens the debate.

Affirmative If you are the affirmative speaker, you will have two burdens in the policy debate, reflecting two major components of the motivated sequence—*problem* and *solution*:

1. *The affirmative must demonstrate that there is a need for a change.* You must establish that there is a problem or set of problems inherent in the status quo. This is the issue of **inherency.** If you are proposing that the state offer new business incentives, you must first establish that there are significant problems that are inherent, or unavoidable, in current state practice.

2. *The affirmative must establish that the proposed plan will solve the problems.* This is the issue of **solvency.** There is not much use in a solution that will not work or that fails to address the problems cited.

Negative If you are the negative speaker, you can respond in a variety of ways, but basically you will still adhere to the problem-solution format.

1. *The negative speaker can show that a **problem does not exist** or that the problems cited by the affirmative are **insignificant.** For instance, you might say*
   We get it. Our respected opponent thinks our state is losing opportunity in jobs and tax *income* by neglecting *incentives.* But look what happened with Zenon. The state sacrificed millions of tax dollars to attract a tech company dependent on unlimited water resources, a company that turned a residential site into an eyesore, and when it went bankrupt laid off 1000 workers, making no amends for our environmental and economic losses. The problem is not a lack of incentives but too many incentives for companies without conscience.

2. *The negative should demonstrate that the affirmative solution will not solve the problem.* For example:
   And if my opponent thinks that an additional $100 million in tax incentives will help fund our schools and fix our roads, just look at how Zenon contributed less than promised to our state. They promised 3000 jobs and provided 1000, and those only after five years. They were guaranteed tax deferrals for ten years, but within eight years, they shuttered the company altogether.

3. *The negative may propose a counterplan.* If you think the problem is a valid one, you can still reject the solution as unworkable or unsatisfactory, as follows:

   Yes, we still are reeling from the recession, and we do need to improve our employment rate, but tax incentives are not the answer. On the other hand, we *can* provide partnerships between our community colleges and potential businesses, offering training resources for the jobs those companies will provide.

Rebuttal

The final speech for each debater typically has three goals:

1. *To state the opposition claims that you question.* This step is the same as refutation in a persuasive speech. You will do this more easily if you have taken notes during your opponent's arguments. Refer to Chapter Seven for suggestions on what to refute, such as your opponent's sources of information or reasoning.

2. *To refute these claims with opposing evidence or an alternative interpretation of evidence.* You will want to say what is wrong with your opponent's claims, whether they are unsupported, illogical, or inaccurate.

3. *To restate clearly and vigorously your own case and appeal for audience agreement.* This can take the form of a summary or recapitulation of your main ideas to refocus your audience on what you believe are the critical issues.

The rebuttal is usually the shortest piece of the debate, but it is crucial for clarifying your position and highlighting the key points you have made.

An informal debate may or may not have specified these debate elements. If the debate begins spontaneously, you can step back and suggest that both participants agree to continue debating according to certain guidelines. Will a moderator enforce time limits? How will the back and forth of speakers be structured? Will speakers be allowed to interject comments at will? You will not want to control the proceedings entirely but to share a clear sense of format. From that point on, you may need to determine independently whether you are affirmative or negative and what your obligations are in arguing your position.

Debate can be unnerving, but more often it is the most stimulating form of advocacy. It vigorously shakes out public opinion to uncover the most viable direction for public policy.

Speeches of Interpretation, Accusation, and Defense

While advocacy applies the principles of policy persuasion, social commentary and courtroom speech most often incorporate propositions of value and fact. Commentary interprets, analyzes, endorses, or criticizes an event rather than encouraging action. Courtroom speaking, especially in legal summations, defines the nature of an event in terms of law.

Social Commentary

Social **commentary**, as a persuasive genre, offers an *interpretation* of events. It provides a context of information as the basis for evaluating an issue. Good political commentary depends on a speaker's "inside" knowledge and background. The commentary's distinctive objective is to stimulate inquiry, thought, and discussion, by rethinking an issue or looking at it in a novel way.

Social commentary often takes the form of satire, engaging the audience through humor to provoke a different perspective or to point out an essential nature of the issue that has not been considered. Professor of Media and Communication, Geoffrey Baym's study[18] of *The Daily Show* (at this writing, more than twenty years running) explores how the show has used satire "to interrogate power," demand accountability, and cast light on "the foibles and character flaws" of political actors.[19] Although *The Daily Show* has trumpeted itself as "fake news,"[20] Baym recognizes in its satire "a discourse of inquiry" that asks unanswered questions about morality and honesty in political life and spurs "deliberation within" audience minds. Whereas advocacy persuades people toward action, commentary probes beliefs about public values.

At some time, you may find yourself in the position of having to make a live statement at a hearing or an on-the-air statement about a cause you have championed. Since you are at the mercy of those granting you speaking time, you want to be able to capture the essence of your views in a few words. Your statement should strive for clarity, precision, and force. You may have time for only a soundbite condensed from a longer speech. It might be the most memorable phrase, such as John F. Kennedy's inaugural phrase, "Ask not what your country can do for you; ask what you can do for your country." For a classic soundbite, many would point to Ronald Reagan's concise stand against communism in 1987 Berlin (a city divided in two by the great wall between communists and free Berliners) when he challenged then Soviet President Mikhail Gorbachev, "Mr. Gorbachev, tear down this wall." President Barack Obama's 2008 campaign soundbite became "Yes we can."

You may have limited, but more than a soundbite's time, to present a social commentary or testimonial, as did Fred Rogers when he defended funding for the first educational television station in the United States. His Pittsburgh program first had been seen in Canada as *Mister Rogers' Neighborhood*, but eventually it became a mainstay of US children's educational television for more than thirty years, right up to Rogers' death in 2003.[21]

Rogers' 1969 testimony addressed a US Senate Commerce Committee, which had withheld twenty million dollars in funding for educational public television, pending their findings in committee. Rogers' testimony occurred on the third day of hearings. It ran only seven minutes, but in that time, he converted a weary and testy Senator John Pastore, committee chair, to his cause. The following transcript of Rogers' address (see footnote for recorded version) shows how Rogers' deep knowledge of children, and his thoughtful considerations about the value and nature of educational programming, made a robust case for dedicated federal funding.

Children Need Quality Educational Programming[22]

Rogers begins by indicating his trust in Senator Pastore's promise to read his entire statement, establishing a climate of good will with his audience.

Senator Pastore, this is a philosophical statement and would take about ten minutes to read, so I'll not do that. One of the first things that a child learns in a healthy family is trust, and I trust what you have said, that you will read this. It's very important to me. I care deeply about children. . . .

He lays the groundwork for his own credibility, providing specific background and data to underscore the scope and import of educational television.

My first children's program was on WQED fifteen years ago, and its budget was $30. Now, with the help of the Sears-Roebuck Foundation and National Educational Television, as well as all of the affiliated stations, each station pays to show our program. It's a unique kind of funding in educational television.

With this help, now our program has a budget of $6,000. It may sound like quite a difference, but $6,000 pays for less than two minutes of cartoons. Two minutes of animated, what I sometimes say, "bombardment."

Rogers delineates the broad range of values that this children's programming offers:

1. *It deals with real issues of childhood development.*

2. *It provides constructive solutions that children can understand and apply—a claim supported with the evidence of previous, exemplary backing for educational television.*

I'm very much concerned, as I know you are, about what's being delivered to our children in this country. And I've worked in the field of child development for six years now, trying to understand the inner needs of children.

We deal with such things as the inner drama of childhood. We don't have to bop somebody over the head to make drama on the screen. We deal with such things as getting a haircut, or the feelings about brothers and sisters, and the kind of anger that arises in simple family situations. And we speak to it constructively. . .

3. *It expresses care for each child.*

4. *It promotes self-esteem.*

5. *It promotes mental health*

Rogers concludes with a concrete application of the constructive caring direction educational television can provide for child audiences.

I'd like very much for you to see it. We made a hundred programs for EEN, the Eastern Educational Network, and then when the money ran out, people in Boston and Pittsburgh and Chicago all came to the fore and said we've got to have more of this neighborhood expression of care. And this is what I give. I give an expression of care every day to each child, to help [them] realize that [they are] unique. I end the program by saying, "You've made this day a special day, by just your being you. There's no person in the whole world like you, and I like you just the way you are."

And I feel that if we in public television can only make it clear that feelings are mentionable and manageable, we will have done a great service for mental health. I think that it's much more dramatic that two men could be working out their feelings of anger, much more dramatic than showing something of gunfire. I'm constantly concerned about what our children are seeing, and for fifteen years I have tried in this country and Canada, to present what I feel is a meaningful expression of care. . .

Could I tell you the words of one of the songs, which I feel is very important? This has to do with that good feeling of control which I feel that children need to know is there. And it starts out, "What do you do with the mad that you feel?" And that first line came straight from a child. I work with children, doing puppets, in very personal communication with small groups.

"What do you do with the mad that you feel?
When you feel so mad you could bite.
When the whole wide world seems oh so wrong, and nothing you do seems very right.

What do you do? Do you punch a bag? Do you pound some clay or some dough?

Do you round up friends for a game of tag or see how fast you go?

It's great to be able to stop, when you've planned the thing that's wrong.
And be able to do something else instead—and think this song—

I can stop when I want to. Can stop when I wish.
Can stop, stop, stop anytime.
And what a good feeling to feel like this!
And know that the feeling is really mine.

At the end of Rogers' brief address, Senator Pastore has embraced these values, when he declares, "I think it's wonderful. I think it's wonderful. Looks like you just earned the 20 million dollars."

Know that there's something deep inside that helps us become what we can.
For a girl can be someday a lady, and a boy can be someday a man."

Transcription by Barbara L. Breaden of Testimony by Mr. Fred Rogers delivered before the United States Senate on PBS Funding on May 1, 1969.

Legal Persuasion

Courtroom (forensic) persuasion most often deals with propositions of fact. Was the death a homicide? Is the evidence admissible? Did the officer obtain a search warrant before entering the house? The format of a courtroom speech follows our basic pattern: an introduction that lays out the point to be proven, a body that "weaves together . . . logic . . . and the deepest passions of human nature,"[23] a summarizing yet moving conclusion.

Perhaps the most dramatic courtroom persuasion takes place in the final summation. Inducted into the Trial Lawyer Hall of Fame in 2011, Moe Levine, calls the summation the "keystone and crown of a case."[24] Yet certain basic principles are critical to courtroom persuasion, not the least of which is audience adaptation. Levine offers practical advice for legal persuaders: to speak to the jury on the highest level of which you are capable, and to impress jurors with the fact that they are there to express the conscience of the community.[25] Of this, says legal writer Jesse Brumbaugh, jurors are "constantly unconsciously aware."[26] Brumbaugh stresses adapting to the jury-audience by establishing common ground. The great error of courtroom speech is failing to adapt to the jury: by revisiting content (an insult to a jury that has listened to an entire case) and by denying them constant and consummate courtesy.

While sociopolitical commentary makes for effective satire, as in Comedy Central's *The Daily Show*, commentary also works by confronting issues directly, as it does in MSNBC's *Rachel Maddow Show*.

In 2015, *The Daily Show's* Jon Stewart[27] satirized then businessman Donald Trump, who had dismissed the war–hero status of Senator John McCain (son of World War II's Admiral McCain), who was shot down and critically injured on a bombing mission in the Vietnam War. A prisoner of war in Vietnam from 1967–73,[28] McCain refused to cooperate with the enemy to win his freedom. Released (disabled by his torture) at the end of the war, McCain went on to become a congressman and a senator, always a staunch defender of US veterans and opponent of torture in military conflicts.

Trump, who had received multiple deferments from military service, mused that even though he was lauded as a war hero, McCain should not be considered heroic, because he wound up captured. "I like people that weren't captured, OK?" Trump explained. Jon Stewart, rather than directly attacking the brazen comment, staged a comic, if macabre, mockery of Trump's position, declaring "I like people who don't get cancer. I like winners. Those are the people whose bodies don't suffer from an uncontrollable division of cells attacking their organs."[29]

Contrast Stewart's satirical approach with Rachel Maddow, who from 2008 vaulted to the top of news commentary. With impressive educational credentials (Stanford University and Oxford), she is precise and articulate, showing

© Juli Hansen/ Shutterstock, Inc.

intellectual confidence in taking on reputable sources, like PolitiFact, a Pulitzer Prize winning fact-checking offshoot of the *Tampa Bay Times*, and holding accountable political figures like Senator Rand Paul.

Maddow both questions and confronts ethical breaches in her commentaries, telling PolitiFact, "You are fired!" for bungling a fact check on President Obama's 2012 State of the Union message[30] and delineating point by point how Rand Paul plagiarized by reading whole sections of *Wikipedia* verbatim—as if his own—in parts of several speeches.[31]

So consider . . .

1. How do both Stewart and Maddow perform the function of commentary to interpret events or provoke thought? How would you state their value claims?

2. What are the advantages and disadvantages of both satire and direct confrontation in social commentary?

3. If you had the opportunity to express your views in a commentary, would you prefer to address the issue directly or satirically? How would the subject, context, and audience affect your choice?

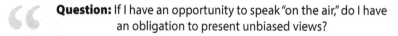

Since You Asked...

Question: If I have an opportunity to speak "on the air," do I have an obligation to present unbiased views?

Answer: This has been a hotly debated issue in the courts from the latter half of the twentieth century into the twenty-first. A 1949 Report on Editorializing by Broadcast Licensees held that broadcasters, or those who speak on their time over licensed airwaves, can argue a point of view if they provide air time to opposing viewpoints. In 1959, Congress amended the Communications Act to formalize the 1949 report. This action became known as the **fairness doctrine**.

From 1969, the courts weakened the fairness doctrine, culminating in a 1989 decision which found that the fairness doctrine often dissuaded broadcasters from presenting any treatment of controversial view-points."[32] In 1996, Congress tried to reinstate the fairness doctrine as part of the new Communications Act, but failed to do so.

In 2011, the Federal Communications Commission officially removed the fairness doctrine from its regulatory books, but in 2014 the FCC initiated a "Multi-Market Study of Critical Information Needs," known as CIN. The commission's objective was to gather research on how news agencies decide which stories they will report—that is, what is their "news philosophy"—and how do they ensure that the community gains access to critical information.[33] The FCC described the CIN project as a voluntary, fact-finding mission, but it raised hackles among news organizations that seek greater separation of government from media coverage.[34]

At this writing, if you are asked to present an on-the-air viewpoint, you have no problem. In fact programs such as PBS' *News Hour* draft spokespeople from diverse viewpoints to represent conflicting sides in a controversy. Depending on a station's profile and mission, broadcasters may feel free to editorialize on the air, but to manage liability, stations most often identify overt editorial viewpoints as individual rather than corporate expressions of opinion. Any discouragement to immoderate expressions of opinion must come from public pressure, opposition, and avoidance of views with which it does not agree—although there are many listeners who seek out disagreeable commentators in order to know the opposing position better.

While today you would have considerable leeway in broadcast commentary, remember that your credibility is perpetually at stake. Excessive confrontation and blatant or venomous bias can undermine rather than advance your cause.

Levine goes on to stress the importance of emotional appeal in courtroom summations, as in the case when he sought damages for a poverty-stricken man who lost his wife in a negligence case. Levine tried, he said, to feel (like Cicero—see Chapter Ten) what the plaintiff felt; this is possible, he said, only by tapping into one's own personal suffering. This fundamental *identification* helps counsel to understand the case and to argue credibly. In the case of the widower, Levine argued:

He did not lose very much, did he, but he did not have very much, and he lost everything he had. Where is he going to get another companion? That is finished. He must live the rest of his miserable life in loneliness. She wasn't much, but she was all he had.

Clarence Darrow[35] was another iconic forensic orator who knew the importance of emotional appeal, as when he concluded a summation saying,

> Gentlemen, it is not for [my client] alone that I speak. I speak for the poor, for the weak, for the weary, for that long line of men, who in darkness and despair have borne the labors of the human race.[36]

The Chicago Seven Conspiracy Trial of 1969-70 involved a group of political radicals accused of conspiring to incite a riot at the 1968 Democratic National Convention in Chicago. In a year of political upheaval over race and war, Martin Luther King had been assassinated, President Lyndon Johnson had withdrawn from the presidential contest over his support for the divisive Vietnam War, and Robert Kennedy, now presidential frontrunner, was shot and killed during a campaign appearance.

Outside the convention, in the parks and streets of Chicago, 10,000 demonstrators gathered in protest but were outnumbered by Chicago police, resulting in police violence and violent pushback from demonstrators. The arrests focused on demonstration organizers, who would appear before a grand jury charged with conspiracy to incite riot. The five-month hearing was bursting with drama and emotion. Defense attorney, William Kunstler's proposition of fact, then, would be "The Chicago Seven defendants intended to protest government policy;" they did not intend to incite riot. He concluded his summation by drawing attention toward the principles of free speech and the place for protest in a democracy.

The Chicago Seven: Silence Will Not Dispel Dissent[37]

We are living in extremely troubled times . . . . An intolerable war abroad has divided and dismayed us all. Racism at home and poverty at home are both causes of despair and discouragement. In the so-called affluent society, we have people starving, and people who can't even begin to approximate the decent life.

Kuntsler begins by identifying the events surrounding the Chicago riots—namely the Vietnam War, race relations, and poverty—as at the core of the hearing

These are rough problems, terrible problems, and as has been said by everybody in this country, they are so enormous that they stagger the imagination. But they don't go away by destroying their critics. They don't vanish by sending men to jail. They never did and they never will.

To use these problems by attempting to destroy those who protest against them is probably the most indecent thing that we can do. You can crucify a Jesus, you can poison a Socrates, you can hand over John Brown or Nathan Hale, you can kill a Che Guevara, you can jail a Eugene Debs or a Bobby Seale. You can assassinate John Kennedy or a Martin Luther King, but the problems remain.

The solutions are essentially made by continuing and perpetuating with every breath you have the right of men to think, the right of men to speak boldly and unafraid, the right to be masters of their souls, the right to live free and to die free. The hangman's rope never solved a single problem except that of one man.

I think if this case does nothing else, perhaps it will bring into focus that again we are in that moment of history when a courtroom becomes the proving ground of whether we do live free and whether we do die free. You are in that position now. Suddenly all importance has shifted to you—shifted to you as I guess in the last analysis it should go, and it is really your responsibility, I think, to see that men remain able to think, to speak boldly and unafraid, to be masters of their souls,

It is those events and conditions, not the protestors themselves, he argued, that are intolerable, even worthy of protest.

The actions of demonstrators, then, were not riotous behavior but legitimate protest.

The defendants acted as social critics, protected by the U.S. Constitution.

The allusion to the John Kennedy and Martin Luther King assassinations would touch a nerve for grand jury members and indeed for anyone living in the period between 1963 and 1970.

The appropriate decision by the court is to recognize the right of free expression, as exercised by those on trial.

The plaintiff proposal to incarcerate the defendants fails to recognize the essence of their intent and does not address the real issue.

The Grand Jury's decision must focus on the definition of the defendants' purpose: to protest government action gone awry.

Both poet Allen Ginsberg and songwriter/ singer Judy Collins had testified to the peaceful intent of the demonstrators. Judy Collins' quote is a line from Pete Seeger's 1955 song to lost innocence and beauty, "Where Have All the Flowers Gone?"[38] *This is a folk song in the classic sense, known deeply and widely in the culture of the time. Most often it was performed with the audience singing along; Kuntsler's reference would reliably cue the song in juror's minds.*

and to live and die free. And perhaps if you do what is right, perhaps Allen Ginsberg will never have to write again as he did in "Howl," "I saw the best minds of my generation destroyed by madness," perhaps Judy Collins will never have to stand in any Courtroom again and say as she did, "When will they ever learn? When will they ever learn?"

All defendants were acquitted on the count of conspiracy to incite riot. Two were sentenced to five years in prison for traveling across state lines with the intent to incite riot, but this decision was overturned on appeal in 1972.[39]

Excerpt from trial transcript, "The Chicago Seven: Silence Will Not Dispel Dissent"

In Summary

You can prepare and deliver a broad range of persuasive speeches using the fundamental principles presented in Chapters Two through Ten. Social and political advocacy are essentially speeches of policy, but then so are sales pitches and often informal debates. As speeches of policy, they call for a problem-solution proof.

Social commentary and courtroom speeches, on the other hand, deal with propositions of fact and value. Each genre has a distinct function. Social commentary interprets and evaluates events, often through humor and satire, while emotional appeal and identification are at the heart of courtroom persuasion.

Endnotes

[1] With permission from Dr. Tim Vogus, Vanderbilt University, Owen Graduate School of Management. You can view the speech at <http://www.youtube.com/watch?v=XUo-Gksrn3Y&feature=youtu.be&t=40m30s>.

[2] Keith M. Eades and Timothy T. Sullivan, *The Collaborative Sale: Solution Selling in a Buyer-Driven World* (Hoboken, NJ: John Wiley & Sons, 2014) 44.

[3] Ibid.

[4] Susan Adams, "How to Sell Almost Anything," *Forbes*, November 25, 2014, 21 August 2018 <https://www.forbes.com/sites/susanadams/2014/11/25/how-to-sell-almost-anything-5/#74075b886440>.

[5] Villarica, Hans. "Maslow 2.0: A New and Improved Recipe for Happiness." *The Atlantic*, 17 Aug. 2011, https://www.theatlantic.com/health/archive/2011/08/maslow-20-a-new-and-improved-recipe-for-happiness/243486/. Accessed 22 June 2018.

6 StartupNation, "Elevator Pitch: Define, Compose, Practice and Polish! (Rise and Repeat)," *StartupNation Media Group, Inc.*, 2010, 22 June 2014 <http://www .startupnation.com/articles/elevator-pitch-define-compose-practice-and-polish-rinse-and-repeat/>.

7 Ibid.

8 Fishkin, James S. "Yes, Ordinary Citizens Can Decide Complex Issues." *The Wall Street Journal*, 4–5 Aug. 2018, p. C3.

9 "Making Deliberation Practical." *Democracy When People Are Thinking: Revitalizing Our Politics Through Public Deliberation*. Oxford UP, 2018, http:// www.oxfordscholarship.com.libproxy.uoregon.edu/view/10.1093/ oso/9780198820291.001.0001/oso-9780198820291-chapter-3?print=pdf

10 Fishkin, *Wall Street Journal*.

11 Tannen, Deborah. *The Argument Culture: Moving from Debate to Dialogue*. Random House, 1998, pp. 8–16.

12 Ibid., 219.

13 Ibid., 218–36.

14 David Brooks, Analysis of Shields and Brooks, *PBS News Hour*, May 30, 2008, 22 June 2014 <http://www.pbs.org/newshour/bb/politics-jan-june08-mcclellan_05-30/>.

15 As an example, when in the summer of 2018 an Iowa student was killed in Brooklyn, NY, by an illegal immigrant, the victim's father, Rob Tibbetts, refused to join a chorus of critics against the US immigration system. "The Hispanic community are Iowans," he asserted, "They have the same values as Iowans. As far as I'm concerned, they're Iowans with better food." The Associated Press, "Tibbetts" father calls Hispanic locals "Iowans with better food," *The Register Guard*, 28 Aug. 2018, p. A4.

16 "Fact Sheet: The Dream Act, DACA, and Other Policies Designed to Protect Dreamers." *American Immigration Council*, 7 Sept. 2017, https://www. americanimmigrationcouncil.org/research/dream-act-daca-and-other-policies-designed-protect-dreamers. Accessed 24 June 2018.

17 It is possible to debate fact and value propositions as well, but because advocacy usually addresses policy decisions, we will examine the obligations of this form of debate.

18 Baym, Geoffrey. "The Daily Show: Discursive Integration and the Reinvention of Political Journalism." *Political Communication*, 21 Aug. 2006, https://doi.org/ 10.1080/10584600591006492. Accessed 18 July 2018.

19 Ibid., 4, 6.

20 "Transcripts." *CNN.com*, 15 Oct. 2004, http://transcripts.cnn.com/ TRANSCRIPTS/0410/15/cf.01.html. Accessed 18 July 2018.

21 "Mister Rogers' Neighborhood: A History." *Fred Rogers Productions*, 10 July 2018, https://www.fredrogers.org/fred-rogers/bio/index-test.php.

22 Rogers, Fred. "Mr. Rogers Goes to Washington, May 1, 1969." *Fred Rogers Productions*, 29 Apr. 2016, http://www.fredrogers.org/frc/news/mister-rogers-

goes-washington-may-1-1969. Accessed 2 Mar. 2018. Transcribed by Barbara Breaden from the video recording.

23 Jesse Franklin Brumbaugh, *Legal and Public Speaking* (Indianapolis: Bobbs-Merrill, 1932), 161 ff.

24 Moe Levine, *The Best of Moe: Summations* (Dobbs Ferry, NY: Glanville Information Services, 1983).

25 Ibid., 221.

26 Brumbaugh, 149.

27 Beginning in 2017, Trevor Noah replaced Stewart as host.

28 See "John McCain captivity in Vietnam, 1967-Original Footage." *YouTube*, 22 Sept. 2017, https://www.youtube.com/watch?v=PhXCc3X0KTw. Accessed 23 July 2018.

29 "Rant-Man." *The Daily Show with Jon Stewart*, 20 July 2015, http://www.cc.com/video-clips/ow94ov/the-daily-show-with-jon-stewart-rant-man. Accessed 22 July 2018. Stewart's satire produced a still sharper bite when in 2017, Senator John McCain was diagnosed with brain cancer. At the time McCain died in August, 2018, he and the President had remained unreconciled.

30 Dylan Byers, "Rachel Maddow: 'PolitiFact, you are fired!' *Politico*, January 25, 2012, 21 June 2014 <http://www.politico.com/blogs/media/2012/01/maddow-politifact-you-are-fired-112342.html>.

31 "Rachel Maddow Attacks Rand Paul for Response to *Wikipedia* Plagiarism Charges: Absolute Incoherence," *YouTube*, October 30, 2013, 24 July 2018 <https://www.youtube.com/watch?v=-5crxJFVTmQ >.

32 Richard Holsinger, *Media Law*, 4th ed. (New York: McGraw-Hill, 1996), 457.

33 Ajit Pai, "The FCC Wades Into the Newsroom," *The Wall Street Journal*, February 10, 2014, 22 June 2014 <http://online.wsj.com/news/articles/SB10001424052702 304680904579366903828260732?mg=reno64-wsj&url=http%3A%2F%2Fonline.wsj.com%2Farticle%2FSB10001424052702304680904579366903828260732.html>.

34 Ibid.

35 Darrow argued many high profile cases but is best known for opposing attorney William Jennings Bryan in the "Scopes Monkey Trial" which considered whether evolution could be taught in public schools. This trial was later loosely represented in a play (later a film), *Inherit the Wind*.

36 Ibid., 990–991.

37 William Kunstler, *Famous American Trials*, 19 June 2014 <http://law2.umkc.edu/faculty/projects/ftrials/Chicago7/Closing.html> For more on the trial, see Douglas O. Linder, "The Chicago Seven Conspiracy Trial," 24 August 2014 <http://law2.umkc.edu/faculty/projects/ftrials/Chicago7/Account.html>.

38 Seeger, Pete. "Where Have All the Flowers Gone." *Genius*, 29 Aug. 2018, https://genius.com/Pete-seeger-where-have-all-the-flowers-gone-lyrics. Listen via the audio link near the top of the web page.

39 "The Chicago Seven Conspiracy Trial," *Federal Judicial Center*, 22 June 2014 <http://www.fjc.gov/history/home.nsf/page/tu_chicago7_narrative.html>.

Theory into Practice

1. If you have the occasion to visit a car dealership or to purchase insurance, take the opportunity to observe sales skills or faults at work.
   a. Does the seller try to identify your "problem" and seek a solution?
   b. Can you tell what level of needs (according to Maslow), the seller perceives as most salient to you?
   c. Is the seller open to your concerns and willing to forsake a preconceived solution to satisfy your needs?

2. If you are involved in a local organization or workplace committee, see if you can identify an opportunity to engage competing sides in informal debate. Do you recognize any of the following debate elements?
   - proposition
   - definitions of terms
   - affirmative and negative speakers
   - proofs of inherency and solvency
   - counterplans

3. Listen to an online (or television or radio) commentary to attempt to
   a. Identify the proposition (usually a proposition of value).
   b. Map out the proof; does it follow a logical structure?
   c. Analyze its stylistic effectiveness. Whether directly confrontational or satirical, does the commentary promote thought and inquiry about the issue?

4. Try sitting in on a court trial.
   a. Determine what propositions are being addressed.
   b. Try to identify the order of the counselors' proofs.
   c. Note the use of emotional appeal in summations.
   d. How do the counselors treat the jury? the judge? What direct appeals are made to them?
   e. Do the counselors try to establish identification between their clients and the jury? If so, how?

Chapter
12 Assessing Speech Effectiveness

To Make a Long Story Short...

The challenge in determining a speech's impact is weighing the blend of subject, speaker, and audience at a point in time.

Key Concepts

- The Toulmin model is a useful tool for assessing a speaker's reasoning.
- Listeners should examine emotional appeals as rigorously as they would examine logic.
- In spite of cultural and individual differences, ethical standards do exist for persuasion in contemporary society.
- Speech criticism analyzes persuasive influence and provides a valuable historical record for significant public events.
- Fundamentally, speech criticism evaluates the speaker, the message, and the audience.
- Exemplary speech criticism evinces the unique blend of circumstances surrounding a speech.

Key Terms

premise	ethical naturalism
claim	ethical relativism
data	pentad
warrant	agent
ethics	agency

Listening to Persuasion

When you are present at a speech, unless you have heard the speaker before, you really don't know what to expect. It takes time to adjust to the speaker, the setting, and the message. Because persuasive speeches want something of us—a change in beliefs, attitudes, or actions—it's reasonable for us to resist the message at first, as a way to avoid being manipulated. Just as we stipulated in Chapter One that persuasion requires the audience's free will, so audiences are free to listen or not to listen, even in the case of a captive audience.[1] Some audience members may want to tune out any persuasive appeal, but at this point in this book, we assume that you will not tune out. You will submit yourself to the message with the purpose of agreeing or disagreeing, getting caught up in the speech or enduring its tedium. To walk the line between uncritical acceptance and irrational rejection, you'll need to get your bearings as a listener, beginning as the speaker did, by determining what the speech is about, its goal, and its proposition.

Why Is This Person Speaking?

If you suspect that a speaker wants to influence you, you probably want to know more precisely that speaker's goal, which might be

> *an argument*—an attempt to alter your beliefs or attitudes;
>
> *a motivational appeal*—a call for you to do something, to take action;
>
> *an emotional appeal*—an enticement to feel a certain way about something or someone.

Figure 12.1 Even when compelled to be present, the audience possesses freedom of thought and the freedom *not* to listen.
©spirit of america/Shutterstock, Inc.

It is helpful to be explicit in identifying a speaker's goal: "She is trying to get me to vote for Perez as governor," or "He wants me to donate money."

In the same way, to help you think clearly about the speech you can pinpoint its proposition and main ideas. And you can spot these by being alert to claims that the speaker emphasizes and returns to more than once. The speaker may offer clues, such as "The most important point I want to make is . . . ." When you hear such a cue, look to see whether this point has been proven by the speech. How do you determine this? By referring to the requirements for propositions of fact, value, and policy speeches.

- Does the proposition of fact speech give adequate reasons for accepting the fact?

- Does the proposition of value speech establish criteria for and justify the value term?

- Does the proposition of policy speech show a real need for change and a workable solution?

Recognize and Evaluate the Speaker's Reasons

Speeches are full of assertions worth evaluating. These points, or **premises**, include claims, propositions, generalizations, or "statements about issues, people, ideas, events, that the speaker advances and wants the listener to accept."[2] But what makes a premise acceptable? Chapter Two offered guidelines for assessing evidence, but Professor Stephen Toulmin gives us a simple and practical tool for evaluating reasoning.

As Toulmin demonstrates in his classic, *The Uses of Argument*,[3] a **claim**, or assertion, requires supporting **data**, the evidence for believing it. Theoretically, without data a listener will reject the claim.

Yet even *with* the data, the listener may not accept the claim. Why?

Let's take an example:

> *Claim:* The proposed rapid-transit bus system will not work.
> *Data:* Regular bus ridership along that route does not support an upgrade to rapid transit.

My data supports my claim, but will this satisfy the audience? Isn't it possible that regular bus ridership is low because the route is excruciatingly slow to travel? Might a rapid-transit route increase ridership? Recognizing that evidence can be brought to bear on either side of the claim, Toulmin adds elements to his model. Let's try our argument again:

> *Claim:* The proposed rapid-transit bus system will not work.
> *Data:* Regular bus ridership along that route does not support an upgrade to rapid transit.

Warrant: Nationwide ridership patterns demonstrate that poor ridership on a regular bus route will not transmute into strong ridership on a rapid-transit route.

Here's another example,

Claim: U.S. entanglement in Middle East conflicts risks a long-term financial commitment.

Data: The U.S. war in Iraq drained the economy for more than nine years.

Warrant: The region's multiple religious sects have a history of prolonged and unsettled conflicts, some lasting decades—and more.

Yes, the Toulmin Model (see Figure 12.2) says that a *claim* should be backed by *data*, but the data should *warrant* the conclusion or claim. The speaker's **warrant** is a statement asserting that the claim follows from the data given. If you believe there are no valid data and warrant, you have good reason for rejecting the speaker's appeals.

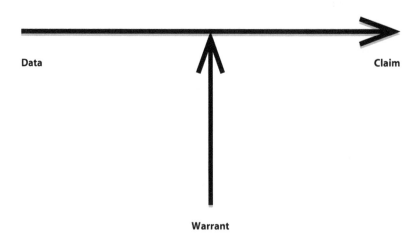

Data

Claim

Warrant

Figure 12.2 The Toulmin Model in its simplest components shows that we depend on supporting evidence (data) to reinforce or justify a claim. The warrant explains how the data lead to the claim.

To the elements of claim, data, and warrant, Toulmin would add a **qualifier** or **rebuttal** that limits the claim (the claim is true "unless a country has agreed to equal representation for all religious sects") and a **backing** to support the warrant (the warrant applies "Because this is the region's prevailing world view: that each sect threatens the well being of others"). Your task as listener (and the task of any speech critic) is to determine whether data, warrant, and other elements of argument are present and sufficient for accepting any claim.

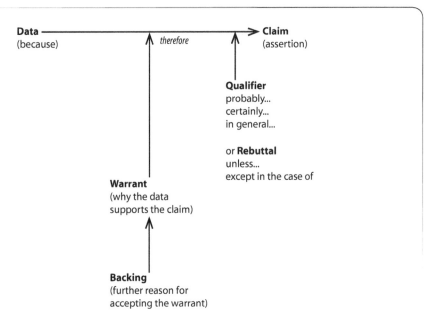

Figure 12.3 A more complete analysis of reasoning with the Toulmin model incorporates backing, qualifier, and rebuttal elements of argument.

Recognize and Analyze Emotional Appeals

Figuring out whether a speaker is reasonable is tricky enough, but listeners face a special problem when confronted by emotional appeals. As Ralph Nichols, the founder of listening as an academic discipline, points out, "Emotions cause deafness."[4] Persuaders can appeal to a host of emotions: fear, avarice, guilt, compassion, loyalty, or contempt. By attaching emotive labels to people, places, and events, the speaker can trigger potent responses. Think of labels that elicit your sharp reaction. Regarding people, you may think of words like *sleaze* or *predator*. Health-related terms, such as *e-coli*, *malignancy*, or *HIV-positive* have potency. In all political eras, the names of political figures, from George Washington to Barack Obama and Donald Trump, have called up emotional reactions. When leaders in the United States have demonized international figures, their citizens often have complied, accepting the demonization, as the names of Fidel Castro, Vladimir Putin, and Osama Bin Laden attest. The difficulty with emotive labels is the trigger factor: labels short-circuit rational evaluation. As an antidote to this tendency, Nichols suggests that we:[5]

1. *Be aware* of words that trigger emotions (such as insulting terms).

2. *Analyze* why labels have an impact on you.

3. *Discuss* with others the impacts of specific emotional triggers.

Finally, when you are exposed to influence, you can take time to reflect on the speaker's appeals and to weigh possible responses. The harder a speaker pushes for an immediate response, the more reticent you should become about responding.

Critical listening is an active process. Rather than being swept away by a speaker's charm, cleverness, or emotional intensity, a student of persuasion will examine the speaker's reasons, seeking data and warrants to support claims. The critical listener will be wary of emotional appeals, reflecting on whether evidence warrants our emotional investment. And the astute listener will recognize fallacies and know that psychological appeal does not validate a claim.

If as a society, we were habituated to critical listening, we could expect two outcomes. First, people would willingly embrace sound arguments for their good and the good of the society, and second, they would become less vulnerable to seductive but unsound claims.

ETHICS WATCH

Of two candidates for governor, Luzarski recently exposed his opponent (Murphy) in a campaign speech. Murphy, a publisher by trade, had published a string of classified ads for child pornography. Murphy happens to be a candidate who touts traditional values as a criterion of public policy; his ads contradict his political platform.

Luzarski's speech graphically describes the content of the pornography

advertised, although the pornographic content was never included in the ads.

Consider, then …

1. What emotional response does Luzarski want from the audience?

2. Does the information given here justify (or warrant) the emotional response Luzarski seeks?

Evaluating Ethics

In the national socio-political conversation we are often presented with evidence of ethical violations. From President Clinton's dalliance with a White House intern in the 1990s to the financial bilking of the American people by Wall Street in the early 2000s to perennial occasions of politicians selling political favors to the highest bidder, our outrage (or weariness) over scandal confirms that we have ethical standards. What is meant by the term *ethics*?

As a starting point, let's consider **ethics** as "a set of rules of conduct or 'moral code.'"[6] Even here we encounter difficulties. **Ethical naturalists** believe there are universal standards of ethical conduct. To an ethical naturalist, what is ethical to an sixty-year-old miner in rural Kentucky is ethical to a nineteen-year-old college student in Boston. **Ethical relativists** claim that ethical conduct depends on the culture in which it occurs and principles within that culture. What is ethical in Yemen could be construed as unethical in New Zealand, and vice-versa. In the United States of the twenty-first century, for example, the central test of ethics has become what conduct provides the greatest good to the majority.

To evaluate the ethics of persuasion, we might consider:

1. *Can ethical speech conduct be separated from circumstances?* Do personal principles negate a universal ethical code?

2. *Is the most ethical conduct for a speaker that which pleases or benefits the most people?* Must a speaker's goal always promote the common good?

To answer the first question, it is undeniable that personal ethical principles conflict and that the persuader in a democratic society, says rhetorical scholar Karl Wallace, is bound to respect diversity of argument and opinion.[7] Yet if we are bound to respect diverse opinion, we are considering diversity an absolute value, so some overarching ethical principles appear to exist, at least within a democratic culture. Intercultural communication scholar William Gudykunst asserts that we cannot avoid making ethical judgments, but that there are certain universal ethical standards, like prohibitions against murder, violence, and deceit.[8] But do governments that use violence to quell violence violate this ethical "universal?" You see how convoluted ethical judgements become.

As for the second question, persuaders in a democratic society are likely to argue that their proposals benefit the majority. However, this is not to say they *please* the majority. The majority may be uncomfortable in broadly allowing gun possession, but they may find the policy preferable to restricting the right of gun ownership. Taxes are another example; they are not pleasing, but they provide public benefits.

Another consideration is this: that a speaker's *proposals* benefit the majority does not mean that the speaker's *conduct* benefits the majority. If you run for Congress promising to cut taxes for the middle class, but you have no real intention of cutting taxes for the middle class, your proposal appears to be beneficial, but your conduct (essentially lying) is not. Your conduct defrauds the voters by denying them the complete and accurate information they need to make a rational decision.

Consequently, persuasive ethics should encompass the following rules of conduct:

1. *Persuasion depends on free choice.* Listeners are free to listen or not, and to accept or reject the speaker's position. As discussed in Chapter One, without choice, by definition, we have no persuasion.

2. *Reasoned choice depends on availability and accuracy of information.* Persuasive speakers are responsible for locating and citing timely and reliable information that is crucial to the audience's rational decision.

3. *Informational accuracy depends on a speaker's honesty and thoroughness.* Plagiarism is unethical because it represents as one's own what is not; we cannot trust information from a speaker who is dishonest (see Chapter Two on misinformation and disinformation and Chapter Four on credibility). Cheating is unethical as well, in the sense that one might cheat listeners by omitting information detrimental to one's cause. A speaker's thoroughness, however, must be limited by the bounds of law; illegally obtained information or information that violates another's rights under the law can be considered unethical disclosure.

What if you have illegally obtained information that you feel serves the public good? This was the question in the case of Edward Snowden,[9] a former CIA employee who in June, 2013, was charged with theft of government documents and with disclosing classified defense information. Yet Snowden's defenders argued that his revelations uncovered a massive government surveillance project that infringed the privacy of all United States citizens. Snowden himself claimed to be a whistleblower, and that the information he disclosed was in the public's legitimate interest. Here we are faced with a pivotal question: Can something benefit the public if it is acquired illegally? This is the stuff of scandals—the belief that the practical needs override the law, or that the end justifies the means.

Is it possible to trust a speaker who has endangered (potentially) one public interest, such as national defense, to expose an illegal government activity, such as violation of individual privacy? Here we are forced to determine which is the graver violation; the end might justify the means on a balance sheet of rights and wrongs, benefits and harms.

4. *Persuaders should defend what they honestly believe to benefit the majority.* This may mean that the persuader should propose what is displeasing if it is eventually beneficial. By displeasing, we mean entailing hardship or discomfort. You may advocate hardship if you believe that the hardship is beneficial in itself or that it will lead to eventual benefits that offset the hardship. This concern for the common good is fundamental to a dialectical approach to persuasion.

Listeners should try to discern whether the persuasive speaker and message reflect ethical standards. To evaluate persuasive ethics, listeners should weigh the persuasive message against these four points. In a democratic society we are protected against unethical speech conduct by virtue of the fact that it is readily uncovered and evaluated by the people and the press. As disheartening and painful as the cycle may be, the great hope is that unethical conduct is visible in the end. This should serve as a caution for those who contemplate shady means; their acts are liable to be exposed to light.

Framing and Phrasing a Useful Critique

It may never occur to us to critique a speech except to say, "Good speech," or "I thought I'd die of boredom." When a persuasive speech impacts a substantial number of people, it makes sense to analyze what happened. Ernest Wrage articulates one of the most powerful values of rhetorical criticism when he claims speech criticism shapes social and intellectual history, since "the ideas, values, and beliefs of a culture are expressed in speeches."[10] Rhetorical critic Marie Hochmuth Nichols writes that the function of the speech critic is to serve society and self by revealing and evaluating the speaker's "interpretation of the world around him."[11] To contemporary rhetorical scholar Sonja Foss, rhetorical criticism improves our communication skill by providing "principles or guidelines for those of us who want to communicate in more self-reflective ways and to construct messages that best accomplish our goals," and "can help make us more sophisticated audience members."[12] When you critique a persuasive speech, you clarify for yourself and others a speech's significance, value, and effectiveness.

How to Critique

As Foss points out, there are innumerable ways to critique a speech. You may ask a question, such as "How did the speaker contend with a hostile audience?" or "Did the speech live up to its hype?" or "Did the audience connect to the speaker's proposal?" Your critique can be limited or broad in scope. It can examine a speaker's use of metaphor or consider where the speech ranks in recent political history. The critic might offer a Marxist or feminist rhetorical analysis. In such cases the critic is examining the speech through a particular lens. Just as when you look at a drop of blood through a microscope its individual cells can be seen in detail, so using a distinct "lens" reveals a perspective not otherwise discovered.

Answer: A critic sensitive to the essence of a speech should try to discover its most significant element. This is perhaps the truest approach to speech study: let the speech guide you. The occasion or context of the speech is the touchstone for gauging its success. The persuasive persona (the speaker's presence) may be a compelling factor, or the message itself. Let creativity begin with the speech itself; let the analysis embedded in the speaker's message speak to the critic.

Traditional criticism judges the speech's perceived effectiveness, through classical rhetorical theory. The critic considers each of the canons of rhetoric and how invention, organization, and verbal style, for instance, contribute to the speech's impact. The critic will ask how ethos, pathos, and logos functioned as forms of proof to answer how well the speaker used the available means of proof.

Kenneth Burke's criticism is based on five elements Burke calls the **pentad**.[13] The pentad focuses on people— 1) what motivates them to speak as they do and 2) why they are motivated by speeches. The pentad is composed of the

act—the speech itself;

agent—the messenger;

agency—what conveys the message;

scene—where and when it occurs;

purpose—why it is delivered.

A Burkeian critic sees the speech as a player in the great human drama of life and views it holistically through the pentad to probe diverse aspects of and influences on its effect.

Of other forms of criticism, **metaphoric criticism** examines underlying perceptions as they are generated and reflected by a speaker's metaphors. **Feminist criticism** questions an established order of human domination, inequality, and stereotyping expressed in a speech. **Narrative criticism** analyzes how speakers present controversies as stories, when they frame issues and conflicts from particular personal and experiential perspectives.[14] As a critic, when you experience a speech either "live," recorded, or transcribed, you are an audience the speech has touched. Bringing a curious and critical eye to the rhetorical experience engages us in the social act of caring about, understanding, and contributing to a society's well being.

You begin the speech critique as you might begin a film review. Your firs step, of course, is to see the film, jot down some notes on its content and it striking features, and finally make a judgment about whether it was any good. With a speech, your best approach may be to record the message. This will allow you to recall what was said, since you will have an accurate record. And since it can be difficult to get a coherent view of the speech as you listen, you will need a way to look back. For the introduction, you may have noted an attention-getter and a proposition. For the body, you may have main points and supporting examples and evidence. At the conclusion, you might note whether the speaker revisits main points and suggests a course of action. As you review your notes you are more likely to uncover the speech's hidden structure.

Your notes might look like those in Figure 12.4, or you could use a critique form, such as those provided at the end of this chapter. See how the sample

Report—facilities head, Jarrett	I. *Gym walk-through: leak, warped floorboards, broken hoops/backboards (kid injured, etc.)*
Who is doing the exploring? Explore for real? Open to options?	A. *Shared responsibility, affects all kids*
	B. *Wants to "explore"*
Check on 3rd point	1. *Pressing "issues" & cost*
	2. *How to approach*
	3. *?? (missed: proposal by March 30?)*
No extra $$? Why hiring new admins? Copy of budget?	II. *Why we're here*
	A. *Probs.*
Cuts possible?	1. *Tax shortfall, no extras—$10M under budget*
Lawsuits?	2. *Safety issues, leaks*
Projected cost/ income?	3. *Cost of repairs*
	B. *Looking @ solutions (timeline?)*
Needed?	1. *Auction (volunteer coord.)*
(Afford repair from these projects??)	2. *Game parking*
(Check on this stat!)	3. *(something about jog-a-thon or wrapping paper?)—ask coordinator*
Seriously?	C. *Can we do it?*
	1. *Ex. Of Cath Schools--$450,000!*
	2. *Need 20 hrs/parent or $1000/family (!) Jog-a-thon?*

Need breakdown: how much from each event!

Get details from E&C

Nice quote from kid: favorite place to be...

III. Next steps

   A. Reminds of events—open to more ideas

   B. Organized by classes—volunteers, fundraising coordinating

   C. See EvaP and CharlotteS, front hall, 8-12, M/Tu/W

   D. Kid in cafeteria story—why we're in this together

Figure 12.4 These sample notes try to capture a presentation at a school board meeting on fundraising for a new gymnasium. This approach to note-taking shows the speech structure on the right, "editorial" notes on the left. The critique will be a blend of reporting speech content and assessing message effectiveness.

notes attempt to follow the outline form we have used in this book and how the writer has jotted down a few editorial remarks while sticking primarily to actual speech content. Speakers do not always follow a strict organization. If you do follow one, however, you will be able to understand why the speaker who deviates from a standard organization is so hard to follow, a point you might mention in your critique, to illustrate for the reader what makes a speech effective.

After hearing the speech and taking notes, think about what you have heard. Ask yourself *what was the ultimate goal of the speech*—anger, sympathy, or action, for instance. Obviously the proposition, if you can detect it, reveals a goal. Then focus on *what the speaker did or did not do to achieve the goal*. Finally, as you prepare to transform your notes into a critique, think about *how the speaker adapts the message to the audience*, and draws them in—or not.

A "standard" speech critique can look at the speaker, the message, and the audience, the historical context, the physical context, the language, delivery, style, or any of a multitude of factors. But a good starting point is to examine the *speaker*, the *message*, and the *audience*.

The questions in Figure 12.5 encompass most of *Speaking to Persuade*. How profound the reader's reaction to your critique depends on the importance of the speech, of course, but also on your goal in writing it and the incisiveness of your analysis. Your most important critical consideration should be to reflect as accurately as you can your impression of the speech's intent, content, and effect.

THE CRITIQUE: WHAT TO ASK

About the speaker	About the message	About the audience
• Does the speaker have a reputation or established *credibility*? • Is the speaker *prepared* to speak, with command of the subject and organization of ideas? • Is the *delivery* fluent and expressive? • Does the speaker adhere to *ethical* standards? • Does an exceptionally positive or negative quality in the speaker stand out?	• What is the *proposition*? How is it made evident? • What points support the proposition? Are these logically or dramatically *organized*? • What *evidence* (data) supports the claims? Is it sound evidence? Does the speaker explain the connection between the evidence and proposition? • Do the speaker's *language* and images support the speech goal?	• Is the speaker tuned in to audience *composition*? Does the audience extend beyond the group present? • Are they homogenous or diverse in *viewpoint*? Do they make their positions clear? • Does the *speaker adapt* to the audience in the intro and conclusion? in use of examples, visuals, emotions, and counterarguments? • Does the speaker adapt to the occasion, setting, and audience response?

Figure 12.5 The observable nature of speaker, message and audience help guide the speech critic to an analysis that suits both content and context.

What Makes a Good Speech?

Clearly, a speech is an oral event, not written words on a page. The following speech by former President Barack Obama took place in the White House briefing room on the heels of the controversial outcome over the 2013 Trayvon Martin case in Florida. In February, 2012, George Zimmerman, a 38-year-old Hispanic neighborhood watch captain shot and killed a 17-year-old African-American high school student, Trayvon Martin.[15] Zimmerman maintained that he was acting in self-defense, while Martin's family and defenders asserted that Zimmerman was not threatened by Martin; his actions were based on racial profiling and dubiously justified by the state's dangerous "Stand your ground" law.[16] More than a year of escalating charges and counter-charges built toward the trial, where on July 13, 2013, Zimmerman was acquitted.

The dramatic backdrop to this speech and its historical moment remind us that what you *read* on this page is not what was *heard* on July 19, 2013. Your perspective becomes more or less detached depending on your ego- and issue-involvement (see Chapter Five) and your distance in time and space from the stream of events leading up to the speech. In reviewing and assessing the speech, you probably come to see its issues as one sees through a different lens from that of the original audience.

President Obama, the first African-American President of the United States—who as chief executive of an entire nation is expected to represent all the people—had not been blind or deaf to the racial overtones of the Martin-Zimmerman case and the sense of injustice felt by African-Americans in particular. Six days after the trial's conclusion, emotions still running at a fever pitch across the country, President Obama addressed his quiet and measured remarks to the White House press corps. This context provides him the opportunity to transmit his reflections to the public at large (it would be dependably broadcast on the evening news), and to sidestep an emotionally charged group in a public arena.

The speech reads well. Of course, it is not easy to critique an unrecorded speech, where you have one shot at its content before it is gone. When you critique written speeches, you may visualize but not know the speaker's delivery, you cannot hear the speaker's voice, and the throb of energy in the air is impalpable. Thus, you should check the delivery of this speech by following the footnoted link. This is not the fiery, dynamic, stump-speaking Barack Obama. You will notice that the President's eye contact does not scan a teleprompter; he is glancing sidewise and downward at first, convincing us that his speech is largely extemporaneous at least, impromptu in part. He is searching for phrases, pausing thoughtfully, at times awkwardly, as he attempts to express himself with accuracy and honesty. His audience of professional journalists would not be demonstrative. They remain reserved and silent throughout the 17-minute statement, reinforcing the impression of this speech as an intimate conversation between concerned people.

Listen to and analyze President Obama's speech by answering as many of the critique questions (Figure 12.5) as you can, but also considering the questions posed in the adjacent column. You may want to read the speech to familiarize yourself with the relevant issues, but try to base your critique on the authentic oral presentation.

Figure 12.6 The White House Press Briefing Room does not ordinarily host a large or rowdy audience. One might say the number of people present is insignificant. But this setting allows the President to temper the emotional tenor of his remarks while still reaching the public at large.

From http://www.whitehouse.gov by Lawrence Jackson, White House Photographer.

Remarks by the President on Trayvon Martin[17]

The reason I actually wanted to come out today . . . was to speak to an issue that obviously has gotten a lot of attention over the course of the last week—the issue of the Trayvon Martin ruling . . . .

Usually the press is assembled to grill the President or Press Secretary on White House action and inaction, positions and silence. Try to get a sense of the President's tone as he begins. As you listen to the speech, what do you notice about his delivery?

First of all, I want to make sure that, once again, I send my thoughts and prayers, as well as Michelle's, to the family of Trayvon Martin, and to remark on the incredible grace and dignity with which they've dealt with the entire situation. I can only imagine what they're going through, and it's remarkable how they've handled it.

The President and First Lady clearly identify with the African-American community. Consider whether this makes the President's address one-sided.

The second thing I want to say is . . . there's going to be a lot of arguments about the legal issues in the case—I'll let all the legal analysts and talking heads address those issues . . . . But I did want to just talk a little bit about context and how people have responded to it and how people are feeling.

You know, when Trayvon Martin was first shot I said that this could have been my son. Another way of saying that is Trayvon Martin could have been me 35 years ago. And when you think about why, in the African-American community at least, there's a lot of pain around what happened here, I think it's important to recognize that the African-American community is looking at this issue through a set of experiences and a history that doesn't go away.

There are very few African-American men in this country who haven't had the experience of being followed when they were shopping in a department store. That includes me. There are very few African-American men who haven't had the experience of walking across the street and hearing the locks click on the doors of cars. That happens to me—at least before I was a senator. There are very few African-Americans who haven't had the experience of getting on an elevator and a woman clutching her purse nervously and holding her breath until she had a chance to get off. That happens often.

And I don't want to exaggerate this, but those sets of experiences inform how the African-American community interprets what happened one night in Florida. And it's inescapable for people to bring those experiences to bear. The African-American community is also knowledgeable that there is a history of racial disparities in the application of our criminal laws—everything from the death penalty to enforcement of our drug laws. And that ends up having an impact in terms of how people interpret the case.

Notice what boundaries the President is drawing around his content. What will he not address? What, then, is his purpose in presenting these "remarks?"

In what disparate ways might the President's personal connection with Trayvon Martin influence the audience? Can you detect a proposition so far in this speech? If not, where does a proposition seem to emerge?

What goal does this list of examples serve?

What knowledge or awareness is the President assuming in his audience? Would his immediate audience know about the impact of certain laws, the death penalty, and drug law enforcement on African-Americans? Would the broader U.S. audience share that awareness that these constitute problems needing resolution?

Now, this isn't to say that the African-American community is naive about the fact that African-American young men are disproportionately involved in the criminal justice system; that they're disproportionately both victims and perpetrators of violence. It's not to make excuses for that fact . . . . They understand that some of the violence that takes place in poor black neighborhoods around the country is born out of a very violent past in this country, and that the poverty and dysfunction that we see in those communities can be traced to a very difficult history.

And so the fact that's sometimes unacknowledged adds to the frustration. And the fact that a lot of African-American boys are painted with a broad brush and the excuse is given, well, there are these statistics out there that show that African-American boys are more violent—using that as an excuse to then see sons treated differently causes pain.

I think the African-American community is also not naive in understanding that somebody like Trayvon Martin was statistically more likely to be shot by a *peer* than he was by somebody else. So folks understand the challenges that exist for African-American boys . . . . And that all contributes I think to a sense that if a white male teen was involved in the same kind of scenario, that, from top to bottom, both the outcome and the aftermath might have been different.

Now, the question for me at least, and I think for a lot of folks, is where do we take this? How do we learn some lessons from this and move in a positive direction? I think it's understandable that there have been demonstrations and vigils and protests, and some of that stuff is just going to have to work its way through, as long as it remains nonviolent . . . . But beyond protests or vigils, the question is, are there some concrete things that we might be able to do?

See if you can pick out several counterarguments in the following segments of the speech.
How does the President defuse those counterarguments?

Is there a persuasive purpose in President Obama's reference to statistical realities? Does this admission increase or decrease the racial divide over the case?

While the first half of the speech has set out to raise consciousness of African-American problems and perspectives, the President shifts here to solutions. Notice what arenas of society he seeks to engage in solutions.

Number one, precisely because law enforcement is often determined at the state and local level, I think it would be productive for the Justice Department, governors, mayors to work with law enforcement about training at the state and local levels in order to reduce the kind of mistrust in the system that sometimes currently exists.

When I was in Illinois, I passed racial profiling legislation, and it actually did just two simple things. One, it collected data on traffic stops and the race of the person who was stopped. But the other thing was it resourced us training police departments across the state on how to think about potential racial bias and ways to further professionalize what they were doing.

And initially, the police departments across the state were resistant, but actually they came to recognize that if it was done in a fair, straightforward way that it would allow them to do their jobs better and communities would have more confidence in them and, in turn, be more helpful in applying the law . . . .

President Obama served as an Illinois State Senator before he was elected to the Presidency in 2008. How does his account of his work there help to make his case? Is there an ethical issue in his statement, "I passed racial profiling legislation?" Here the President addresses solvency issues; do you think he effectively undercuts opposition to his proposed solutions?

Along the same lines, I think it would be useful for us to examine some state and local laws to see . . . if they are designed in such a way that they may *encourage* the kinds of altercations and confrontations and tragedies that we saw in the Florida case, rather than diffuse potential altercations.

I know that there's been commentary about the fact that the "stand your ground" laws in Florida were not used as a defense in the case . . . . And for those who resist that idea that we should think about something like these "stand your ground" laws, I'd just ask people to consider, if Trayvon Martin was of age and armed, could he have stood his ground on that sidewalk? And do we actually think that he would have been justified in shooting Mr. Zimmerman who had followed him in a car because he felt threatened? And if the answer to that question is at least ambiguous, then it seems to me that we might want to examine those kinds of laws.

Would the President's turning the tables strategy be persuasive to his broad national audience?

Number three—and this is a long-term project—we need to spend some time in thinking about how do we bolster and reinforce our African-American boys. And this is something that Michelle and I talk a lot about. There are a lot of kids out there who need help who are getting a lot of negative reinforcement. And is there more that we can do to give them the sense that their country cares about them and values them and is willing to invest in them?

Here, again, the audience is drawn into a kitchen-table conversation between the President and First Lady. Assess the value of this strategy.

I'm not naive about the prospects of some grand, new federal program. I'm not sure that that's what we're talking about here. But I do recognize that as President, I've got some convening power, and there are a lot of good programs that are being done across the country on this front. And for us to be able to gather together business leaders and local elected officials and clergy and celebrities and athletes, and figure out how are we doing a better job helping young African-American men feel that they're a full part of this society and that they've got pathways and avenues to succeed . . . .

Notice how many times in this speech, the President has repeated that he and others are "not naive," as a way of acknowledging that other points of view exist and are relevant. Does this technique establish understanding of diverse segments in U.S. society?

And then, finally, I think it's going to be important for all of us to do some soul-searching. There has been talk about should we convene a conversation on race. I haven't seen that be particularly productive when politicians try to organize conversations. They end up being stilted and politicized, and folks are locked into the positions they already have. On the other hand, in families and churches and workplaces, there's the possibility that people are a little bit more honest, and at least you ask yourself your own questions about, am I wringing as much bias out of myself as I can? Am I judging people as much as I can, based on not the color of their skin, but the content of their character . . .?

He arrives finally at a personal appeal to action, not just for the press corps gathered here, but for those at their computer screens and in living rooms across the country. Does the President's easy allusion to Dr. Martin Luther King's "I Have a Dream" speech intensify the importance of his remarks? ("I have a dream that one day my four little children will live in a nation where they will not be judged by the color of their skin but by the content of their character.")[18]

And let me just leave you with a final thought that, as difficult and challenging as this whole episode has been for a lot of people, I don't want us to lose sight that things are getting better. Each successive generation seems to be making progress in changing attitudes when it comes to race. It doesn't mean we're in a post-racial society. It doesn't mean that racism is eliminated. But when I talk to Malia and Sasha, and I listen to their friends and I see them interact, they're better than we are—they're better than we were—on these issues. And that's true in every community that I've visited all across the country.

And so we have to be vigilant and we have to work on these issues. And those of us in authority should be doing everything we can to encourage the better angels of our nature, as opposed to using these episodes to heighten divisions. But we should also have confidence that kids these days, I think, have more sense than we did back then, and certainly more than our parents did or our grandparents did; and that along this long, difficult journey, we're becoming a more perfect union—not a perfect union, but a more perfect union.

In 2008, Obama campaigned under the banner of "Hope." Does his "Things are getting better" argument ring true in the case, as he describes it? The President once more references his family conversations, again setting the tone of a "fireside chat," as Franklin Delano Roosevelt conducted when President in the 1930s and 40s.

What ultimate terms do you think the President is inferring as national aspirations? This "more perfect union" reference to the Preamble of the United States Constitution heightens again the speech's importance and takes it beyond the press briefing room, placing its issues as central to our nation's founding. ("We the people of the United States . . . in order to form a more perfect Union . . .")[19]

A speech critic's final consideration is, naturally, was the speech effective? Did Barack Obama achieve his ends with his reflections on the Trayvon Martin case in 2013 America? In the short term, polls conducted between July 17 and 22, 2013, revealed a gaping divide between black and white Americans over the outcome of the trial,[20] but those polls began *before* the speech took place. They would not be a sound indicator of public reaction *following* the President's message.

On the other hand, it is noteworthy that protests to the verdict in the Trayvon Martin ruling were largely peaceful in the weeks to follow. Did the thoughtful and sympathetic tone of the President's speech assuage anger among African-Americans; did they feel they had been heard and their voices validated by his remarks? Did he anger Zimmerman supporters apparently mostly white, with his rhetorical position? Could he have expressed his thoughts and his proposals more diplomatically or connected more surely with all those who heard him?

The Trayvon Martin case will doubtless be cited, interpreted, and evaluated for years to come. Since this case, more high-profile interracial shootings have occurred in the United States. Yet it was the Trayvon Martin case that sparked a #BlackLivesMatter movement that continues to organize and act in US society, balanced by counteracting WhiteLivesMatter and AllLivesMatter hashtags.[21] For this reason, Obama's remarks about Trayvon Martin easily apply to the status of race relations in the United States well into the twenty-first century, and well beyond the culmination of Obama's presidency—a sign of his speech's ongoing relevance and potential longevity.

A speech, that real live event, is a moment in time, a moment in history, when people share a message, agreeably or disagreeably. The words above tell us what people talked about on July 19, 2013. The speech reveals a story of real people with real concerns that may look surprisingly familiar to later generations and eras. Literature possesses this effect of perpetual timeliness, and so do music and art. But speeches convey our social and political reality with the words and fury of a speck in time. They show us audiences long since dispersed along with expressions and events we have ceased to think about or that we continue to ponder. They show us that speaking to persuade is true and relevant action at the very core of democratic society.

In Summary

Persuasion makes no difference when no one listens; but listening to persuasive speeches is vital when we perceive the significance of a moment in time or that a speaker's words impact our lives. Evaluative listening includes recognizing the speaker's goal, proposition, and reasons as well as reflecting on the message's long-term impact.

Speech effectiveness cannot be isolated from the speaker's ethics. Our society is probably no more unethical than any other, for our public sense of ethics does affect how we respond to speakers and their ideas. The most fundamental ethical standards in our society include free choice, honesty, accuracy, and the common good.

A speech evaluation in the form of a written critique is an important journalistic tool, but it is also critical to political movements and historiography. The critique is a means of understanding public influence and interpreting it for a wider audience. Various critical methods provide a lens for viewing the speech act, a significant historical event that participates in shaping the heart and mind of a society.

Endnotes

[1] It has been argued, however, that an audience *is* unduly influenced by the message when they have been forced to attend a speech in the employer-labor union context. We would submit in this case that the principles of coercion are at work here; audience members are free to *think* as they see fit, even when forced to behave as the employer prescribes. See Roger C. Hartley, "Freedom Not to Listen: A Constitutional Analysis of Compulsory Indoctrination Through Workplace Captive Audience Meetings," *Berkeley Journal of Employment and Labor Law* (2010): 31), 62-125.

[2] Andrew Wolvin and Carolyn Coakley, *Listening*, 5th ed. (New York: McGraw-Hill, 1995), 340.

[3] Stephen Toulmin, *The Uses of Argument* (Cambridge, 2003), 94 ff.

[4] Ralph Nichols and Leonard A. Stevens. *Are You Listening? The Science of Improving Your Listening Ability for a Better Understanding of People* (New York: McGraw-Hill, 1957), 90.

[5] Ibid., 101.

[6] Raziel Abelson and Kai Nielsen, *The Encyclopedia of Philosophy*, ed. Paul Edwards (New York: Macmillan, 1972), 81.

[7] Karl Wallace, "An Ethical Basis of Communication," *The Speech Teacher* 4.1 (1955): 9.

[8] William Gudykunst, *Bridging Differences: Effective Intergroup Communication*, 4th ed. (Thousand Oaks, CA: Sage, 2003), 308. Gudykunst's contention becomes complicated when we consider cultural defenses of violent actions as self-protection, and murder, as in suicide bombing, a way to a transcendent good. Likewise, is it unethical to deceive an enemy to protect innocent people?

[9] Michael Ray, "Edward Snowden: American Intelligence Contractor," *Encyclopædia Britannica*, June 17, 2018, 28 July 2018 <https://www.britannica.com/biography/Edward-Snowden>.

[10] Carl R. Burgchardt, ed. *Readings in Rhetorical Criticism*, 3rd ed. (State College, PA: Strata Publishing, 2005), 1.

[11] Marie Hochmuth Nichols, *Rhetoric and Criticism* (Baton Rouge, LA: Louisiana State Univ. Press, 1967), 78.

[12] Sonja Foss, *Rhetorical Criticism: Exploration and Practice*, 5e. (Long Grove, IL: Waveland Press, 2018), 8.

[13] Kenneth Burke, *A Grammar of Motives* (Berkeley, CA: Univ. of California Press, 1969), xv ff.

[14] See Foss for thorough discussions of these and other critical approaches.

[15] For more background on this case, see "Trayvon Martin Shooting Fast Facts," CNN U.S., February 22, 2014, 18 July 2014 <http://www.cnn.com/2013/06/05/us/trayvon-martin-shooting-fast-facts/>.

16 Statute 776.013, *Home protection; use of deadly force; presumption of fear of death or great bodily harm*. The 2013 Florida Statutes, Online Sunshine: Official Internet Site of the Florida Legislature The law states: "A person who is not engaged in an unlawful activity and who is attacked in any other place where he or she has a right to be has no duty to retreat and has *the right to stand his or her ground and meet force with force, including deadly force if he or she reasonably believes it is necessary to do so* to prevent death or great bodily harm to himself or herself or another or to prevent the commission of a forcible felony." 18 July 2014 <http://www.leg.state.fl.us/statutes/index.cfm?App_mode=Display_Statute&URL=0700-0799/0776/Sections/0776.013.html>.

17 James S. Brady, "Remarks by the President on Trayvon Martin," Office of the Press Secretary, The White House: President Barack Obama, July 19, 2013, 18 July 2014 <http://www.whitehouse.gov/the-press-office/2013/07/19/remarks-president-trayvon-martin>. This is the written version of the speech. For the video see "President Speaks on Trayvon Martin," *YouTube*, July 19, 2013, 29 August 2018 <https://www.youtube.com/watch?v=MHBdZWbncXI>.

18 Martin Luther King, "I Have a Dream . . ." National Archives and Records Administration, August 28, 1963, 18 July 2014 <http://www.archives.gov/press/exhibits/dream-speech.pdf>.

19 *Constitution of the United States*, Charters of Freedom, The U.S. National Archives and Records Administration, 18 July 2014, <http://www.archives.gov/exhibits/charters/constitution_transcript.html>.

20 Alana Levinson, "Polls Show Wide Racial Gap on Trayvon Martin Case," NPR, 2014, 19 July 2014 <http://www.npr.org/blogs/itsallpolitics/2013/07/22/204595068/polls-show-wide-racial-gap-on-trayvon-martin-case>.

21 Trymaine Lee. "Analysis: Trayvon Martin's Death Still Fuels a Movement Five Years Later." *NBC News*, 26 Feb. 2017, https://www.nbcnews.com/news/nbcblk/analysis-trayvon-martin-s-death-still-fuels-movement-five-years-n725646. Accessed 28 July 2018.

Theory into Practice

1. You can check a local news source to locate a scheduled speaking event. Take along a notepad or tablet for documenting your thoughts on the following evaluative listening steps:
   a. Does the speaker *intend* to influence you—rationally, motivationally, or emotionally.
   b. See if you can pinpoint the speaker's proposition and main points.
   c. try to keep track of evidence (or its absence) for the speaker's claims.

2. With a selected opinion piece (printed, if it's online),
   a. Underline each of the writer's claims.
   b. Circle the data supporting each claim.
   c. Write *w* over the warrants that link the data to each claim.

3. Try to *outline* a speech as you listen to it, as in the sample critiquing notes given in this chapter. If you find you cannot outline it, consider if this is because the speech is not well organized and the speaker difficult to follow.

4. Write a brief (two to three-page or 500 to 750 word) traditional critique of the Obama speech.

5. Choose another method of criticism and rewrite the critique.

Critique for a Generic Persuasive Speech

Speaker: _____

Subject: _____

Date: _____ Place: _____

1 = undeveloped, 2 = developing, 3 = adequate, 4 = competent, 5 = proficient

Speaker:

Prepared? Extemporaneous delivery?	1	2	3	4	5
Establishes credibility?	1	2	3	4	5
Control of space/time?	1	2	3	4	5

Message:

Proposition clear?	1	2	3	4	5
Organizational clarity?	1	2	3	4	5
Support?	1	2	3	4	5

Audience Awareness:

Introduction/conclusion?	1	2	3	4	5
Signposts?	1	2	3	4	5
Counterarguments/refutation?	1	2	3	4	5
Physical delivery?	1	2	3	4	5

Comments:

Critique for a Fact or Value Persuasive Speech

Speaker: _____

Subject: _____

Date: _____ Place: _____

1 = undeveloped, 2 = developing, 3 = adequate, 4 = competent, 5 = proficient

Speaker:

Prepared? Extemporaneous delivery?	1	2	3	4	5
Establishes credibility?	1	2	3	4	5

Message:

Proposition clear?	1	2	3	4	5
Appropriate proof?	1	2	3	4	5
Support from authorities?	1	2	3	4	5
Visual aids?	1	2	3	4	5

Audience Awareness:

Introduction/conclusion?	1	2	3	4	5
Signposts?	1	2	3	4	5
Counterarguments/refutation?	1	2	3	4	5
Nonverbal elements?	1	2	3	4	5

Comments:

Critique for a Policy Persuasive Speech

Speaker: _____

Subject: _____

Date: _____ Place: _____

1 = undeveloped, 2 = developing, 3 = adequate, 4 = competent, 5 = proficient

Speaker:

Prepared? Extemporaneous delivery?	1	2	3	4	5
Establishes credibility?	1	2	3	4	5

Message:

Proposition clear?	1	2	3	4	5
Motivated Sequence?	1	2	3	4	5
Evidence?	1	2	3	4	5
Visual aids?	1	2	3	4	5

Audience Awareness:

Introduction/conclusion?	1	2	3	4	5
Signposts?	1	2	3	4	5
Counterarguments/refutation?	1	2	3	4	5
Nonverbal elements?	1	2	3	4	5

Comments:

Glossary

action—a behavior

ad hominem—a fallacy involving an attack on personal characteristics rather than on the substance of a person's views; Latin for "to the man" or "to the person"

advocacy—speaking to propose policy change

affect displays—nonverbal expressions that show emotion

affirmative—the debater favoring or defending the proposition

agency—the means used to convey a message

agent—the messenger

anticlimax order—the strategy of placing the most significant arguments first in the speech and least important ones last

appeal to conformity—fallacy arguing that one should adhere to a position or adopt an action because of its popular appeal

attitude—a predisposition or inclination to act in one way or another in response to controversy

attribution— 1. the act of citing the source for one's information 2. an audience's perception of a speaker's motives

audience alienation—the act of repelling audience agreement, often unintentionally and usually through the speaker's insensitivity to the nature of the audience

belief—an idea central to one's worldview

brainwashing—a systematic process of coercive indoctrination to impose a set of beliefs

canon—guideline or precept, as in the canons of rhetoric, which serve as guides or stages to speech preparation

chronemics—the use of timing, time of day, and historical time to convey meaning

claim—an assertion

climax order—the strategy of placing weak or less important arguments early in the speech and more powerful arguments later

coercion—exertion of force, restraint, pressure, or compulsion

cognitive dissonance—a state of mind where one's beliefs, attitudes, or actions conflict

cognitive restructuring—to reduce speech anxiety, a method of identifying anxiety-producing self-statements and replacing them with coping statements

commentary—a genre of persuasive speech (often satirical) that evaluates and interprets events to stimulate inquiry and novel perspectives

common topics—perspectives or questions asked about a controversy in order to analyze it; perspectives on a subject or ways of looking at a subject; also known as *topoi*

consubstantial—alike in substance, the experience of common sensations, concepts, images, ideas, and attitudes with another

controversy—a subject on which people disagree

counterargument—an assertion opposing a speaker's claim

credibility—believability; *ethos*

critical thinking—the process of analyzing and evaluating information

data—reasons or evidence; statistical information

deduction—a form of reasoning that derives particular truths from general beliefs

deliberative oratory—the speaking characteristic of legislative bodies, concerned with setting policy

democracy—a form of government where rule is exercised by the people governed, rather than by a totalitarian leader; a state characterized by the people participating in governance directly or through their representatives

demographic information—objective information about audience externals, such as age, gender, education, income, and so on.

devil-term—ultimate term for something considered by the public or a sizeable group to be negative or offensive

dialectic—the process of discovering sound ideas through discussion, questioning, and evaluation of conflicting perspectives

disinformation—deliberately false information circulated to mislead or influence others

ego-involvement—the belief that a subject is important to one's well being

epideictic oratory—speech characteristic of eulogies or other ceremonies, usually asserting praise or blame, upholding or opposing a value

ethical naturalism—the belief that ethical standards are independent of personal or cultural perceptions

ethical relativism—the belief that ethical standards depend on personal and cultural perceptions

ethics—standards of conduct; a moral code

ethos—the speaker's image; credibility

euphemism—an indirect, milder word substitute for a harsh, unpleasant, embarrassing, or unflattering reality

evidence—any support for a conclusion or to substantiate one's claims as believable

extemporaneous—a delivery style characterized by thorough and thoughtful preparation but using brief, unmemorized notes to retain spontaneity and a conversational tone

fairness doctrine—a 1949 Federal Communications Commission policy, formalized in the Communications Act of 1959, that required broadcasters to air all points of view when reporting on a controversy

fallacy—a vulnerable argument or reasoning pattern

false cause—fallacy that argues because something occurred first, it caused what followed; also known as *post hoc ergo propter hoc*: after this, therefore because of this

faulty comparison—fallacy that assumes that because things are alike in some respects, they are alike in many or all respects

forensic oratory—speech characteristic of the courtroom, usually to determine questions of fact.

gender-neutral—terminology that does not specify gender

gender-specific—terminology that indicates gender

god-term—ultimate term for something considered by the public or a large group to be a good or an ideal

hasty generalization—a fallacy of reasoning that occurs when one jumps to conclusions, relying on too few specific instances in drawing a general conclusion

homophily—the audience's perceived similarity of the speaker to themselves

identification—a speaker's demonstration of commonality with the audience

illustrator—gesture used to depict a verbal message

image—a succinct verbal construction to convey thoughts and emotions in an instant

imagism—a poetry movement in the early twentieth century characterized by economy and precision of words and by using images as instruments of thought

impromptu—an unrehearsed delivery style characterized by very brief, even momentary, preparation

inclusive—non-restrictive; in language, use of terms that reference, respect, and incorporate diverse individuals rather than limited, elite, or *exclusive* groups

induction—a form of reasoning whereby particular instances lead to a general conclusion

inherency—the issue that establishes whether a problem is avoidable or unavoidable given the status quo

inoculation theory—theory that an audience exposed to a speaker's opposing arguments will resist subsequent persuasion away from that speaker's position

invention—one of the five canons of rhetoric; the process by which a speaker discovers ideas and arguments to defend a position

invitational rhetoric—rhetorical communication characterized by a speaker's openness to a listener's perspective, with a goal of reciprocal understanding toward a mutually satisfying outcome

issue-involvement—the belief that a subject is important even though it does not affect one personally

latitude of acceptance—a range of attitudes at the agreement end of an opinion scale

latitude of rejection—a range of attitudes at the disagreement end of an opinion scale

Likert scale—a form of questioning that indicates attitude along a range of attitude positions

long-term memory—an aspect of the human memory system whereby unlimited information can be retained indefinitely

metaphor—a language device characterized by calling a thing what it is not

misinformation—inadvertent falsehood without the intent to mislead

mnemonic device—memory aid or technique

monotone—having limited vocal range or inflection, usually including a variation akin to approximately three whole notes on a musical scale

motivated sequence—an organizational scheme for proving a proposition of policy, by following the steps of attention, need, satisfaction, visualization, and action

narrative—a historical record or story; rhetorical technique of telling a story to enhance audience interest and engagement

narrative criticism—analysis or interpretation based on a historical or dramatic story line as context

negative—the debater opposing the proposition

optimum pitch—one's natural pitch level (as from low to high on a musical scale); the pitch best suited to the vocal structure for an individual voice

pathos—emotional appeal or proof

pentad—a group of motives used to analyze speech behavior and effectiveness; composed of act, agent, agency, scene, and purpose

persona—a person's overall image, a blend of appearance, personality, and character

persuasion—the intentional verbal act that attempts to influence the beliefs, attitudes, and actions of listeners

plagiarism—using another's words or work without attributing them to their original source; passing off another's words as one's own

polarization—description of a socio-political climate characterized by a population's divergent and staunchly opposed points of view

political correctness—the use or imposition of inclusive terms to sensitize society to discrimination

premise—a reason for accepting a conclusion or an assumption in an argument; a claim

preparation outline—a manuscript or full-sentence construction of the speech using outline notations

primacy—the effect on persuasion of first-speaker position in a series of speakers

primary source—the original source of information about a subject, or the source closest to the original

propaganda—the deliberate and systematic attempt to promote, shape, and manipulate cognitions or perceptions, often toward a doctrinaire point of view

proposition—the thesis statement of a persuasive speech; a proposal that an audience adopt a point of view or follow a course of action

proposition of fact—an assertion that something exists, has existed, or will exist

proposition of policy—an assertion that something should or should not be done or that an action is necessary or unnecessary

proposition of value—an assertion that evaluates a person, policy, or thing

proxemics—the speaker's use of space or speaker-audience distance

public deliberation—evidence-based group discussion among demographically and politically diverse individuals, for the purpose of devising workable solutions to public problems

purpose—the goal or reason for giving the speech

puzzlement-recoil stage—the stage in interpreting a metaphor when the listener experiences confusion and searches for meaning

qualifier—phrase or statement to express reservations or to make an assertion less absolute

rebuttal—the refutation segment of a debate

reasoning—forms, ways, or patterns of thought

recency—the effect on persuasion of last-speaker position in a series of speakers

recollection—the ability to retrieve stored information in one's memory

refutation—demonstration that a claim or argument is not valid

refute—to disprove an argument

regulator—gesture that attempts to control audience response

retention—information storage in the memory

rhetoric—the art of persuasion

secondary source—a secondhand account; information one or more steps removed from the original source of information

semantic differential—a method of audience analysis where one reveals attitude toward a term by choosing from a range of descriptors of that term

short-term memory—a conception of the human memory system, that its limited capacity requires continual rehearsal for retention

signposting—the technique of telling an audience what the speech will cover, what it is presently addressing, or what has been addressed

social judgment theory—theory of persuasion claiming the speech's effectiveness depends on audience perception of the speaker's position in relation to theirs

solvency—the issue that establishes whether a proposed solution is workable and will solve the problem

soundbite—vivid or striking public statement that distills into few words the essence of a viewpoint

speaking outline—speech notes written in brief phrases or single word outline entries, rather than in full sentences

stereotyping—a fallacy characterized by hasty generalization, but applied to groups of people

systematic desensitization—a method of enforced deep muscle relaxation in response to anxiety-producing stimuli

tenor—in a metaphor, the thing given meaning by comparison

topoi—Greek word for the common topics

tribalism—the act of exclusive loyalty to a like-minded social, cultural, or political group; opposing or rejecting cooperation with those outside one's "tribal" affiliations

ultimate term—a word or phrase considered by a cultural group to be an ideal (god-term) or an offense (devil-term)

vehicle—in a metaphor, the analogy used to carry the meaning

warrant—a statement, often implied, establishing that a claim follows from the data given

working memory—term used to describe the cognitive process used to store and manipulate information temporarily, as with short-term memory

Index

abolition, of slavery, 19
accusation and defense speeches, 278–282
ACLU. *See* American Civil Liberties Union
action
  cognitive dissonance and, 12
  definition of, 12, 144
  as outgrowth of beliefs and attitudes, 12
ad hominem arguments, 179
advocacy, speeches of, 264–268
affirmative position, in informal debate, 276–277
Affordable Care Act, 98
agonism, 273
American Civil Liberties Union (ACLU), 150–151
American Psychological Association, 207
Ancient Greece, 17, 52, 236, 245. *See also* specific Greek philosophers
Ancient Rome, 52. *See also* specific Roman philosophers
anti-immigration issues, 96
anxiety. *See* speech anxiety
appeal to conformity, 179–180, 186–187
appeal to popular sentiment, 179, 180
Apple Keynote, 249
arguments
  analysis and repair of speaker's credibility, 83–103
  Aristotle on, 84
  common topics and, 67–76
  evaluation of, 295
Aristotle, 18, 19, 40, 52, 84, 85, 119, 221
assertion, 69
attitudes
  of audience about proposition, 121–124
  of audience about speaker, 112
  definition of, 11
  in sales presentation, 269, 272

social judgment theory of, 122
  of speaker toward subject of speech, 115–116
attraction, as credibility aspect, 86
audience polling, 111–113
audiences, 151. *See also* evaluation
  analysis of, 107–126
  attitude of, about proposition, 121–124
  attitude of, toward speaker, 112
  demographic information about, 108–109
  ego-involvement of, 113
  emotional appeals to, 119
  evidence requested and received by, 40–41
  experience of, 113, 117–118, 120
  finding information about, 113
  issue-involvement of, 113
  knowledge level of, 112–113
  questionnaire for, 113–116
  questions to ask about, in critique, 301–302
  speaker's identification with, 198–199
  speaker's modification of proposition based on, 124–126
  stereotypes about, 110
authenticism, 19
authentic persuasion, 16–17
authority, as a common topic, 71

Baidu, 45
Baym, Geoffrey, 279
beliefs, definition of, 11
Berinato, Scott, 248
Bing, 45
body action, of speaker, 242–244
body of speech
  outline of, 147–148
  visual aids for, 253
Bowerman, Bill, 6
brainwashing, 14, 121
Burkeian criticism, 302
Burke, Kenneth, 18, 20, 93, 198, 202, 302

Bush, George H. W., 89, 179, 193
Bush, George W., 89–90, 200, 274, 297

canons of rhetoric, 20–21
causal reasoning, 174
cause and effect, as common topic, 140
cause-effect method of organization, 139–140
chart, 248–249
  for visual aid, 248
Chinese culture, classical, 18
chronemics, 246
Cicero, 52, 68, 222, 223, 236, 244, 245, 284
claim, definition of, 296
climate-change skeptics, 182
climate control, 246–247
climax order, 151
Clinton, Bill, 57, 89, 90
Clinton, Hillary Rodham, 57, 298
coercion, definition of, 16–17
cognitive dissonance, 12, 144
cognitive restructuring, 230
commentary, 279–280
common topics
  definition of, 69
  examples of, 71–75
  function of, 69–71
  list of, 75–76
  memory and, 74, 224–225
  survey, 138
Communications Act of 1959, 284
comparison
  as common topic, 71
  faulty comparison, 182–183
  reasoning using, 174–176
conclusions, in persuasive speech, 155
conformity, appeal to, 179–180, 186
consubstantial, definition of, 198
controversies
  considerations about, 32–33
  defining purpose of persuasive speech, 35
  definition of, 33